ON FOOTBALL

ON FOOTBALL

JAMES LAWTON

FOREWORD BY
JOHN GILES
EDITED BY
IVAN PONTING

dewi lewis media

ON FOOTBALL
by James Lawton

This edition first published in the UK in 2007 by
Dewi Lewis Media Ltd
8, Broomfield Road
Heaton Moor
Stockport SK4 4ND
www.dewilewismedia.com

All the texts by James Lawton in this book first appeared
in *The Independent*, except for 'It Was Everything And More'
which was published in *The Daily Express*

> Edited by
Ivan Ponting

> Design and Artwork Production
Dewi Lewis Media Ltd

> Print and binding
Biddles Ltd, Kings Lynn

ISBN: 978-1-905928-02-6

10   9   8   7   6   5   4   3   2   1

CONTENTS

FOREWORD   JOHN GILES

A wise man once said: "The trouble with common sense is that it isn't so common." There is no doubt, though, that it shines from the work of Jim Lawton, where it underpins crucially a glorious writing talent unequalled, I believe, in modern sports journalism.

It's a precious commodity, this common sense. Without it, all the sparkling words in the world amount to nothing. Down the years I have known plenty of terrific writers whose clever phrases dance across the page, but who tend to ruin the effect by purveying rubbish. To put it bluntly, they don't know what they're talking about, and they achieve little more than exposing their own ignorance.

Then there are the guys with an excellent knowledge of their chosen sport, but who struggle to express themselves, leaving their puzzled readers to wonder precisely what point they're trying to make.

Happy to say, Jim Lawton inhabits a different universe from either of these unfortunate stereotypes. He starts from a position of immense intelligence and he is tremendously aware of what is going on, both in sport and in the wider world. Importantly, he's a good listener, too. When being interviewed by Jim – and I've had that privilege frequently – he never needs you to labour the point. If I'm rabbiting on, which is not unknown, he'll bring me back to earth, probably employing a favourite Irish saying: "Don't milk the cow twice, John" comes the courteous but firm Lawton reproach whenever I start to meander.

Integral, too, to his enduring success is his genuine love for his subject. There are lots of fellows who write about sport for their living and to them it's just a job. To Jim it goes much deeper; in his case, we're talking about passion. I think that comes through in his columns, whether he's holding forth on football, cricket, boxing, golf, rugby, tennis, the Olympics, any and every sport – and the fact that he is so versatile is yet another aspect of his excellence.

There are more: for example, his integrity, his judgement and his refusal to be carried along by whatever might happen to be the latest fashion. A pertinent case is his coverage of the 2006 World Cup. During the year leading up to the tournament, when England were winning a few matches despite playing badly, he wrote what he saw rather than what people might have wanted to hear.

When it would have been far easier to hedge his bets and go with the general jingoistic flow, he outlined clearly what he considered to be the fatal flaws in the Sven-Goran Eriksson regime and highlighted the absurd lionising of David Beckham. Consistently he was the voice of reason in a sea of ludicrously inflated expectations, strong enough to swim against the tide while advancing cogent reasons for doing so. He was never vindictive, always according unto Beckham his considerable dues, but pointing out simply that his celebrity had overtaken his ability. It was a joy to all realists to read Jim's columns at the time, and even more instructive to review them afterwards, in the wake of England's chronic failure to perform.

I'd like to emphasise, too, that he is not one of those distressingly partial journalists with an axe to grind. Football fans, and even some people inside the game, can be notoriously touchy where their own club is concerned, but Jim is utterly neutral. No matter what followers of Arsenal or Manchester United, Liverpool or Chelsea, might fancy from time to time, he merely tells the truth as he sees it, without fear or favour.

Beyond all that, of course, the man is a truly brilliant writer. Infallibly he gets to the heart of the matter and, once there, he expresses himself eloquently, yet in a way which everyone can understand, which has to be the first requirement of any successful communicator. His command of the language is exceptional and his style is uniquely entertaining.

Lest anyone accuse me of bias, let me own up that Jim is a good friend of mine. I encountered him first in my days of playing for Leeds United, got to know him better when we were both working in Vancouver in the early 1980s and later enjoyed producing a weekly column with him for the *Daily Express* over more years than either of us care to remember. I found him to be a grand fellow, notable for his generosity of spirit and a lack of cynicism which is not present in everyone with such vast experience of reporting on international sport.

However, I would never allow personal regard to cloud my judgement of an individual's professional achievements. Having made that clear, I have no hesitation in commending this collection of his columns from *The Independent* unreservedly. I'd say Jim Lawton has total credibility with all fair-minded observers of the football scene, and he has earned it by sustained sureness of touch over a long period. He is a consummate artist who sits at the very pinnacle of his profession.

John Giles, September 2007

IT WAS EVERYTHING AND MORE

James Lawton says farewell to the Daily Express
Published: 24 May 2000

When Ernest Hemingway brought to a close *Death In The Afternoon*, his treatise on bullfighting and life, he said that if it had been enough of a book it would have had everything in it.

It would have had the grain blowing in the wind, the taste of the cold white Rioja poured from the big jugs, the Prado art museum packed with Goyas and looking like a college building, and how it was when the matadors went swimming with the girls of the night in the river beneath the big trees where the rooks peered down like sentinels.

Forgive me for quoting my boyhood hero but this is my last column for the *Express* and if it was enough of a piece it would, indeed, have everything in it. It would have the best part of 30 privileged, thrilling, desperate, haunting years which went by so quickly that now, when I come to reflect upon them, it is rather like playing back a fast-reel film racing off its spool.

But then there are so many frames frozen forever. How could you forget the sight of Bill Shankly getting up on the table in his little office beneath the big stand at Anfield and clenching his fists together and then spreading them wide and declaring that his latest, young Liverpool were going to go off like "a bloody bomb in the sky"?

Or getting drunk with Malcolm Allison and Joe Mercer on a scouting mission to Coimbra, a town in Portugal, where Big Mal delivered the deathless advice: "When the bedroom spins, all you have to do is put one foot on the floor."

Or being commanded by Muhammad Ali to have breakfast with him in a cabin in his training camp in Deer Lake, Pennsylvania, after being told by one of his aides: "We haven't seen a writer here for days. Ali was getting restive because he has so much to say."

Or the icy feeling in your stomach when you saw Viv Richards marching up the rickety steps of the press box in Antigua, when he should have been leading the West Indians, and you knew that it was you he was coming to see with hot anger gripping his huge heart.

Yes, there are some things you'll never forget. You could not forget the despair of walking among the dead in the killing field of Hillsborough on a sunny spring day. Or the hollow feeling that came in the Korean dawn when it was clear that Ben Johnson, who 48 hours earlier it seemed had sprinted to the very stars, had been stripped of his Olympic gold medal.

You couldn't forget the last Tour de France of 'The Cannibal', Eddy Merckx. Nor the name of the obscure *domestique* you saw fall in the valley and gash his head horribly, and then, hours later, saw again, straining up the Road of the Cross to the peak of Alpe d'Huez with blood seeping through the bandages which swathed his head. It was Lopez Corill.

You couldn't forget waiting with Tommy Simpson's widow at the monument they built 20-odd years after his death which came when his heart was pushed beyond all limits by blind courage – and the contents of the empty phials they found in his baggage. When you think about it, there are so many things not to forget.

George Best, the dark-eyed, shy kid playing his first game at Old Trafford, tracking back to his penalty area, robbing an attacker, swivelling, looking up with the aplomb of a veteran and sending a 50-yard ball inch-perfect to Denis Law, the reaction of the crowd so delayed because what he had done was so stunning. Bobby Charlton, imperious as a galleon on a high sea, sending cannonballs through the enemy masts. Law, lacking only a pirate's eye-patch, plundering goals. Nobby Stiles, as myopic as Mr Magoo, sniffing out the points of danger. John Giles and Billy Bremner running Leeds. Ian St John, who Shankly said would have made a great middleweight, ferocious as a fighting cock. Bobby Moore oozing class.

Shortly before he died, on assignment in Poland for his radio station, Moore was concerned that some colleagues and I would lack for refreshment on an overnight drive from Poznan to Warsaw. He went to his room and delivered up the last of his duty-free. Who better to drink to in the depths of a starless Polish night?

There are so many fights you cannot forget. Ali-Shavers in Madison Square Garden, when the great man was beginning to slide but still had the grace and courage to repel a young, harder-hitting man. Hagler-Hearns, which for less than three rounds burned like a shooting star. Duran-Leonard 1, an epic triumph of will over the highest talent. Leonard-Hearns 1, possibly the greatest fight I ever saw. Lewis beating Holyfield a second time, remembered not for the fight but what it meant to a decent man and a worthy champion.

Boxing occupies a lot of that fast-reeling film, for the best and the worst reasons. There is Mike Tyson, whose scabrous origins you observed in the company of a young New York City policewoman-social worker who couldn't keep the tears out of her eyes when she talked of the conditions which a man like Tyson is expected to survive, whole and reasonably balanced, occupying a great swathe of the time you spent filling this space.

You saw just about all of him, his rise, his fall, his tortured writhings in the light of fame that slipped so quickly into notoriety. You saw him baiting Tyrell Biggs – "he was so frightened he screamed like a woman" – beaten in Tokyo by Buster Douglas after days of hellish disintegration; stand trial for rape in Indianapolis, emerge, eyes blinking, from prison in a frosty dawn; and none of this prepared you for the moment he bit the ear of Evander Holyfield.

You also saw Michael Watson and Gerald McClellan condemned to wheelchairs and darkness, and when you saw that you wondered if the candle of the old game was spluttering towards an end.

Angst and joy run so strongly down the reel. The joy of Maradona's mastery in Mexico, untouched, you have to say, even by his cynical hand of God; the exuberance of the Brazilians in Spain in 1982 before they imploded against Italy and the sound of their samba died against the blare of Lancias and Fiats down Las Ramblas in Barcelona.

If it was enough of a column it would indeed have everything. It would have dining on a mountain top above the city of fire, Tbilisi in Soviet Georgia, and Sebastian Coe winning in Moscow and Los Angeles; it would have Michael Schumacher and the late Ayrton Senna in the rain, and Gower and Botham in the sun.

It would have the old Fred Trueman conning me into the belief that he had evolved a brilliant new bowling technique when really he was merely fanning the last embers of his talent. It would have Andre Agassi outlasting the haunted Croat Goran Ivanisevic.

Indispensably, it would also have the patience of the readers. I thank you all, including Angry of Bedford. Without him, I might have believed I had died and was living in heaven.

BIG MAL BATTLING TO END THE TORMENT

Published: 03 June 2000

Nearly 30 years after the first slippage of his fame, when fellow celebrity Michael Parkinson described him as "possibly the least tranquillised Englishman alive," Malcolm Allison experienced a series of sharp role reversals this week. He received withering lectures from Francis Lee, Mike Summerbee and Colin Bell, the three players who most perfectly expressed the force of his outrageous but stunningly brilliant annexation of English football as coach of Manchester City in the late Sixties.

They brought fruit and Havana cigars – but no champagne or brandy. Allison, 72, is drying out in a Priory Clinic. He was driven there last weekend, 24 hours after the *Daily Mail* paid him £600 for the right to ransack what was left of his life. It wasn't much. Said the *Mail*: "He was one of sport's most flamboyant figures with a penchant for Bunny Girls. But now Malcolm Allison reveals he is on the verge of suicide."

In fact he was on the verge of rescue, but one which Lee most forcefully pointed out was entirely dependent on his own will to pull back from a Prozac -and-cognac fuelled descent into despair and self-pity.

Lee, the former Manchester City and England star who had laid the foundations of a multi-million pound business before the end of his swash-buckling playing days and had a successful spell as a racehorse trainer, told Big Mal: "You made Belly and Mike and me do a lot of things we didn't want to do. You made us work so hard we spewed up. You never stopped kicking our arses; you made us achieve things as footballers we never dreamed were possible. You were bloody incredible, I don't believe there has been a better pure football coach. You changed our lives. Now you have to change your own. We're here to help, but you have to do the real job."

It was Lee who guaranteed the cost of Allison's treatment – the most decisive move in a remarkable reclamation effort by a network of friends who, as they went about their daily business, had been unaware that a man who had so coloured their lives, so regularly pointed them to the stars, was sliding ever closer to an abandonment of pride.

The process started two years ago when he was fired from a North-east radio station for "obscene" language, slips which had accompanied an increase in the drinking which would eventually persuade his long-time partner Lynn, and mother of his 10-year-old daughter Gina, to change the locks on the semi-detached house they shared until recently in the village of Yarm, where he had settled after his last, convulsive big-time manager's job at Middlesbrough. That was the trigger for what amounted to swift disintegration. He spent three weeks coaching young players in Romania, a project which started optimistically but quickly slid into disillusionment. He reflected, over a cheap glass of brandy, that once Gianni Agnelli, the owner of Fiat, had invited him to coach Juventus with the promise of a private plane to fly in his Mayfair friends at the weekend.

Back in Yarm, he broke into his former home, drank a bottle of wine and was arrested by the police. Two weeks ago he travelled to London – ironically as a guest of the *Mail* – for the annual Football Writers' dinner in the West End, but, unaware that a group of friends, finally alerted to his plight, were waiting to take him into a private room to discuss his situation, he had a liquid lunch – he doesn't remember where – and found himself on a train back to the North-east. He caused a disturbance and would have been thrown off but for the calming presence of an acquaintance on the train. He arrived at his former home by taxi, demanded to enter and was again arrested. He later told friends he had spent four days in a police cell. He spent one night in custody. He was effectively homeless. But he had a friend, a steadfast one indeed.

Tony Zivanaris is a 58-year-old Cypriot-born hotelier and property developer who briefly served on the Middlesbrough board in the early Eighties. He was thrilled by Allison's vision of football and tolerant of his excesses. After he parted from the club with some acrimony, Allison once ran up an £11,000 bill at Zivanaris's Baltimore hotel, and a member of staff called the owner, nervously, to report that he was checking out with the bill unpaid. "Let Malcolm go," said Zivanaris. He later received a cheque posted from Kuwait. Through his latest crisis Zivanaris was the man who stood between Allison and the street. His staff prepared meals for Allison, served privately, cajoled him from the bar when fellow guests, seizing on faded celebrity, insisted on buying champagne. Last Sunday Zivanaris told Allison that he had a friend, but one who had a duty to point out certain realities. Malcolm Allison could still be a good man, perhaps even a great one, but not in the old way. The Bunny Girl days were over. That was another life, but he could still contribute in some way to a game that still gripped his imagination, and about which he still knew so much. Zivanaris then had his driver take Allison to the Priory, complete with a new dressing gown and pyjamas and slippers.

After Zivanaris's pivotal help, there has been plentiful evidence of the enduring impact of Allison's work as the revolutionary coach of Manchester City, his rage to shake the national game out of its shibboleths which started when he was a boy at Charlton Athletic railing against outdated training schedules and old-fashioned gear and then as the supreme barrack-room lawyer at West Ham, when the young Bobby Moore seemed to dog his every footstep.

Gordon Taylor, chief executive of the Professional Footballers' Association, has conferred with his old Bolton Wanderers team-mate Lee, and promised help with the "restructuring" of the life of a fallen hero. Says Taylor: "We know that when a player's career ends it often has the effect of a cold shower. Malcolm knew so much success as a coach, was such a great man in the game, you imagine his shower has gone on for a long time." David Bernstein, chairman of Manchester City, has also lent a sympathetic ear. He says: "I know Malcolm a little, he has been our guest at Manchester City, and I like him a lot. I also know what he did for this club, what an important part of our history he is." Terry Venables, whose coaching career was launched by Allison at Crystal Palace the day he was required to tell him, painfully, that it was time for him to quit as a player, has also rallied to the cannon-pocked banner.

Summerbee, who has a shirt business, visited Allison this week to take a fitting – and to reinforce Lee's message. "Even now, after all he's been through, I still don't believe there is anyone in football with a sharper brain, a more complete understanding of the game. I've told him that it's a tragedy he's still not involved; maybe it is a little bit of the game's fault, but also Malcolm's. He's got to come out of that place in charge of himself, with his pride back and I wouldn't be surprised if someone doesn't say, at this late hour, 'wait a minute, this guy could help.' Not as a manager, of course. Malcolm never really was a manager. He was a coach, a glorious coach. When I arrived at Maine Road I was proud to wear that pale blue shirt, but I was also a bit scared. In no time at all, he had me running around full-backs as if it was my right."

But then that was the easy part. The tough job was quelling the furies, the sheer lust that came with his discovery that in the game he adored he had found an extravagant expression of his nature. The scuffling days as a professional gambler, and as a club owner in Tin Pan Alley, which followed a year in a sanatorium after the discovery that tuberculosis had taken away a lung and ended his West Ham career, gave way to a riot of achievement. He coached the undergraduates of Cambridge University, discovered Tony Book, ageing stone mason and semi-pro at Bath and turned him into arguably the best uncapped full back in the history of English football, carried Third Division Plymouth Argyle into the semi-final of the League Cup, and then Joe Mercer, a great name recovering from a harrowing time as manager of Aston Villa, took him to Maine Road. The rest was tumultuous history. When City won the 1968 title with a breathtaking run to the line, beating Spurs and the great Dave Mackay, and Newcastle away in the last two matches, Allison declared: "Next stop Mars." He never made it to Mars, though he nearly died trying. This week his friends were encouraged to see him somewhat nearer earth. He reported: "I'm going to make a record recovery." He had just won the clinic's evening quiz. Naturally.

I'M ASHAMED TO BE AN ENGLISHMAN

Published: 20 June 2000

It had to happen. It couldn't go on, not all that vomiting of a nation's pride, that dreary, lemming-like trampling of the sensibilities of foreign cities and towns, whose citizens huddle together in shock and disbelief when the English football "fans" leave their calling-cards of beer stains and broken glass.

Indeed, there can be only a few small regrets in the wake of the decision taken by Uefa, the European football authority, to put the hooligans on notice that they are just one riot away from causing the banishment of their team from the European Championship currently being played in Belgium and the Netherlands.

Naturally, there is concern for the betrayal of the team, who won a famous victory over their most bitter rivals, Germany, last Saturday night, even as revulsion at the behaviour of their invading compatriots was hardening into an official resolve to take action.

But if the plight of the players is sad, it cannot be equated with the outrage now being felt in the sophisticated city of Brussels and the small industrial town of Charleroi, the latest victims of a rampage that is now nearly 30 years old. There is also the matter of the name of England across the sports world. Grimly, it is now synonymous with a breakdown in civilised behaviour.

The roots of football hooliganism reach back to the early Sixties, when Everton fans, returning from a match in Sunderland, took over a train travelling between Leeds and Liverpool. I happened to be on that train – and in the Feyenoord stadium in Rotterdam 10 years later, when Tottenham followers ran amok in the city and then fought Dutch spectators and police at the cost of 200 injured; the great Spurs manager, Bill Nicholson, appealed for calm on the public address system, adding in a breaking voice: "You people make me feel ashamed to be an Englishman."

There is neither time nor space to list all the occasions when that emotion of Nicholson has come back as hard and raw as the first time you saw the mad-dog ravaging of some great boulevard or village street abroad.

Yes, Uefa is right; it cannot go on, and if there is one overwhelming regret, it is that a committee of European football bureaucrats have done for England what national honour insisted it should have done for itself.

Uefa has moved toward closure of England's shame, and it is a small irony that, in doing so, it has heaped a little more reason for shame on to the nation which incubated a disease so fiercely and exported it with not much more than an official shrug.

Certainly it is hard to believe that just a few weeks ago Jack Straw, the Home Secretary, was lecturing Belgian and Dutch officials on the need for firm action against the hooligans. Lock them up, said Straw, omitting only to add that it would be to our great convenience if they also threw away the key.

The time for such evasions of responsibility is surely over; and if there are now cries from within football that the game is carrying responsibilities that properly belong to all of society, the Football Association should perhaps be invited to discuss the injustices of life with the burghers and the people of Brussels and Charleroi. They bargained for football tournaments, a festival of sport, not an effusion of hatred and random violence and the numbing sense that their lives had, for a little time at least, been put on hold while a sinister phenomenon displayed itself with grotesque pride.

If the Uefa decision appears draconian, it is not; it is rather a snapping of patience, a belated conclusion that what a large group of socially dysfunctional English men and boys bring to football is simply no longer acceptable. It never was, of course, but maybe there was a belief that the malignancy would pass if it wasn't prodded too hard, that in time the world's game would, because of its power to bring joy, sooner or later expel the problem.

That was the optimistic thought that provoked Uefa to lift its ban on English clubs imposed after the tragedy of the Heysel stadium – as it was then known – in Brussels in 1985, when 35 Juventus fans died during the Italian club's European Cup final with Liverpool. The hope was that the English virus had died, that a hard streak of violence had found new outlets in Saturday night pubs and Ibiza disco strips. It was an unpretty but hopeful thought, though now shattered utterly by the yobbish, racist alliance that has attached itself to the England team and that sports the flag of St George not as an emblem of pride but as a rallying point of hatred and contempt for all foreigners.

Now the Government, still absurdly trailing its hopes for the campaign to host the 2006 World Cup, has been pushed into a corner out of which it can emerge only by the frank admission that, despite a torrent of warnings, it has done too little, too late. Uefa has said that platitudes are worn out and only action will do. If this action involves the exile of England's team and even that of the hugely profitable high-profile clubs from the megabuck European competitions, it is a price that will just have to be paid.

The alternative – a continuation of the anarchy that in Belgium and the Netherlands gives all Englishmen pariah status – would represent nothing so much as a failure of both national will and conscience. Passports have to be lifted, as they were in Germany after the violent excesses of some of their fans during the World Cup in France two years ago – and civil libertarians may have to be told, finally, that large sections of civilised societies hitherto uncontaminated by the violent slobbishness of England's virulent minority of fans are in need of a little protection, too.

Those most concerned with hooligan rights are certainly warmly invited on a random fact-finding journey back through the years. They could start on that train rattling over the Pennines. They could see a little of the terror that came to the trapped, innocent passengers, the anguish of a young man attempting to protect his girlfriend from brutish advances, the horror of a middle-aged woman as urine seeped into her compartment, the ashen faces of parents clutching at their children.

They could look into the expressions of disbelief on the faces of Rotterdam people that sunny day when cafe tables went flying, glass shattered and suddenly every corner of the street was filled with a previously unknown menace. They could see streets cleared in panic in Cagliari and Dusseldorf and they could see what I saw from the balcony of a hotel room overlooking the old port of Marseilles. They could see evil foment over a long day of drinking and then the first scuffles and fights and the volleys of beer cans and glasses and the riot police forming up and loading the tear gas, and later they could see the kid with his throat slashed and all the time hear the chants of "In-ger-land, In-ger-land", and they might think again about their insistence on the preservation of such niceties as allowing the authors of such behaviour out into the world.

Much more recently they could have seen how it was in Brussels before the English arrived. They could have seen the amiable Swedes drinking beer and debating the possibilities of their opening game with Belgium. They could have seen them slipping unobtrusively into the life of the city. They could have seen how it is supposed to be when nations gather to play football, rather than make their own, rancid version of war.

The idea of England's footballers being sent home is indeed one of terrible sadness, but sometimes in life sacrifices must be made. For the sake of the country's name, this is such a one. The shame has to stop.

HARSH REALITY OF ENGLAND POVERTY CRUELLY REVEALED

Published: 21 June 2000

England's Euro 2000 campaign finished pretty much as it started, in tactical chaos and a numbing failure to understand that what passes for soaring entertainment in the Premiership is a much lower flying currency indeed in a market where the imperative is not circus but patience and control.

There is another problem, and it was cruelly underlined by a Romanian team which had been dismissed, quite stunningly it seems to those outside the hard-dying tradition of English triumphalism, as a token barrier on the way to a quarter-final with Italy this Saturday. Romania, right from the start of a game which England needed only to draw – only to draw! – invested in the degree of skill and movement which are staples of the European game. England, as always, sailed on waves of John Bull determination, that peculiar hubris which so relentlessly prevents a sustained look in the bathroom mirror, and at the end of the draining night they were once again stirring not so much into a harsh reality but a wounded sense of injustice.

The wounds are, of course, self-inflicted. They come from a failure to deal with the nature of a challenge that has been beyond the English game more or less permanently since Sir Alf Ramsey imposed his regime of order and consistent preparation back in the Sixties. That's a long time to neglect a lesson imposed with magnificent discipline and glorious results.

The resulting decay was grimly evident here last night. That England were involved so tightly in the outcome until the last convulsive minute, when Ioan Ganea drove home the penalty that came from a catastrophically mistimed tackle by Phil Neville, was an extraordinary testament, no more and no less, to the fighting instinct of the English footballer. But what it said about his ability to compete at a high level of the game beyond the impetus provided by his traditional spirit, the poverty it revealed, yet again, in the matter of controlling a match in which an advantage had been hard won, was bleak indeed.

It is said that behind the riches of the Premiership there is a rather desperate case of Third World football poverty.

In this tournament only aged, atrophied Germany were beaten. Both Portugal and Romania, who caused scarcely a frown when their names came out of the hat as England's group opponents, fell briefly under the weight of England's competitive power but they rose above it with the steady application of confident skill. They moved into space; they had players free to gather the ball; they had easy skills to extricate themselves from the tighter places. They exhibited the confidence which comes when you know you have mastered the subtleties of a game which is only allegedly simple, which in truth is a wonderfully elaborate test of skill and ingenuity. Here, in this sometimes sublime area, England were again exposed as bankrupts.

It may have been a chilling surprise to the English fans, so many of them dramatically reformed by the weight of the ultimatum from Uefa, European football's governing body, which had brought a surreal peace to the streets of this Belgian town before the game, but it was not as though England's approach to this tournament had not been littered with disquieting clues of uncertainty about both personnel and tactics. But always there is that cussed streak in an English football team, however outgunned in technique or outfought in tactics.

When Alan Shearer scored from the spot and Michael Owen raced away to put England into the lead on the stroke of half-time, the English end of the ground was in peaceful tumult. "We're not going home," they sang, but of course they were. Romania had never lost trust in their superior ability to pass the ball and find the hurtful places deep in England's defence.

The blame will inevitably centre on Kevin Keegan, and it has to be said that his approach to this tournament always seemed to owe more to the forces of hope, chance and speculation than a real effort to bind England's limited resources into a practical fighting force.

There were signs of disarray, dismayingly, even in the final, perfunctory practice match in Malta a week before the start of these European championships in which England's record, apart from the run to the semi-final at home four years ago, has become an open-ended disaster.

The lack of certainty has seeped into every corner of the team's campaign, and though victory over Germany provoked some hope, the reality always was that Romania would prove far more difficult opposition than most around the England camp imagined.

They were without their old war chief Gheorghe Hagi, but he has been a fading force for some years now and last night his place was taken by the clever, thrusting young Adrian Mutu. Hagi was hardly missed when Romania poured confidently on the goal of Nigel Martyn and took the lead direct from a curling cross from another bright youngster, Cristian Chivu. England's response was typically belligerent and for a while they rallied strongly. But always there was a shortfall in touch and confidence and at the end the Romanians' patience brought a dividend devastating to English hopes.

The winning goal carried a hard blow of reality. It said, as the Portuguese goals did last week, that England's football will probably get worse before it gets better. England came into this match with apparent confidence – and a pledge that they would battle strongly against the revived Italians in Brussels on Saturday. But it is an old English story, one that has become congealed by recurring failure.

Keegan will take the heaviest blows now, but he is as much victim as culprit. He operates in a world of English football which has put excitement and profits before a real effort to come to terms with the demands of winning on the international field.

This was a defeat, the meaning of which stretched beyond still another failure in a major tournament. It was a rebuke which must be heeded if the free-fall is not to continue.

HATRED 1 DIGNITY 0
– A FAMILIAR SCORELINE

Published: 31 October 2000

Could anything provoke quite such instant despair at the moral condition of English football as the sight of Stan Collymore inciting a mob of Leeds United fans? Yes. It is the sight of a mob of Leeds United fans inciting Stan Collymore.

Talk about a soft-headed target. Examples of Collymore's psychological inadequacies are too many and too wearisome to recount here; enough to say that the likelihood of his doing something fleetingly brilliant at the opening of the latest phase of his long football misadventure was exceeded only by his capacity to make poison out of gold.

The Leeds chant was, though, fairly vicious even from a section of humanity which cheerfully sings of the Munich air disaster when Manchester United provide the opposition.

"Stanley's going mad," brayed the mob. Maybe, but he's not exactly on his own.

Bradford's decision to enlist his help, a move accompanied by a "public warning" for the unfortunate manager Chris Hutchings from chairman Geoffrey Richmond, is quite bewildering. Beyond, however, the desperation of an outgunned football club shedding its most viable asset, decent professional values, is an even more depressing prospect. It is the relentless brutalisation of what used to be a cornerstone of popular culture. The truth is that outside of the odd insulated executive box, watching a football game in England now more often than not involves at least passing contact with hell.

The horror runs deeper than even the single malignancy of racism. The need for a campaign against racism is not unique to English football. In Italy concern is growing rapidly, along with the growth of fascism in the north of the country, and in the last week or so several leading players have spoken out against the depressing trend. But the Collymore incident was not, at least in any central way, about racism, though don't be surprised if the eternally self-indulgent Collymore again raises the issue. It was about sheer unspecific hatred, pure, raging animosity against anyone who does not happen to be part of your "team".

So Collymore who, whatever you think of his behaviour, has recently undergone treatment for "depression," is yelled at that he is mad. George Graham is abused by Tottenham fans, who when they're not at football presumably lead reasonably rational lives, but scream at their manager for no better reason than that he was once an employee of Arsenal. And, as Michael Parkinson pointed out to a national television audience at the weekend, David Beckham has his wife categorised as a whore and cancer wished upon his young son. It is unfortunate for football that people capable of such evil also call themselves fans of the game. But then football cannot free itself from all responsibility.

Back in the Seventies, when Elland Road was closed for a month following a crowd riot, I went along to the game that followed the announcement of the closure, which was to start at the opening of the following season. I went as a fan, got on the bus in the city centre and spent two or three of the most disagreeable hours of my life. It was a night of herding and humiliation, of urine running down the terraces, of great swaying surges and breath-snatching panic. There was not much dignity to be had, and still less offered, and perhaps nor would there be until tragedies at Bradford and Hillsborough shook English football into the latter half of the 20th Century. The brutalisation just did not happen on its own. It was cultivated more easily in the slum conditions.

We see the legacy with horrible clarity every week now. We see the abuse of Beckham, the random booing of any opposition player. We saw Alan Shearer reviled at Ewood Park, where he was a demi-god for so long, when he returned to Blackburn as a Newcastle player in a cup tie last season. Shearer scored twice and said they were the most satisfying goals of his career. Such is a routine travesty of the values of a game which conquered the world with its beauty and its accessibility for all shapes and sizes and talents.

The pictures of the hate-filled Collymore and his tormentors were enough to make you shudder for the future of the game. They made utterly poignant the memory of those days when fathers took their sons not only to cheer the home team but admire the skills of famous visitors like Matthews and Finney. Once an uncle took a nephew to Chester for a game against Crewe Alexandra. It was not, even then, the high point of the nephew's sporting life for already he knew the terrain of Goodison Park and Wilderspool, the home of Warrington Rugby League Club and their mythic wing threequarter Brian Bevan. Why Chester v Crewe? Because Crewe had a great man playing out his last days in the game, the sleek winger Frank Broome, formerly of Derby County and England.

He did not have a great game but he produced an echo or two of the past and he was clapped on and off the field. He had respect. He had dignity. He had passed through, with distinction, a game and a life which had not learned hate.

That was a little less than 50 years ago, but on Sunday afternoon at Bradford it might have been a thousand.

HODDLE HAS YET TO HEED LESSONS OF HIS FAILURE

Published: 06 February 2001

Glenn Hoddle's reinstatement as a football icon has been impressive in several ways. He has brought a little Premiership security and some pleasing football to Southampton and up to now – or rather until his outpourings to some of last Sunday's prints – he has sounded like a reasonably well adjusted fellow occupant of the planet.

A touch of humility was always going to be the best thing he could have taken from his fall as England manager; that, and some sense of how he had put in place the forces of his own destruction. But Hoddle's rehabilitation plainly has some way to go.

Take, for example, his astonishing offer to his successor Sven-Goran Eriksson. "There are a few things I could tell Sven-Goran Eriksson. Not about football, because he will have to make his own decisions, but I would be willing to offer advice on matters which might help protect him."

The brain reels. Does Eriksson, after 20 years of successful operations in some of the most sophisticated areas of European football, really need to be told that it would not be smart to install a faith healer as a key member of his staff. Or to betray, for profit, his closest dealings with players. Or to chop and change his team and his tactics almost from game to game. Or to claim that it was a masterstroke to leave Michael Owen on the bench until 20 minutes before the end of a losing performance against Romania in the 1998 World Cup. Or to question the state of mind of one of his most gifted players, David Beckham, days before the start of a World Cup campaign which, we had been told, had seen the "best ever" preparation of an England team.

A preparation which had included right up to the dawn of action a Paul Gascoigne who had become a parody of a professional football player.

If that is a wearisome listing of some of Hoddle's mistakes as England manager, it does not include the Football Association's stated reason for his dismissal, which was the re-airing of crackpot views about the past sins of handicapped people. Hoddle could have been sacked for half a dozen legitimate reasons, and that's not including one which is routinely employed by leading football nations – a failure to get beyond the last 16 of the World Cup.

"Revisionism," we should know by now, is a staple of football thinking. It explains why so many re-tread managers re-emerge in top jobs. Time, it seems, forgives almost everything, but Hoddle wasn't so wise to strike such self-serving levels in his recent interviews. His attempt to rewrite history had come a little quickly. But then, on the other hand, he could point to considerable success over his Sunday morning cornflakes.

With the honourable exception of one newspaper, most took Hoddle's comments at face value. In this version of events Hoddle was a winning manager cut down because he had been "misquoted". Of his final three games, two had been won and one drawn. One of the wins was in a meaningless friendly with the Czech Republic, another was a wretched 3-0 performance against Luxembourg, and the draw was a harrowing goalless home game against Bulgaria in qualifying for Euro 2000, a disastrous result for England after being cut to pieces by Sweden in Stockholm.

All of this is history – recent, vivid, painful history – and if values and truth were not so easily twisted in the football world there would be absolutely no need for its recounting. Hoddle has created that need by his attempt to recast events in his own favour. He says he was betrayed by the Football Association, and he would never consider returning to the England job as long as his betrayers remained in office. This is an astonishing statement of arrogance. Hoddle's failure in the England job was profound.

For all his knowledge of the game, and the aura he carried as a player of some distinction, he seemed incapable of embracing the core of the job, which is to establish trust and confidence with his players, to provide a pattern of play and expectation that was consistent. Instead, he constantly referred to the need of his players to take new things on board. He played Steve McManaman at right wing-back. Alan Shearer and Michael Owen, who was in breathtaking form, scarcely played together before the onset of the World Cup. But all of this is pushed to one side now. He lost his job, he claims, because of betrayal at the FA and because of a view of life that sounded so warped it would have been better left completely unsaid, rather than returned to with such disastrous consequences.

None of this deflects from Hoddle's promising work at Southampton and nor is it likely to prevent a likely return to Tottenham Hotspur at the end of the season. Hoddle has played a cool, effective hand at The Dell, but he should remember the advice of Kenny Rogers. He should know when to hold them – and when to fold them. All the revisionism in the world cannot alter one fact.

As England manager, Glenn Hoddle was an utterly busted flush.

UNITED MUST PAY THE PRICE FOR DOUBLE STANDARDS

Published: 10 February 2001

It was vulgar of Manchester United to parade their wealth in New York this week and, apparently, rather confusing to New Yorkers. But then if money can buy you a lot of things, especially in football, there is no price tag on class.

What was particularly sad, for those of us who still get lumps in our throats when we think of his majestic passage along the peaks of the game, was Sir Bobby Charlton's walk-on role as a barker for what, when you boiled it all down, was a shirt deal which would have hardly caused a stir down Petticoat Lane.

It meant that United could flog their over-priced souvenir gear at Yankee Stadium and the Yankees would have the same privilege at Old Trafford. The Bronx, I'm told, was not *en fête*. Nor was Chorlton-cum-Hardy.

Sir Bobby, stung by suggestions that United were again trumpeting their marketing brilliance at a time when the rest of the Premiership were holding up their hands at the futility of trying to compete against them, delivered a lecture against the perils of envy. He declared: "Money is not a dirty word. To remain at the top of this sport you have to make money. We know how to do it and so do the Yankees. We are trying to be first, that's all. If it upsets people, it is because they are trailing behind and don't like it. The good of the game is paramount."

It is scarcely necessary to go too deeply into why United occupy the centre of such a huge market which stretches all the way to the Far East. Or to say that it has little or nothing to do with slick salesmanship. They have a story of tragedy and romance, of pain and resurrection and flights of pure football beauty – and for more than a decade now it has been augmented by superb management and virtually unbroken success on the field. The sports world has of course changed hugely and no one has been better placed to exploit it than United because of yesterday's glory and today's point of achievement. But this week's commercial triumphalism wasn't merely coarsely self-congratulatory. It was dangerously pitched at a time when the cream of United's dressing-room is hammering on the door for major pay rises.

While United bask in their rather prosaic business relationship with the

Yankees, they might just delve a little deeper into Charlton's assertion that United and the Yankees are linked by a shared and perhaps mystical knack for turning a buck and a quid.

The owner of the Yankees, despite an occasional outburst of sentimentality, is a man of legendary hardness. George Steinbrenner, who made his initial wealth in the shipbuilding business, is keen on money, no doubt – but he is also besotted by baseball because it can be both a cash cow and a white steed. What he understands is that success on the diamond is everything, and that United's commercial wizards would scarcely be on first base if they didn't have a winning product. This is why the odds are that Steinbrenner will shortly agree to an eight-year contract, worth upwards of $120m (£82m), with his brilliant short stop Derek Jeter. While Jeter is a splendid short stop, a position which requires the reflexes of a cat and the nerve of a gunfighter, it is fair to say that he is not as central to the marketing of Yankee products as David Beckham is to those of United. But then, it is reasonable to ask, how is it that Beckham's reported desire for a salary of around £5m a year, which is considerably less than Jeter's current rate for the job, has provoked a cry of "anarchy" from United's chief executive, Peter Kenyon. It would seem that while it is perfectly acceptable for United to squeeze every cent and penny out of their marquee names – indeed it is apparently "brilliant" business – those who create the wealth, and the selling power, and a value nearly twice as great as that of the Yankees, are criticised for "greed" the moment they ask for a more realistic share of the profits.

Steinbrenner, if he had the time, would be stunned by the sheer nerve of his new business associates.

He would also be amazed by the capacity of one team to so dominate a championship without even a passing nod to the disastrous prospect of a collapse in competitive values. It's true that the Yankees have now carried three straight World Series, but this is in a league which understands that ultimately it is only as strong as its weakest link. This is why Steinbrenner joined with fellow Major League owners a few years ago and sweated out extended strike action by the players. Such unity of purpose was not conspicuous in English football, of course, when United went off to pursue a few dollars more in Brazil last year at the expense of the FA Cup.

The baseball owners stood together then, but of course they didn't have to answer to the City of London and the shareholders. Not out of the essential sweetness of their natures, or that any of them were steeped in the values of the Eton playing fields, the gnarled old baseball bosses held a line which they believed marked out the common good. They did it because they couldn't seriously contemplate the alternative, which was of a handful of clubs buying up all the best players and making a farce of the idea of a competitive league. Here, though, United's hold on the Premiership intensifies to the point where their eventual membership of a European Super League is seen as a formality. No doubt Bobby Charlton is right when he says that United are merely acknowledging the primacy of money as the overwhelmingly decisive factor in the new age of English football. But to charge all who question the situation, who pine for the days when the field was rather more level than the north face of the Eiger, with a simple case of envy is to miss the point.

United will shortly have to pay the price for their financial aggrandisement. They will have to meet the demands of the Beckhams and the Giggses without a whisper of the word greed. Money, says Sir Bobby, is not a dirty word. Not certainly on the lips of a United shirt huckster, so you have to wonder why it would be so on those of someone who creates the demand for the product. Greedy footballers, some say. Even as they, at least literally, sell the shirts off their backs.

SCHOLES LETS DEEDS ON FIELD DO HIS TALKING

Published: 09 March 2001

In the eyes of Paul Scholes' relatively small but increasingly passionate fan club, he did rather more than rescue Manchester United from humiliating defeat in Athens this week. He defined, quite beautifully, what it is to be a consummate professional in an age of instant celebrity and slavishly honed public relations. When Scholes speaks, which is rarely, it is usually to utter a few self-deprecating remarks on his way to the nearest bolt-hole. Yet on the field his eloquence is as relentless as it is unfancy. He is, more than anything, a brilliant throwback to those days when a professional was happy to be judged on what he did rather than what he said.

In a week when new, and essentially just, transfer regulations provoked all kinds of legitimate fears about the durability of the old relationship between a star and a club's following – and when the "retirement" of Stan Collymore makes its own forlorn statement about the size of the current gap between rewards and achievement – Scholes again announced himself as a man of insistent action.

His injury-time goal grabbed the headlines but the watching England coach, Sven-Goran Eriksson, would have been most impressed by the sheer tenacity of Scholes' effort as Panathinaikos literally ran rings around most of his team-mates. When Eriksson launched his new regime against Spain last week, he said: "I wish I had 25 players like Paul Scholes."

This week Sir Alex Ferguson would have been pleased with at least half a dozen in the mould of the Salford boy who, when it was put to him that he had chosen a rum trade in which to be shy, smiled broadly and said in exaggerated North Mancunian: "Yeah, it's a problem, innit?" But for whom?

Not Scholes, certainly. He says: "I get all I want from football on the field. Basically, I'm a very shy person. I don't know why this is, but it's a fact. I don't worry about it. It doesn't get in the way of my football." Inevitably, there was a point of harsh comparison this week in the performances of Scholes, who was never less than relevant to the action, and that of his superstar team-mate David Beckham.

Even as Beckham's form dwindles to all but nothing, his publicity swirls on.

While two-year-old Brooklyn Beckham's birthday party soared, inevitably, into a picture splash in the tabloids and glossy magazines, Scholes' son Aaron Jack showed up with his rather glum-looking father as a bit player in another publicity-orientated Beckham family show. But the role reversal was rather dramatic in the stadium in Athens.

While Beckham's presence was again worryingly slight, Scholes' refusal to accept second place was finally rewarded when a fiercely struck shot flew into the Panathinaikos net. So, you might say, what? The point is that somewhere along the line values have become rather severely twisted.

Beckham, it seems, has won himself a place in the regard of the public and the media out of all proportion to his achievements. His marriage to Posh Spice, his presence in an all-conquering United team, his willingness to promote himself at almost every opportunity, and his undoubted natural gifts, have inevitably created huge celebrity. But at what point does the fame intrude on football judgement?

Certainly it is interesting to speculate on how long Beckham's captaincy of England, which was presented to Eriksson as something of a *fait accompli*, would survive performances as inept as the one in Athens. It is fair to assume that Eriksson, desperate for signs of authority, of needle-sharp form, before the big game with Finland later this month, was privately appalled by Beckham's zero influence on Wednesday's game.

In the most basic area of statistics, goalscoring, the international records of Scholes and Beckham simply do not stand comparison. In 38 games Beckham has scored one, a beautifully flighted free-kick against Colombia in the World Cup. Scholes has scored 10 goals while making seven fewer appearances. It is true that Beckham has played mostly wide on the right, and that his crossing and free-kicks have often been tremendous assets to the team. But from where does the great disparity in fame and appreciation come? Not, surely, in any serious assessment of the relative contributions of the two players to their club and their country.

At the end of last season's title campaign, Ferguson said it was hard to say who was his most influential performer – Scholes or captain Roy Keane. Meanwhile, Beckham makes documentaries, sells picture books, puts in a public application for the captaincy of his country, and re-states his ambition to be voted the world's No 1 footballer; all of it, we have to presume, coming in the absence of an authoritative voice demanding a little less profile and rather more performance. If such a voice is to be heard, and surely the chances are that it will come in a Scottish accent, you have to suspect that now is the time.

Certainly Ferguson's disillusionment with his team's performance in Athens could not have been more plainly stated. But for the pyrotechnics of Fabien Barthez, and the resilience of Scholes and Keane, United would surely have been thrashed. As it is, they remain on course for another formal annexation of the Premiership title and another shot at the European Cup.

In the big arena of Europe, United's chances of success clearly hinge hugely on the willingness of the rest of the team to take the hard road of Scholes and Keane. In one of his more loquacious moments, Scholes made a stab at assessing his strengths as a footballer. He said: "I like to think I can make chances and score goals. That's it really. The first thing I do when I get the ball is look up and see what run the centre-forward is making and, if he's in, there's no point in looking for someone else if there's a chance of playing him through. If that's not on, I have to make sure that I protect the ball and get it to one of my team-mates."

That, from Scholes, is a speech, a declaration of ambition, a lurch into the airwaves of publicity that he so distrusts. It is also, as it happens and perhaps not coincidentally, the vital, basic code of all great footballers.

HODDLE RISKS ALL IN SPURS' TRAVESTY OF GLORY GAME

Published: 31 March 2001

Tottenham's new owners and Glenn Hoddle might be said to deserve each other. If George Graham had been an impudent office boy he could scarcely have been fired with less style or dignity, and Hoddle's much trumpeted Christianity plainly does not include any squeamishness about stepping into the shoes of dead football men.

In just over a year he has now blithely inherited the jobs of two excellent managers cut down with stomach-wrenching cynicism by their clubs.

Still, we should probably put a cap on the moral outrage. Anyone who follows modern football in the hope of finding a decent measure of finer feeling, not to mention altruism, is going to give himself a severely hard time. Perhaps the more intriguing question concerns that which passes for a mature thought process in the mind of the average Spurs fan.

Whatever his IQ, or the distinction he has achieved in his own business, it seems that the mere click of the White Hart Lane turnstile is enough to send him into wild and, when you get round to proper analysis of it, rather disagreeable fantasy.

Most football fans love their team, and often their affection can amount to a mild form of mental disorder. But if Manchester United fans believe fanatically in their right to win, if Liverpool, whose tradition makes that of Spurs look puny indeed, tend to fall back on rather mordant wit, the Tottenhamite makes his own childlike world. He is a bit like a troubled adult who pines for an idyllic youth which, tragically, did not really exist.

In Tottenham's case it did, of course, albeit briefly and before most of the current following were either born or out of short trousers. Blanchflower and Mackay, White and Jones were something indeed, and then, rekindling that glory there was Greaves and later, fleetingly, Gascoigne. Hoddle straddled the days of achievement and those of yearning. He inhabited the fantasy without ever making himself, either for Spurs or England, a fulcrum of success. He was a vision in a world of football Camelot, a wanderer in a field of endless dreams.

This week it has been reported that Hoddle could have a budget stretching up to £50m. If he doesn't now, he will know soon enough that he will need every penny of it. If he is a hugely popular figure at White Hart Lane, he also carries a terrible burden. He is a man who has to do rather more than win a few football matches. He embodies the dream and, if he cannot make it happen in real life, who can? If he fails, the fantasy game could, finally, be over.

Graham in a way facilitated Tottenham's dreaming. As long as he was there, with his Arsenal connection, his financial constraints, he could be the symbol of frustration, the man delaying the dream. But with Graham gone, reality kicks in. The fans have their man of destiny and the owners no longer have Graham to kick around.

So having helped to drive out a football man of Graham's quality for no better reason that he once happened to work, brilliantly, for Arsenal, and that most Saturdays the caperings of the celebrated David Ginola were a frontal assault on what he expected of a hugely rewarded individual engaged in a team game, the Tottenham fan now explodes with joy at the arrival of the messiah, Hoddle. Waiting for this arrival, the Spurs fan has sometimes resembled a cargo worshipper of the South Pacific, but now the tide is in he might do himself a favour, and give the rest of us a little peace, by actually inspecting quite what it has brought. The truth is there is something ugly on the shoreline.

It is one of the shoddiest episodes in the history of English football. It is a mixture of irrational mob prejudice against Graham, cloying sentiment for Hoddle, and crude manipulation by the new boardroom. Nor should Southampton's contribution to this travesty of the glory game be minimised. They cut adrift their manager, David Jones, who had done so much to build the club's security, even as he first embarked on a campaign to clear himself of criminal charges that, soon enough, were thrown out of court. Hoddle was handed the job of Jones, who, it was said at the time, was taking a leave of absence.

Now Southampton's chairman, Rupert Lowe, is demanding the best part of £1m compensation for the loss of his "caretaker". He is also asking Tottenham to pay the bonuses Hoddle earned at Southampton. It is against the background of such behaviour that John Barnwell, of the League Managers' Association, pleads again for some regulations governing managerial contracts. It is a cry made empty by the repeated failure of Barnwell's members to act in the common interest. A simple declaration that no member of the LMA would accept a job while its previous occupant's contract was unresolved would help, but repeatedly the proposal has gone without support.

There is always the self-interest factor which Hoddle just recently has come to embody. He may well feel, as so many Spurs fans do, that he is simply fulfilling his destiny to lead Spurs back to where they fondly believe they belong, that mythic place where victories are always accompanied by dreamily perfect style. Hoddle of course has never lacked self-belief. Once, as a young player, he scored a beautiful goal at White Hart Lane. Wide on the right, he produced a shot that dropped exquisitely inside the far post. Later, the Burnley winger Willie Morgan speculated that Hoddle might have intended a cross. The young hero was indignant. "It was top skill," he said, puckishly.

It was simple then. He had only to play to express himself. Now he has to deliver on the hopes that he has helped to nurture down the years. It is something to occupy his ambition for some time and no doubt it will fuel new enthusiasm at White Hart Lane. Meanwhile some of us will be inclined to simply let them get on with it. It is their business and they are welcome to it. They probably don't understand why it is a little too murky for some tastes.

FERGUSON BLINDED BY A ROMANTIC ILLUSION

Published: 22 May 2001

When the angst eases a little Sir Alex Ferguson will maybe realise he is in good company. Also, perhaps, that he is the author of his own plight. Whatever you do in football there comes a day when the chief beneficiaries of your best work – and was there ever such an opulent gang as the one that will count its shareholdings when Ferguson finally stomps his way out of Old Trafford? – cannot wait to see the back of you.

Sir Matt Busby's financial pay-off for making United a legend was a small share in the club gift shop given to him long before anyone realised it could be one of the best earners since the Mob dreamed up the numbers racket. Busby did get an office down the corridor and a presence which deeply complicated the operations of his successors, Wilf McGuiness and Frank O'Farrell, but then, in a way which Ferguson, untouched by the kind of emotion generated by the crash at Munich, could never be in these rougher days, he was uniquely untouchable. However, Busby too was short-changed. It is simply the way it is in football, always has been and always will be.

Bill Shankly walked around with his broken heart on his sleeve when his day was done at Anfield. Busby wrote to Stan Cullis of how wretched he felt about human nature the day Wolves sacked the man who brought world-wide attention to the Black Country. Leeds didn't lift a finger when Don Revie left for the England job, scarcely a surprise considering that one of the directors had wondered out aloud: "Why is it that the manager gets all the credit around here?" Jock Stein, like Ferguson at United now, was offered little or nothing when his time was through at Celtic Park. Derby County players threatened to hack down the boardroom door with an axe, but Brian Clough was still a goner. We could go on for some time, but the point is scarcely in need of reinforcement. Football in this country has always taken the best of a man and spat out the rest.

Why, you have to wonder, did Ferguson think his situation would be any different? Maybe because he remains out on his own in terms of performance, because when you look for reasons why United became the richest sports franchise in the world you begin and end with him. This last season he had the

Premiership won so many weeks before his rivals for the manager of the year award, Gérard Houllier and David O'Leary, settled their dispute about not who would finish second but third. Ferguson did it so so easily, too easily, too effortlessly perhaps for his own good, and when he happened to fall at the quarter-final stage of the League of Champions the reproaches were directed, legitimately, not at his door but those of the directors who had so palpably failed to provide him with the means to strengthen a team plainly in need of fresh sustenance at the highest level.

Ferguson's classic mistake was to feed in all the pluses of his situation and forget the one overwhelming minus. He forgot the ultimate rule in a business where so easily you can become impaled upon your own success. You can only negotiate from strength and Ferguson threw most of his away when he set a date for his own retirement. Suddenly all Ferguson's glory, all the profits he had created, were more or less wiped away.

The King, this most obstreperous of rulers, might not be dead but soon enough there would be a new one. That inevitably changed everything.

More than anything, the Ferguson business makes clear to us again the great division in football, one that has been relentlessly emphasised by the march of the plc ethos. Compared to the average businessman, there is something child-like about even the most sophisticated of football managers. It is a necessary component of their success. However practical they are about the nuts and bolts of winning football, they cannot erase a romantic streak. They believe that the nature of a club's success, and their contribution to it, is self-evident and that inevitably they will get their rewards. As we have seen once again at Old Trafford, it simply doesn't work like that.

Because it is so obvious to most of us why United have been such winners, because we remember how it was before he arrived with his one-eyed zeal, it may seem outrageous that in the stream of leaks from the United boardroom we have been fed so many mind-numbing statements, notably the suggestion that Ferguson would never sell one of the club's team strips. The one that caused me most bleak amusement was the hint that Ferguson was wanting "silly money" in exchange for his services as a "club ambassador." Silly money? If United paid Ferguson £1m a year to the day he died, no doubt as crusty and unforgiving as ever, they would still be able to measure surreal profits from the day he walked into the building.

But we should not be so surprised by the club's current position. If Ferguson had so much trouble getting decent pay rises at the peak of his success, and when he had to wrestle the board so hard for vital transfer seed-money, at a time when the chief shareholder, Martin Edwards, was talking about "the fans in suits" who occupied the boardroom and of the sanctity of the club's pay structure while collecting vast profits for share sales and planning to deliver the club to Rupert Murdoch, why would he expect smooth negotiations for a sweetheart retirement deal? Why did he expect to be embraced as a key member of the board, a wise head who would continue to help in putting distance between United and the rest of the English game? It was because he was a football man. Because he was so immersed in the present he forgot so much of what had happened in the past. Football parades itself as an escape from the realities of real life. But that is for the terraces and the executive boxes. Down below, football meets those realities. And the old football men, however great, always lose.

FANS SUFFER CAMPBELL'S WORLD-CLASS DOUBLE TALK

Published: 29 May 2001

Sol Campbell is not the first plutocrat footballer to take us all for fools and he certainly will not be the last. But he has achieved a kind of distinction these last few months. He has more consistently than anyone in his situation said one thing and done another without even a hint of shame.

He has talked about his passionate involvement with Spurs while all the time doggedly refusing to sit down and talk even in the vaguest terms about the possibility of his signing a new contract. In the process he deeply undermined the management of George Graham, who, so ludicrously as it turns out, had his loyalty to the Tottenham cause compared unfavourably with the super-zealot Campbell. Double-talk may be an institution in football, but no one pushed the convention harder than the big centre-half. Self-interest, even in the jungle of plc-driven football, should have some limits, and if they do exist Campbell has surely flown beyond them.

In one respect he is just another rich player attempting to stake out his true value in an overheated market. The fact that his reported demands of Spurs would have paid him roughly two and a half times Roy Keane's salary, thus rendering it blatantly absurd, does not interfere with that basic truth. Where the blood recoils at the situation Campbell and his agent have fashioned over long months of double-talk is the scale of the hypocrisy.

We all know the Campbell mantra by now. Money, he says relentlessly, is not the important thing; indeed it is nothing compared to the thrill of playing in the great theatres of European action, and this ambition, we are further led to believe, has created a terrible conflict because, as we know by heart now, Campbell is passionate in his feeling for Spurs.

It turned him into a rallying point of rebellion against the unpopular management of Graham. It led to a stream of assurances that he was a pivotal part of Tottenham's future. No one, it seemed if you listened to Campbell, cared more about the club's prospects. He was at one with the yearnings of the most passionate White Hart Lane fan.

Now, after his negotiating position has become public, he declares: "This has been the hardest decision of my football career. It has been a prolonged one because I wanted to give the club every opportunity to have inputs into my future. I will be 27 in September and need to be playing in the major European club competitions sooner rather than later. My decision has been based purely on football. My commitment to the club is there for all to see."

There is a lot to see, no doubt, but commitment without the reinforcement of a telephone number salary cheque is not the most visible. Indeed, if Campbell did not appear to be such a solemn individual, you might say there was a wonderful touch of the arch in the key phrase: "I wanted to give the club every opportunity to have inputs into my career." Clearly he meant the kind of inputs which tend to come in a Securicor van.

Having failed to come up with the booty, the Spurs negotiators were plainly dead. David Buchler, the club's vice-chairman who was so affronted by Graham's suggestion that he was perhaps not the ultimate expert on the ways of football, now declares that Spurs need to build a team "absolutely committed" to the future. We should wish him the heartiest good luck. Commitment is the cheapest word in football. We know that if only because it was scarcely ever off the lips of Sol Campbell, the man who had to tear himself away from Tottenham out of the sheer love of the game.

Yesterday Uefa, the game's governing body in Europe, announced a study into the possibilities of a cap not on individual salaries but a club's total payroll. Mr Buchler should not hold his breath.

FOOTBALL IN DIRE NEED OF A MORAL COMPASS

Published: 08 January 2002

Sam Hammam, who is some people's idea of a football folk hero, witlessly stimulates disorder in a football ground notorious for housing some of the nastiest fans in the game.

David O'Leary, who has more faces than Eve, and more positions than the Kama Sutra, complains that his 21-year-old serial offender Alan Smith, sent off for the sixth time, is cruelly imprisoned by his past. He then goes into the car park and has a row with Hammam that requires his chairman, Peter Ridsdale, to step in.

Claudio Ranieri is outraged at the idea that he should have thought twice before including in his squad, and eventually sending on to the field, John Terry, who a few months ago was stripped of the England Under-21 captaincy for his part in a drinking spree which outraged American travellers at the time of the New York terrorist attacks and now faces charges of affray and assault following an incident in a night-club less than 48 hours before an FA Cup tie at Norwich.

Chelsea's chairman Ken Bates is reported to have brusquely dismissed a Norwich fan who questioned the validity of the decision, but his famously blunt conversational style is not the issue here. However it was couched, the choice of Terry ultimately required his approval and this is the man who last week was extolling the intellectual superiority of his player Graeme Le Saux, saying how someone who often appears capable of provoking mayhem in a nunnery is more sinned against than sinner.

For weeks now the charge against football is that it is in dire need of a moral compass, some means of finding its way through to a consensus of decency before anarchy takes an absolute hold. But the blundering goes on, and all the while there is a lack of even one voice to say unequivocally that the national game has degenerated to gutter level. It means that each day football begins to resemble a little more some vast unedifying scrum, some spiritually-formless ground zero. Why? Is it simply a matter of greed and selfishness, a complete failure to understand that there is a point where self-interest becomes self-defeating? At root, yes.

Football lacks class. Football lacks respect. Most of all, it lacks intelligence. One of the problems shared by the morally dim – a condition which of course does not prevent progress of the ambitious and the acquisitive in areas where a sure instinct for right and wrong is not essential, the City of London and football boardrooms being two notable examples – is that they are never able to draw a limit on their tendency to believe that however outrageous their actions or statements there is always someone mug enough, or cynical enough, to go along for the dubious ride. The current disastrous downturn in football's image is accentuated by a mass of evidence that this may be true.

Thus we had Hammam, whose cavortings during his Cardiff City side's victory over Leeds set an appalling example for those fans who eventually spilled on to the field and made the closure of the ground seem like an absolute formality, praised in the Sky TV studios as a wonderful character by his former manager and match "analyst" Bobby Gould. Tell that to Dave Bassett, the manager effectively driven out of Wimbledon after taking them from non-League to the top flight. Tell it to the janitorial staff at Upton Park who had to clean up the obscene graffiti left by Hammam's "Crazy Gang" on a dressing-room wall. Tell it to all those appalled by Hammam's fervent sponsorship of the player he thought of "like a son", the long-time football thug Vinnie Jones.

Tell it to Joe Kinnear. Tell it to the fans who believed Hammam when he said Wimbledon FC was his life rather than his fortune, which he guaranteed when he flogged the club off to some Norwegian businessmen. Tell it to the birds.

O'Leary, who yesterday launched his book, *Leeds United on Trial*, of which he says he is so proud in the face of suggestions that it may well be the shoddiest literary enterprise since Glenn Hoddle's *World Cup Diary*, is angered by the fact that Smith is paying a price for his reputation.

As if Leeds are not the club who above all others in present circumstances should venture into the subject of natural justice with the circumspection of a bomb-disposal squad, O'Leary complains bitterly that the elbow thrown by Smith at Cardiff's Andy Legg did not warrant a red card. Perhaps a yellow card, then. That certainly would have triggered an interesting talking point in that earlier in the game Smith was caught on video aiming a petulant kick at Legg.

Smith has an appalling record – as O'Leary has accepted from time to time – which demands not special pleading but an understanding that too many liberties have already been taken. Last spring Smith was dismissed from a European Cup semi-final in Valencia for a dreadful, two-footed lunge at an opponent at a point in the game when the issue was no longer in doubt.

Leeds had paid heavily for the absence of Lee Bowyer, suspended on the eve of the game by Uefa, the governing body of European football, for an equally sickening offence, a stamping of the Valencia player Juan Sanchez in the first leg.

Despite the dancing of such disciplinary skeletons, O'Leary's emphasis at Cardiff was not on Smith's latest lack of professional control but the widespread deficiencies of referees, who, according to the manager, now lead lives of previously unimagined ease. Where, you had to wonder once again, was the football man willing to accept his own responsibilities before reminding everyone else of theirs?

Not at Arsenal, where one of the game's brightest individuals, Arsène Wenger, points out that his team's more competitive form this season coincides with a sharp increase in yellow and red cards. This was said in the wake of Thierry Henry's emotional rampage at Highbury recently, when he was so outraged by refereeing decisions he had to be restrained by his team-mates. At what point does a passion for success become a breakdown in professionalism? How many suspensions at any one time are acceptable to a club intent on winning major prizes? The whole argument is a nonsense, and its source is dismaying. Wenger's football belongs with the angels. His ideas on discipline should be kicked into the street.

Football may just argue that it is an easy target for a society not exactly redolent with moral vigour. But, if it does that, it misses another point. Football is a privileged world, of vast reward but also relentless attention. It needs saving not from its enemies but its apologists. That Sam Hammam, David O'Leary and Ken Bates should be able to operate in such a moral vacuum, that they should be granted credibility rather than unremitting scorn, is one huge part of the problem.

Hammam claims that he was simply behaving "normally" at Ninian Park. He always goes behind a goal before the end of a game. His intentions in running on the field were not to provoke a riot. Perhaps not, but did he think about the possible effect? Does O'Leary believe that his torrents of selective moral outrage have not yet been measured against his handling of the Bowyer-Woodgate affair, and the personal profit he will make from it at the bookstall, or that his platitudes still have the power to beguile anyone but the simple-minded? Does Ken Bates think that in the case of Terry he represents anything but appalling expediency?

Sooner or later the football tribe must stop to consider such questions, but it is hard to be optimistic. To solve a problem you first need to recognise it. Unfortunately, it is something that takes a little wit.

JONES AND WRIGHT EMBODY SICKNESS OF CELEBRITY GAME

Published: 15 January 2002

One of a number of obscure experts wheeled on to Channel Four's *100 Greatest Sporting Moments* show sneered that the 1953 FA Cup final, in which the late Sir Stanley Matthews dazzled and moved the nation, featured 13-stone players and a three-stone ball. Could anything have been more gratuitously offensive? Yes, I am afraid so. It was the identity of the man who did the wheeling. It was Vinnie Jones.

Having Jones associated with some of the finest moments of sporting history would be funny in a forlorn, one-off sort of way if it wasn't accompanied by the news that Ian Wright, whose disciplinary record as a professional footballer was in many ways just as wretched as Jones's and who did a Saturday morning radio show of such stupefying banality that the only safe reaction is to pull into the nearest lay-by and take a deep breath, is being hailed as the future of BBC television.

Wright has been been awarded a show at a reported fee of £700,000 – entitled *Right Here - Wright Now* – and this ringing endorsement from a source inside the Corporation: "Ian's got the right mix of chat, savvy, wit, openness, enthusiasm and credibility. Men want to be like him and women want to shag him."

This probably says more about some of the people in charge of our licence money than Wright, who does at times display a touch of skittish charm not totally disabled by his frequent inability to utter a coherent sentence. It is also true that Wright, unlike Jones, could actually play football.

Where they can be bracketed is in the way they so perfectly reflect the triumphant earning power of some of the more distorted values of today's celebrity game.

We really shouldn't pussyfoot here. If football had been properly run at the time of their worst excesses, Jones and Wright would have been drummed out of the game.

Wright would certainly not have been awarded a fat fee by the Football Association for a series of TV advertisements aimed at improving the game's image among young people – at a time when he was operating under a suspended ban for disciplinary offences. He was a brilliant striker, a record-breaker at Highbury, though some good judges felt that his late arrival in the professional game had given him a deep-seated insecurity on the field. If this was so, the effect was at times appalling. He abused referees and provoked fans, and when he once declared that his vision of leaving Arsenal was to do so in leathers and astride a Harley-Davidson it was suggested the Hell's Angels might be facing some PR problems. Now the thought seems quaint.

Wright is, consummately, a man of his age. Lionised at the TV Centre, an inflaming presence in the hearts of the nation's womenfolk, a man to be admired and envied, how brilliantly he has outrun his critics. This is not a surreal fantasy dreamed up by Wright while beating up the Guildford by-pass on his Harley. This is not the wish list of a *Big Brother* reject. This is happening, to Ian Wright and to us.

Jones's demeanour, Channel Four surely cannot have forgotten, was relentlessly thuggish. The career-wrecking tackle he performed on Tottenham's Gary Stevens is still capable of making the blood run cold. Jones boasted of his ambition to tear off the ear of Kenny Dalglish and spit down the hole, a sickening idea in itself and scarcely softened by the habit of the Wimbledon team of covering the old sign over the players' tunnel "This is Anfield" with spittle. He squeezed Paul Gascoigne's testicles as he augmented his hard-man image. In fact Jones's reputation as an "enforcer" is mocked by players of an older generation. Said one this week: "Tommy Smith and a dozen others I could name off the top of my head would have broken Jones's leg without him knowing until he came out of the anaesthetic. He was a phoney player, and a phoney hard man."

A good actor, though, they say in Hollywood. Fine. Let him play the celebrity thug. He did it in football long enough, some would say up to Oscar levels, but does anyone begin to have an idea why he would be chosen to celebrate the deeds of men like Muhammad Ali and Pelé, Roger Bannister and Don Bradman? Is it that celebrity, however fleeting, however hollow, is everything now and that name and face recognition can be separated so easily from what they actually represent?

Apparently so. A particularly angry letter, even by the standards of the *Racing Post*, last week railed against the selection of Jones as greyhound racing's Man of the Year. What had he done, apart from owning a dog, to deserve such an award? The answer was simple enough. He had become a celebrity. He had won a long race started back in the Eighties, when his

Wimbledon Crazy Gang – the pride of the rabble-rousing football profiteer Sam Hammam – volleyed their spit at the sign which Bill Shankly, in his cranky way, saw as an intimidatory symbol of what was important in the game: work and bearing and talent. Wimbledon spat out their contempt for such an idea. They would make their own sporting world, and of course they did. It didn't mean anything in football terms, it didn't produce a Great Sporting Moment, but it made Vinnie Jones.

One morning last week Terry Wogan was extemporising in his folksy fashion. "Is Stanley Matthews dead?" he asked. "Is Tom Finney dead?" Did anyone care? The tone of Wogan's voice suggested not. It's something that is liable to happen in a business which makes superstars out of a Vinnie Jones and an Ian Wright – a business which gathers together a mound of great sports footage, opens up its website to the voters, and hands out Vinnie Jones another nice little earner.

Is Tom Finney dead? No. But there must be times when, along with others of his generation, he can hardly tell the difference.

SPECTACLE OF GINOLA IS NEVER QUITE IN FOCUS

Published: 12 February 2002

Some of us will take a lot of convincing that John Gregory "destroyed and humiliated" David Ginola during the player's unhappy sojourn at Villa Park. This scepticism in response to the player's anguished recollections was rather reinforced on Sunday by the sight of him performing for his new club, Everton. As my wife said with a slight but still disturbing catch in her voice, he looked about as beaten-down as Adonis strolling into a singles bar.

What happened at Villa seemed pretty straightforward. Gregory had Ginola imposed upon him as one of chairman Doug Ellis's plays to the gallery. Ginola was a cut-price celebrity picked up to appease the peasants. If they couldn't have the bread of nutritious team-building, they could have a slice of cake.

Gregory had two decent choices. He could tell Ellis what to do with his initiative and walk away. Or he could treat the player with respect while trying to exploit the residue of his talent. Instead, he chose a third course. It involved a dismissively casual use of Ginola while peppering him with cheap shots.

It never looked liked working, and it is hard not to sympathise with some of the Frenchman's complaints. He hated the sneers about carrying "baggage" and the more or less permanent cold shoulder. If Gregory considered him superfluous to his needs, and that was the relentless message he sent out, there was still scope for a dignified handling of the situation.

There will, though, always be a complication in the relationship between a manager and a player. It is the huge regard such a performer builds for himself on the terraces. A Ginola offers colour and romance and spectacle. These are all important aspects of the professional game, but when Ginola claims to be the "last of the great entertainers" he misses an important point. Gregory's preoccupation – as was that of Ginola's boss at Tottenham, George Graham – was not with side-shows but the progress of a winning team.

There was a big difference, however, between the approaches of Gregory and Graham. The latter was quick to say that the player carried himself impeccably, worked in training and off the field never gave him reason to complain. The problem was on the field, where Ginola could no more satisfy Graham professionally than a busker might Sir Thomas Beecham.

Ginola, like another supremely gifted player who was also a misfit on the international stage, Matt Le Tissier, has proved capable of superior vaudeville. But consistent, relevant performance? The verdict has to be no, a reality scarcely grazed by the mind-numbing fact that a few years ago both the football writers and the players elected him Player of the Year. How did that happen? It was the purest whimsy.

God save us, no doubt, from a world without whimsy, but in the imperatives of any competitive business, it has to be a matter of degree.

Ginola's basic problem, one that cut dead his international career with France eight years ago, is that his beautiful touch is unsupported by a proper positional sense. Almost invariably he is ahead of the ball. Nine times out of 10, it seems, he has to perform great natural skills just to get into a starting position that great players make for themselves by instinct. A useful comparison can be made with Ginola's new team-mate Paul Gascoigne. Even with the etiolation brought by the years of waste, Gazza's sense of position is still pretty much at genius level. It is something that is hard to learn, and probably impossible at Ginola's stage of development.

So why would a knowing old pro like Walter Smith attempt to rescue Ginola's career as he has Gascoigne's? Because in his position, Smith will take what he can. He will mix and match and tinker as best he can. Ginola came to Goodison Park on a free, and if he has technical deficiencies he also has a God-like demeanour, some extraordinary basic talent and, when he isn't being pressed into a demeaning corner, a notably agreeable disposition.

Smith, be sure, will get something out of Ginola. He will coax his spirit, respect his pride. Gregory baldly dismissed such requirements.

With luck, Ginola will help Everton out of trouble. What he will never be able to do, you have to suspect, is contradict the assessment of Graham and Gregory that he was not likely to do a lot for the development of a seriously ambitious team. Also beyond him is any serious blurring of the line between a great entertainer and a great player. At least this must be the position held to by anyone who has been fortunate enough to see a fair measure of great players. Pelé, Di Stefano, Maradona, Cruyff, and, when his head was on securely, Best never sought to provide great entertainment. If the simple option was on they would take it. Skill was applied not as a luxury but a component of a game which inevitably produced moments when only the highest quality of play could produce the desired result.

We all have our favourite moments of football entertainment. Bruising though it was to the English psyche, Maradona's decisive goal in the Azteca Stadium in Mexico City was probably the most stunning passage of play. It was complete and consuming, and it came from somebody who was at the heart of the game. That's a place, sadly, where David Ginola is never likely to be.

KEANE IS NOT THE SOLE CULPRIT IN COLLISION OF GRAND EGOS

Published: 28 May 2002

Somewhere in the tortured thinking of the Irish midfield player Roy Keane and his country's manager, Mick McCarthy, something went missing.

It was not pride, heaven knows. They have been like fighting cocks in the matter of keeping face. They have slugged it out in the television studios and in the newspaper columns, and in Keane's case for a profit that would keep a large family in his native Cork in some luxury for several years.

After day-long rumours yesterday that a deal was being struck behind the scenes, that Keane would apologise on Irish national television and McCarthy would be presented with a compromise which he could accept, at least for the duration of the World Cup, the nightmare scenario was replayed all over again. Keane said he had nothing to apologise for, he had been talked into his newspaper columns by his agent, and that the rightness of his original decision to walk out on the team had been confirmed by the approval of his family.

How neat for Keane, how good for the conscience, but at this latest point of self-justification it is surely easy enough to identify that missing element. It is a moment of thought and care for the yearnings of an entire nation. However we may question the validity of the sporting metaphor when applied to the realities of life, we know for a livid fact that a light went out in the spirit of Ireland when Keane stormed away from the World Cup camp.

No doubt the wound will heal soon enough, but for the moment it is angry and Keane's television appearance can only have served as a shovel-full of salt. Keane said that playing in the World Cup was the biggest thing, but he gave McCarthy no room to move. Certainly no more than McCarthy had given him when he first erupted so angrily last week.

Both men have ferociously defended their own position, and no doubt conventional wisdom would insist that McCarthy, if he was to continue as manager of the team, had no option but to follow such a course. It is true – but only to a point. Keane's anger had triggered the crisis but it was not its only cause, and it is why there is a such a split in the reaction of the Irish people. McCarthy was plainly the winner of the publicity battle before Keane stomped into view of the cameras again yesterday, but it is idle to pretend that the player can comfortably be assigned all blame.

What inflamed him so catastrophically that hot morning on the training field? What sent the water bottle crashing to the ground? It was not, even the worst of critics would have to concede, entirely the arrogance of one great but troubled player.

It was also about the frustration of a superb professional who had done, the most casual observer of Ireland's march to these World Cup finals could confirm, more than anyone around him, who went to work seriously and found something out of his worst dream.

A training field so hard it threatened fresh aggravation to the injuries he had carried without flinching for most of the season. A chaos of organisation which left the training kit in the team hotel. A bitter sense that some of his late-drinking colleagues might be less focused on the challenge than himself.

His complaints have been well aired, of course, and none of them excuse the extremity of his reaction. But, if they are not an excuse, they are a reason which may well resonate among some of those Irish fans so sickened by the loss of their team's most striking asset. In a football age of huge rewards and sometimes questionable commitment, Keane's explosion is bound to draw a little sympathy.

He was not caught in a night-club at 3am. He was apprehended on a training field that he considered an insult, raising a fist at standards which he long ago left in the slipstream of a phenomenal career.

That was certainly the case for the defence when Keane spoke to the nation at the eleventh hour. But, if Keane so violently deplores certain trends in the game he has made his personal battleground, he simply wallows in the fashionable principle that, whatever attitude you strike, whatever cause you argue, you do it on your own behalf.

That is all it came down to when Keane went before the television cameras last night. If the player must face the consequences of that, McCarthy himself cannot be too sanguine about his fate over the next few weeks.

When Ireland face Cameroon in their opening match they have to deal with a team of potential brilliance who have lost just one game of their last 17, which include the winning of the African Nations Cup. Their German coach, Winfried Schäfer, has created the sense of a team, and England felt the force of it in Japan last weekend when they struggled to salvage a draw. And the Irish have to do it without their one world-class player. McCarthy will say so be it, but did it really have to be?

It is a little too simplistic to say that the coach had only one course to follow. Could he have been a little more placatory at the outset, did he have to make the issue one between Roy Keane and himself and the rest of the squad, many of whom had reason to feel grateful to their coach for their presence on that foreign field? Was it enough to put Keane in his place and keep him there? There will be no quick verdict in the jury room of Irish public opinion, and really it is hard to see how there could be. Ultimately, Keane shaped the crisis and he has now shown little inclination to break it down.

He told Ireland that his conscience was clear and all the backroom deals that have ever been made across the length and breadth of his native land could offer no easy way out.

As Keane proclaimed his innocence, as McCarthy no doubt waited to further shore up his position, you could see more clearly than ever that this is not a battle of conscience but ego and pride.

It meant that now any breaking of the deadlock, any fudging of the issues between Roy Keane and Mick McCarthy, would constitute a farce. Together they travelled a short but bitter road of anger and pride and intransigence. It has made for the mother of football controversies, but it has left the team to whom they were both supposed to be committed a raggedy orphan indeed.

It would have taken a big man to give an inch, and maybe Keane and McCarthy will one day get round to reflecting upon that. But all the signs are that the World Cup of 2002 will be long gone by then. It may also occur to them that it can never be brought back.

ENGLAND SURRENDER TAMELY TO GAME'S FADED MASTERS

Published: 22 June 2002

The sun beat down mercilessly on England yesterday – and so must the judgement after Brazil, reduced to 10 men and at times, it seemed, down to the dregs of their fabulous football history, won 2-1 and staggered perilously on in pursuit of a fifth World Cup.

Defeat for Sven-Goran Eriksson's men was not the matter for indictment. The crime was in the way it was allowed to happen. The quarter-final, and England's best chance of winning the game's greatest prize since Sir Alf Ramsey's team beat the world in 1966, was not yielded in unremitting battle. It was surrendered, in spirit, in wit, and in the end even in basic competence.

That must be the hard and inevitable verdict on an England team that dared us to believe they could conjure a stunning triumph after surviving the Group of Death, running the favourites, Argentina, into the ground and almost casually cuffing aside Denmark, the conquerors of the reigning champions, France.

But it was hope that shrivelled in the heat here. It was hope that, despite the burst of irrigation provided by Michael Owen's superbly taken goal after the Brazilian defender Lucio had allowed the ball to bounce off his thigh and into the path of the Englishman they feared most, turned, step by leaden step, into a shattering illusion.

The Brazilian goals that destroyed England were executed, by Rivaldo and Ronaldinho, with all the panache that has fuelled the legends of their national game, but both of them had their roots in basic English error. The first came when David Beckham leaped over the ball and allowed it to flow, with the help of a mistimed tackle by his Manchester United team-mate Paul Scholes, to the feet of Ronaldinho, who fed Rivaldo with a perfect angle to drive the ball low past David Seaman.

Ronaldinho, inflamed by self-belief now, delivered the killer blow with a free-kick which will always torment the memory of Seaman, who would later tearfully apologise to the nation. Ronaldinho, who minutes later was harshly dismissed by the Mexican referee, Felipe Ramos Rizo, for a tackle on Danny Mills, claimed that it was entirely his intention to float the ball over the head of Seaman, who had strayed critically off his line. His claim was supported by his captain, Cafu, who said he pointed out the English goalkeeper's dangerously vulnerable position just seconds before his team-mate struck the ball. But these were the details of England's defeat. The meaning of it went deeper, and cruelly so.

It was about a sad failure to seize not just a moment filled with huge promise but an understanding of the rhythm and bite that is required at the highest level of the game.

Eriksson, who will surely survive yesterday's débâcle as the man who won qualification to these finals against the odds, produced victories over Germany and Argentina and then registered as his first credential as an international manager the impressive one of reaching the quarter-finals and going out to Brazil, admitted that his team had looked tired and had not displayed either the patience or the variety of passing which might have seriously tested 10 men fighting to close down space in the draining heat.

But much more damning was the view from the Brazilian dressing room. The goalkeeper Marcos, who had been required to produce a string of spectacular saves earlier in the week against Belgium, said: "I'm exhausted by the tension of the game, but not by England. In all the time we had just 10 men [35 minutes], they didn't give me one moment of concern. I didn't have a shot to save. I could hardly believe it."

Ronaldo, who complained of tiredness to his coach, Luiz Felipe Scolari, at half-time and was withdrawn shortly afterwards, said: "I'm not worried about not scoring against England – the boys had everything under control, and I'm saving a few goals for the semi-final and the final. Belgium gave us a far harder game. They tested us in defence and they put us under constant pressure. From England there was very little apart from Owen's goal."

That was England's shame. To lose is one thing. To lose absolutely, to lose physically and tactically and morally is quite another.

At the finish of the game Beckham signalled for his players to join him in a salute to all the English fans, native and Japanese, who came into the fierce sun with their faces daubed in the red and white paint of the cross of St George and cheered and sang long after it was obvious that Brazil, the faded but still recognisable masters of the game, could easily survive the loss of one man and, who knew, possibly more. But the England players seemed reluctant to join Beckham in any parade, and who could say they were not right in the reading of the mood of this ground and perhaps a nation back home which had been brought to a fine point of anticipation?

England had been the chameleons of this World Cup. Sterile, long-ball speculators against Sweden, superbly motivated in beating the Argentinians, pragmatic against Nigeria, and almost lordly in their smash-and-grab assault on Denmark, this was to be their moment of truth. It would be the truth about England's potential, and the quality of Beckham's leadership, and the ability of Paul Scholes and Nicky Butt to confirm their status as world-class operators at a pivotal point in a World Cup which seemed be beckoning them forward with rare promises, and the defensive composure of Rio Ferdinand and Sol Campbell.

But the truth was unwelcome in its harshness. It said that we had put too much faith too early in Eriksson's imposition of new values. Beckham has plainly been required to operate at much less than proper fitness here, and it may have been his concern at fresh injury that induced his little leap over the ball and away from the crucial action. But the symbolism of it was terrible. You do not surrender the ball to Brazilians. You fight them on every inch of the field because if you do it hard enough, relentlessly enough, you might just put a few question marks against their assumption that they will always find a way to win.

England did not begin to make such an interrogation, and the emptiness of their game and their spirit was all the harder to accept after the sight of Owen seizing so voraciously on the clumsiness of Lucio. The moment Owen found space with the ball in front of Marcos you knew it was a goal, and you thought you knew that England were on their way.

Brazil, surely, were broken, all their fears about the soft underbelly of their defence against sustained pressure blazing into disabling life.

But it never began to develop like that. Owen, as well as Beckham, was clearly only on the edge of fitness, and as anything like a proper service to his feet failed to materialise, so dwindled the threat he had represented so menacingly to Brazilian hearts.

The Brazilian hearts, as it turned out, were much more steadfast and though Ronaldinho misses the semi-final against either Senegal or Turkey, the chances are that he will get another opportunity to inflict his mesmerising touch and thrilling speed in the final in Yokohama a week tomorrow. He could yet prove himself the player of this World Cup. Such a possibility is painfully academic for England now as they fly home stripped of the glory they said they could almost taste.

There is little comfort to offer them in the bitterness of their retreat. It was a defeat, they will have to accept, that they fashioned for themselves.

England surrender tamely to game's faded masters

BOY WITH WORLD AT HIS FEET STRIDES INTO A MINEFIELD OF FAME

Published: 22 October 2002

Forty eight hours on, the blood still pulses with the thrill of young Wayne Rooney's goal. But now, perhaps inevitably, there is a little ice in the veins. Ten days after the appointment of his new, big-time agents, his signing-on ceremony for Everton is delayed for at least a month.

On Saturday morning he was a big, wonderful prospect. On Saturday night he was a property, one, if this was your business, you wouldn't want to rush into a sentimental and perhaps cut-price signing ritual. Business is business, and it doesn't really matter that the kid is only 16 years old.

Old enough to keep a level head? Old enough not to be dazzled, and becalmed, by an earning power which means that whatever happened he would leave the game a rich man – after one goal? Old enough just to keep on playing as though it was precisely what he was born to do? These are questions which will not figure in his first professional contract.

First, though, there was the goal that changed everything so quickly. It has fired up so many memories of those moments which are most precious in sport, the kind that brought the charge when you first saw Muhammad Ali, or the turn of Nijinksy's hoof, or Brian Lara sending the ball like a bullet past a stationary cover point.

Sometimes sport takes you into its confidence. It shows you something quite stunning – and beyond any misinterpretation.

Rooney's goal beat the best team in England and if you had any doubts about its quality, and what it could mean to the future of the game in this country, they were surely largely dispelled by the widely reported reaction of Arsenal's manager, Arsène Wenger.

Understandably his eulogy of the goal, and the potential of the boy who scored it, has been given massive coverage, and rightly so. In the black and white of newsprint, Wenger's unequivocal statement that Rooney is the most naturally talented young Englishman he has ever seen was dramatic enough. But to be around him when he said it was to increase the effect. Wenger's response flew so far above the usual disingenuous post-game reflections. He had been beaten but also thrilled by that thing most guaranteed to excite a football man, especially one with Wenger's reputation as the manager with the golden signing arm: evidence of unique talent. So Wenger's eyes glowed even more brightly than his words.

But if that exhilaration stayed in the blood yesterday, there was also something else. It was that familiar chill which came with the news that Rooney's signing of professional terms with Everton had been put on hold.

Earlier this month Rooney's football affairs were taken over by the agency Pro-Active, which is the firm of Paul Stretford, who came to most early notice with his stewardship – if this is not a contradiction in terms – of the career of Stan Collymore. This is, of course, in itself no reflection on the professional expertise of Mr Stretford. Indeed, it might be said that Collymore's football life was so volatile its proper control would have probably tested not only a squad of agents and motivational experts but also a middle-sized regiment of the line.

Still, the sudden juxtaposition of the names of Rooney and Collymore is unfortunate. It is, at the very least, a crushing reminder that the mere possession of outstanding talent is so far from a guarantee of success in today's game. Collymore was an extraordinary prospect. He operated at a time when Alan Shearer was head and shoulders above all English strikers, but there were times when Collymore made a nonsense of that status. He scored a goal at White Hart Lane, while admittedly some years older than today's Rooney, which was received in awed silence. He was a giant stunted by his erratic nature – and his opulent times.

The prospects for Rooney on the face of it appear so much better. He is devoted to football, his younger brothers are already on his trail, and in David Moyes he has a young Everton manager whose passion and decency are already bywords in the game. But then he is just 16 and it is said that Paul Gascoigne lived for football when he was that age; it was his buffer against an unpromising world. George Best was the supreme football animal, sleek and brilliant, and his appetite to play was so immense that he remained the outstanding trainer at Manchester United even on those frequent occasions when he arrived straight from the pub.

The force of celebrity did in Best; that, and the fact that Manchester United were slow to see its ravaging effects on their stunning asset. When Frank O'Farrell took over at United, Best's fate was just about settled. He went off on a drinking spree in Marbella while the rest of the team toured Majorca and Israel. O'Farrell said: "I worry about George in 20 or 30 years' time. He still has his fame and his looks but how will he be when they have gone." Well, the fame never left and Best, as the grand old man of football rebellion, has never been one for regrets.

Gascoigne may not be so philosophical and it is no harder recalling the words of his Tottenham manager, Terry Venables, than those of O'Farrell. "Sometimes," said Venables as Gascoigne's career careered from one crisis to another, "I look at the face of Maradona, I see all the pain in it and I just hope I don't see the same look on Gazza's face down the road." Venables had briefly known the chaos of Maradona's life in Barcelona, where the ill-starred Argentinian already had an entourage which included a barber and a priest.

Such self-destruction is plainly not imminent in the life of Wayne Rooney, and it would be naïve to believe that a talent of such obvious weight would not already be automatically in the hands of high-powered agents. Yesterday's news merely broke the spell of Rooney's goal and that sense that maybe for a little while the pattern of decades of accumulating wealth and changing priorities in our football players had been pushed aside by the simple need of a young man to play the game for which he is so brilliantly equipped.

At least one old pro, deeply impressed by the young man's presence on the field, is prepared to be optimistic. He says: "There is no doubt that the atmosphere around football today often works against a kid keeping focused simply on his game and letting the rewards look after themselves. But a lot of the talk about careful handling of young talent really misses the point. I'm sure David Moyes is a fine young manager, he has a great reputation for honesty, but whatever he does, whatever the club does, or the boy's agent, the most vital thing of all is the boy's character.

"You cannot wet-nurse a kid for 24 hours. You cannot make him something he isn't. George Best threw his career away because that was his instinct, and he couldn't really fight it. The same is true of Gazza. Maybe this kid is different. Maybe he can put all the other stuff on one side and get on with the game because that is the most important thing to him. Looking at him on the field, there is reason to believe this might just be so. Michael Jordan and Tiger Woods are drenched in money. But they want to win, they still want to be the best."

It is, anyway, something to hope as the money men calculate the value of the goal that briefly made football stand still.

CANTONA'S ELEVATION AN INSULT TO FOOTBALL'S TRULY FAMOUS

Published: 03 December 2002

You may have wondered, as I did with some fervour, precisely which collection of idiots voted Paul Gascoigne into the new Football Hall of Fame ahead of eight members of England's one and only World Cup-winning team – not to mention several legions of brilliant Scottish, Welsh and Irish players who took the trouble to nurture and protect their extraordinary gifts.

Remarkably, one phone call yesterday yielded the full list of shame, which, fascinatingly as it turns out, is not largely comprised of gibbering disc jockeys, radio phone-in hosts and former political spin doctors. In fact, those yay-saying for Gazza might fairly be described as a potential brains trust of the battered old national game.

However, in a committee room seething with knowledge and experience it was decided that Gascoigne, the man-child wrecker of a thousand dreams, had superior claims to a place in the first shrine of the English game than Gary Lineker, the second-highest all-time scorer for England who went through an entire career without a single yellow card; the magnificently enduring Alan Shearer; and Sir Geoff Hurst, who many will no doubt remember scored a hat-trick in a World Cup final.

The panellists are fairly described as "distinguished" by the organisers of the poll, the National Football Museum which, not inappropriately, is housed in the Tom Finney Stand at Deepdale, home of Preston North End, the former "Invincibles" and founder members of the Football League. The names are Sir Bobby Charlton, Sir Alex Ferguson, Sir Bobby Robson, Sir Tom Finney, Jackie Charlton, Jimmy Armfield, Brian Clough, Alan Hansen, Jimmy Hill, Mark Lawrenson, Gary Lineker, David Platt, Jim Smith and Terry Venables.

A formidable gang, indeed, but we surely have to ask what they were all thinking about? One sees the influence of Ferguson, no doubt, in the choice of Eric Cantona as one of the first 22 male players to be ushered through the doors of permanent fame (there is, incidentally, not a whiff of controversy in the choice of the sole woman, Lily Parr, who scored more than a thousand goals for the Dick Kerr Ladies and once drew a crowd of 50,000 before an anxious Football Association closed down the rival petticoat peril.)

Ferguson, of course, sees Cantona as a huge talismanic factor in the building of his own regime at Old Trafford, but a more objective view might be that, whatever the Frenchman's value to Manchester United, a career record that included eight dismissals and an assault on a spectator sits rather uneasily in any pantheon of the game. The French will again be aghast at the English aggrandisement of a player they never forgave for costing them a World Cup place and generally behaving like an overgrown brat. It is also true that under any hard and comprehensive analysis Cantona, despite his psychological value as a catalyst of a new, young team, scarcely flies through any test of history. Hands up anyone who remembers him getting more than an odd kick in any of United's big European games?

At this point it may be worth reporting an anguished phone call from one panellist yesterday. He was so unenthusiastic about the choice of Gascoigne – whose contribution to Lazio, Rangers, Middlesbrough, Everton and England was shockingly slight after his catastrophic, self-destructing performance in the 1991 FA Cup final – and Cantona that he demanded that his name be omitted from the list of voters. When told that it would be impossible to grant his request, he groaned slowly, but, as one pointed out, he knows who he is... some other voters might be seen to be in need of providing documentary proof.

You may ask, who really cares? The short answer is anyone who has a feeling for football and understands the old truth that if you do not understand, and respect, what happened yesterday you are unlikely to have much of a clue about what the future should hold. Gordon Taylor, the chief executive of the Professional Footballers' Association, was at Sunday's celebration and is enthusiastic about the concept of a Hall of Fame.

Though diplomatically non-committal about the selections of Gascoigne and Cantona, he remains a supporter of the idea of recognising the great men of football's past. "The first time I saw a football museum was in Belgrade in 1988," recalls Taylor, "and I was very touched when I went to the Red Star stadium and saw that a centrepiece of the museum was a tribute to Manchester United, who played their last game in the city before the Munich disaster. I wondered how it was that United could be honoured in a foreign land in such a way and not in their own country. So in principle I'm a great supporter of this Hall of Fame."

The principle is fine, but the practice is in danger of becoming an insulting farce. Few could argue with the majority of the original selections – voted in along with Gascoigne and Cantona were Gordon Banks, George Best, Dixie Dean, John Charles, Bobby Charlton, Kenny Dalglish, Peter Doherty, Duncan Edwards, Tom Finney, Jimmy Greaves, Johnny Haynes, Kevin Keegan, Bryan Robson, Denis Law, Nat Lofthouse, Billy Wright, Stanley Matthews, Peter Shilton, Bobby Moore and Dave Mackay.

The trouble is that the choices of Gascoigne and Cantona sabotage any sense of a bottom-line standard. Both players had huge gifts, but under consideration here is a body of work – a consistency of achievement and discipline which is plainly lacking in both careers.

If you have a Hall of Fame, you also have to have a bank of memory and research. It cannot be a random and in this case flippant thing. If you have a first selection of six managers – in Sunday's case Sir Matt Busby, Brian Clough, Ferguson, Bob Paisley, Sir Alf Ramsey and Bill Shankly – how can you ignore the claims of Herbert Chapman, the father of Arsenal; Stan Cullis, who led English football into the wide world of international club football with his superb Wolves team; and Bill Nicholson, architect of the great Spurs Double-winning side?

You cannot really do it. If the work of Chapman, Cullis and Nicholson is not recognised now, when will it happen?

You cannot have a Hall of Fame which plucks out talented but historically slight figures like Gascoigne and Cantona and ignores a century of much deeper achievement. It is too much of a job to speak for all the ghosts of football but let us remember a few... Billy Meredith, Alex James, Hughie Gallacher, Cliff Bastin, Eddie Hapgood, Raich Carter, Wilf Mannion, Neil Franklin, Jimmy Delaney, Johnny Morris, Jack Rowley, Stan Pearson and Charlie Mitten (just to mention one Manchester United forward line), Johnny Carey, Tommy Lawton, Roy Bentley, Ivor Allchurch, Cliff Jones, Danny Blanchflower, Joe Mercer, Stan Mortensen, John White, Bobby Collins, Bobby Johnstone, Roger Byrne, Liam Whelan, Billy Bremner, John Giles...

None of these names were recognised by the Hall of Fame. What can you do? Just sigh and assure a member of a "distinguished" panel defining the greatness of English football that his secret is safe with me.

WEST HAM SADLY NOT ALONE IN SELLING SOUL TO SAVE THEIR LIVES

Published: 11 January 2003

When Lee Bowyer first arrived at West Ham, mouthing, in terms that made the flesh crawl, his platitudinous (albeit short-term) loyalty to the club of his roots, my friend the Hammers fan could not have been more outraged, or more emphatic that his team would no longer be included in his plans for Saturday afternoons.

"That's me, finished," he declared. "West Ham have meant so much all those years since my dad first took me to Upton Park, but I'm not prepared to support them now, not after the signing of Lee Bowyer."

He meant it, too. Gosh, how he meant it. He talked about how his wife, an American bemused by his passion, had been obliged to call him at all points, and through all time zones, with the football results. At first she had faltered over exotic names like Aston Villa and Tottenham Hotspur, but now, when she came to the West Ham result, she had all the inflection of James Alexander Gordon. But no more. Sod that.

You don't put a toerag in the shirt worn by Bobby Moore or Geoff Hurst or Martin Peters. You don't sign a Bowyer on the day when television is showing reruns of the nauseating stamping that brought him a six-match ban from Uefa, less than two years after a three-match suspension for a similar action in the first leg of a European Cup semi-final. You don't compromise everything you are supposed to stand for because a live body, and, to be scrupulously fair, a not unaccomplished player when he's up for it, becomes available and might just keep you the right side of the £16 million-odd a year TV bounty that automatically separates a Premiership club and the rest of football at the start of a season.

The trouble is that in today's football you do all of those things. When you look at a Bowyer, you are not interested in his antecedents but what he can do for you. Can he keep you among the live men walking around with a bit of change in their pockets? If you think he can, that is really all that matters. OK, some of your black players might not be thrilled to be playing alongside him. All right, the CV's not something you would unfurl with a flourish. The abuse of Asian staff in a McDonald's is not too edifying. His former manager David O'Leary's bald announcement that Bowyer was "a liar" and had dragged Leeds United's name into the gutter might, in other circumstances, provoke a pause. But, no, not now.

There is no recent precedent for principled stands against dwindling values. When Eric Cantona attacked a fan at Selhurst Park, he was defended by Manchester United, where Tommy Docherty was once hounded out of office for falling in love with another man's wife.

When Cantona attempted to repeat his assault on a TV cameraman, Sir Alex Ferguson said the photographer deserved anything that came to him. An unbridled attack on a supporter, however provocative he might be, would normally be an invitation to instant dismissal, and perhaps that would have happened had Cantona been a fringe player rather than the catalyst of United glory who also happened to sell a ton of souvenir shirts.

West Ham were already somewhat down this road when they signed Bowyer.

They did, after all, pick up Paolo di Canio after he had assaulted a referee, a fact that remained true even when you noted that the official had reacted rather like a refugee from a knock-about scene at the school pantomime. For all Di Canio's pyrotechnics at Upton Park, his value to the club overall, when you weigh his approach to discipline, his pathetic away form and his willingness to undermine any manager he plays for, and not least the incumbent at West Ham, Glenn Roeder, must be highly questionable.

Nor would a full-blown kick at the head of a fallen opponent at the training ground endear a player to a club which had any genuine connection with the best of its past. But cries that, in any decent organisation, John Hartson would have been marched off the property and had his contract cancelled after he booted Eyal Berkovic made no impression on the Upton Park boardroom. Hartson's goals could keep the Hammers up and there was his price in the market to consider.

You don't have to travel far from the Hartson outrage to the signing of Bowyer. It's just a hop, step and a jump over the sensitivities of those West Ham fans who talk about the club as though supporting it is part vocation, part privilege; and maybe the journey is made easier when someone such as Trevor Brooking, a great name of the past and a major sports politician these days, sums up Bowyer's last year or so in the game as a "torrid time". No high priest of euphemism can have been disappointed with that.

What West Ham have calculated on during these last few days is maybe the bleakest certainty of all. It is that if Bowyer, as well he might, does the business over the next few weeks, he will be embraced by more than a malignant minority on the terraces. When Bowyer played conspicuously well for Leeds last season, as he successfully defended himself against charges of racist-inspired assault, but not without incurring that damning assessment from his boss, there was no cooling of his popularity; quite the reverse. "Bowyer for England" was the chant.

Be prepared for such a chorus from Upton Park if Bowyer helps the Hammers escape from their downward spiral. My friend will not be adding to the din but, after reflecting on his initial, gut response, he will be sitting in the stand. "If I handed in my season ticket, three people would be fighting to sit where I have down the years," he said. "Habits die hard and, who knows, we might come through this to a better time."

He might see again the old values, and young players imbued with the spirit of Bobby Moore rather than the darkest night. You can only wish him luck. He doesn't need telling he shouldn't hope for too much.

ERIKSSON'S ROAD LEADS ENGLAND TO OBLIVION

Published: 14 February 2003

It is now self-evident. The promise of Sven-Goran Eriksson is in ruins. The Little Englanders who seemed so peevishly insular when they railed against the appointment of a "foreigner" have, at least in this specific case, been proved right. The Ice Man has melted before dismayed eyes.

There are degrees of defeat. Most defeats can be worked upon by a coach who is on top of his job. He can pinpoint areas of weakness. He can get an under-performing player back to some of the fundamentals that may have been blurred or neglected.

He can recognise telling slides in efficiency in certain areas of his team. He can break it all down and underline precisely where things are going wrong. He can embrace the fact that sometimes you can get a lot stronger at a broken place.

But you cannot do a whole lot with what happened to Eriksson's England this week, when they lost 3-1 to an Australian team who were playing together for the first time in 14 months. You cannot rebuild on shifting sand. You just have to watch all the particles blowing in the wind.

This truth was irresistible on a cold, bewildering night at the ground where Bobby Moore used to proclaim so imperiously with every stride and tackle and pass the value of a proper football education.

Of course, Eriksson is to some serious degree a victim of difficult circumstances. Sir Alex Ferguson and Arsène Wenger are ferocious in their refusal to give England, or any international team, any more use of their players than is absolutely necessary. We cannot blame a Scot and a Frenchman for this. They are merely doing their jobs and their unyielding stance on the club-and-country issue was never likely be softened by the sight of the Premiership marching into the Football Association's Soho Square offices and taking over the show.

But that does not justify Eriksson in his descent to the status of a Premiership lap-dog, systematically reducing all England preparation for competitive football to farce. If he cannot stage build-up games that do not insult both the public and the players who are involved, that do not shamefully devalue the international caps that used to be a prize but now come down like confetti, he should settle for three-day training sessions. He could play practice matches. He could stop games after 20 minutes, re-cast the teams, work on something new. He could tell Rio Ferdinand that looking a million dollars on the ball does not relieve you of the need to make tackles worth more than six cents – which was around the value of the unsuccessful effort the £30m defender made to stop Harry Kewell for the second goal.

What happened at Upton Park surely represented the end of a road that is plainly going nowhere. What could you do with the appalling performance of the "first team" in the first half? How could you relate it to the more optimistic scamperings of Wayne Rooney and Jermaine Jenas and their mates in the second half? You couldn't. There were no joins. Eriksson talked defensively of poor finishing and defensive mistakes. He was sounding as though he had been involved in a serious football match. He did not kid anyone and when the questioning sharpened there was quite a bit of evidence that he still had some way to go before he convinced himself.

While the Republic of Ireland's new manager, Brian Kerr, was talking about a mere "start" to his job after an impressive victory at Hampden Park, you could not help remembering the style of Eriksson's opening game in a friendly against Spain at Villa Park nearly two years ago. He started as he plainly meant to carry on, sending in a barrage of substitutes, which effectively robs a team performance of any shape or real meaning. As a start, Eriksson's approach was shrewd enough: deflect responsibility, reduce the significance of any one early defeat, go carefully. But eventually, surely, he needs to show us a team which, step by step, is moving forward.

Much was recently made of the pursuit of a new coach when Eriksson's assistant, Steve McClaren, decided to concentrate on his task as Middlesbrough manager. Why was such importance attached to what should be very much a supporting role? The England manager is necessarily a full-time observer of the national game – and no one can question Eriksson's annual mileage – and a part-time coach. But what does Eriksson do when the players are prised away from their clubs? What is his style, his priorities? We may never know. More vitally, nor may his players.

The word is that his input is not high. He is not a Ferguson or a Wenger. He does not rage at the gods. He peers impassively from behind his professor's rimless specs.

The sadness now is that his style promised so much. After the emotion-charged days of Kevin Keegan and Graham Taylor, and the egocentricities of Glenn Hoddle, he was a waft of common sense and sophistication. He rescued World Cup qualification. He was in charge of a hallucinogenic night in Munich. But the tail-off has been long and depressing.

Exploiting the unlikely success in Munich proved desperate work. Robbie Fowler rescued a nervy performance against Albania, David Beckham a much worse one against Greece. The opening game of the World Cup brought tactical chaos that degenerated into long-ball hoofing. A shadowy Argentina were beaten, with impressive bite and spirit – but only after Eriksson's original team was re-cast, and given width with the replacement of the injured Owen Hargreaves by Trevor Sinclair.

Denmark imploded in the round of 16 – a benefit which was squandered terribly against a 10-man Brazil, who in the previous round had laboured, with controversial assistance from the referee, past a lively but scarcely luminous Belgium.

The line on the graph which continued to dip in a poor performance against Slovakia and an abject one against Macedonia this week reached its lowest point in defeat by Australia. The Aussies picked their way through a shambles. Being who they are, naturally they made the most of it. They enjoyed themselves in the ruins of Eriksson's reign. No doubt, and probably sooner than later, they will be seen as the new boys of international football who shouted that the King had shed the last of his clothes.

THE LIGHT GOES OUT
FOR VENABLES

Published: 22 March 2003

As Terry Venables drove home to London yesterday, nursing wounds that may never heal enough for him to return to big-time football, he could only grimace at the last irony of his ill-starred eight-month reign at Leeds United.

Twenty-four hours before he was sacked by the club's floundering chairman, Peter Ridsdale, Venables and his wife, Yvette, had agreed to buy a house in a Yorkshire village next to a stud farm near Wetherby racecourse.

If Venables – whose stand-in replacement is Peter Reid, who has himself twice fallen off the managerial roundabout at Manchester City and, earlier this season, Sunderland – does elect to return to a television studio, the abandoned house in the Dales will serve well enough as a symbol of an itinerant football life which many will say was marked more than anything by missed opportunity – by doors which closed at the wrong time, adventures which were too quickly conceived and, maybe, too rapidly aborted.

At Leeds, though, justice insists that even his most relentless critics have to recognise that he was mostly a victim of circumstances which flew utterly beyond his control.

However, ambivalence will inevitably cling to any appraisal of a football career which has always carried the promise of high achievement – and certainly had its moments – but now may well be over without the under-pinning of the Premiership title which he allowed himself to dream might just be possible at Elland Road before near half his dressing-room was sold off without a hint of consultation.

John Giles, who walked away from football management at an early stage after some initial success at West Bromwich Albion and a brilliant playing career at Leeds, may yesterday have delivered the most telling epitaph of Venables' misadventure at his old club.

"In football terms," said Giles, "it seems to me that Terry was a victim of his own mind – most in the game finish up as just victims of football."

That last belief, you have to believe, coloured every phase of Venables' football career from the moment he hung up his boots at Crystal Palace after successful stints at Chelsea, Spurs and Queen's Park Rangers and representing his country at every level, including amateur.

The street-smart brain of the Dagenham-reared Venables, it seemed, took in the whole sweep of football management almost at one glance. He saw what happened to managerial titans like Stan Cullis, Matt Busby, Jock Stein, Bill Shankly, and Don Revie. He saw Stein die of a heart attack on the touchline after being offered the job of pools promoter by Celtic, the club he had lifted to the stars. He saw Shankly die of a broken heart. He saw Revie spend his last days filled with the pain of illness and angst over his final days in football. He saw Busby eke out a modestly rewarded retirement. He saw Wolves, out of a clear blue sky, order Cullis to drop off the keys of his club car and remove his personal effects.

Venables saw all that and swore he would never be caught in such a denouement. It meant that he was never up for the long march, the kind of trawling for glory which eventually brought Sir Alex Ferguson all of football's glittering prizes but no guarantee of proper financial rewards and lifetime financial security until his high-powered Irish racing friends, John Magnier and JP McManus, bought a slice of Manchester United.

So Venables chose a policy of hit-and-run, one which, in recent years, followers of Crystal Palace and Portsmouth have bitterly claimed was conducted at the expense of the financial security of their clubs. Venables angrily disputes such charges, saying that at Palace he merely entertained, and then demanded the honouring, of the extravagant offers made to him by the failed entrepreneur Mark Goldberg, and that at Fratton Park he was dealing with the family of the man who first planted the seeds of his ambition to own his own club.

It was during his second managerial assignment – at QPR – that the owner, Jim Gregory, who subsequently took control at Portsmouth, advised Venables that he should buy his own club so that he would be in full control of his own destiny. The idea hooked into Venables and he could never let it go. It led him to his personally disastrous partnership with Sir Alan Sugar, who came out of football with a £33m profit and a knighthood and with a finely honed vendetta against the man who had given him his window of opportunity. Venables made some mistakes of his own, including acquiring some business colleagues with CVs that made alarming reading, and his own idea of himself as a modern Elizabethan who could write novels, storm the City and maintain a consistently winning hand in football died hard and damagingly, not least when he was banned from holding a directorship.

Here, certainly, was the fuel for the categorisation of Venables as a "Cockney chancer" and a tide of criticism that at its most hysterical pitch can only be described as disordered. The truth, for all his misjudgements about the way the world might evaluate his actions, lies elsewhere. It is, heaven knows, a not uncomplicated truth.

At Barcelona, where he won the league title after years of dominance by Real Madrid and came within a penalty shoot-out of winning the European Cup, his feelings about the vulnerability of the football man were heavily reinforced. He knew he was one of an expendable line, another roll of the club president's dice like Johan Cruyff and Cesar Menotti and Bobby Robson, and soon enough he was at Tottenham, and having his best players sold and, on the morning of the day he won the FA Cup, arranging a rescue meeting under the unforgiving gaze of a creditor bank.

As Giles observed, Venables had a mind to see the pitfalls of football management in a way that the great managers did not. They served their time in the tunnel and, because of their passion and their narrower obsessions, came out covered in public glory and private regrets.

There was the paradox which so many times ambushed Terry Venables. He saw the problems but he thought he could beat them by giving himself options. Perhaps too many options; at least more than a Stein or a Busby or a Ferguson ever had to confront.

He won respect as coach of England and Australia, but suffered some cruel fate. At the Football Association he could never shake the image in which his critics insisted he be draped. He was putty in the hands of the crudest makers of caricature, but you never heard a player say a bad word about him, and at Middlesbrough a few years ago he made a great statement about his enduring ability to inspire a broken team and shape coherent tactics.

For a while the Leeds fans swallowed the "Cockney chancer" reputation whole, but Venables stayed around with considerable dignity and those who reviled him came to see him through different eyes. They saw a man who cared about what he was doing, a man of pride who rode the disappointments of his first deflating months at the club, when, unquestionably, he had reason to be disappointed with his impact on a squad which was still stocked with great ability.

Yesterday all that became another inconclusive chapter in the football life and times of Terry Venables. Regrets for the sometime crooner at Hammersmith Palais? Not too few to mention, no doubt, but then he does not have to suffer the burden of carrying the heaviest one of them all. He never ran before unpromising odds. He always tried to win the battle on his own terms, something even the greatest of football managers, in the end, never quite achieved.

HONOURS UNEVEN FOR 'FORGOTTEN FIVE' AS BECKHAM 'MERITS' A HIGHER AWARD

Published: 09 June 2003

Three years ago Alan Ball, George Cohen, Roger Hunt, Nobby Stiles and Ray Wilson went to Buckingham Palace to receive the MBE – the most modest gift of the honours system.

It was 34 years after they had helped to win the World Cup on the greatest single day in the history of English sport. Many people, including the players themselves, were not so much gratified as relieved. However belatedly, a scandal of neglect had been put to bed.

When Cohen was notified by Downing Street he detected almost a tone of embarrassment. How would he react to the award? Cohen said: "I would say thank you very much." He was also told there had been some difficulty in contacting him. "We got your number from Nobby Stiles," said the official. Cohen thought it did not say a lot for the Secret Service.

After handing out the MBEs the Queen said, somewhat reflectively: "It's been a long-time".

The reaction of the "Forgotten Five" was muted, though that evening they had a fine dinner in a five-star hotel near the Palace and Cohen said to his team-mates and friends: "Let's celebrate that day we will never forget – and the fact that unlike Bobby [captain Moore] we are still around to share this honour with our families." Cohen had by now fought off cancer three times.

All of this put into a certain perspective the weekend news leak that David Beckham, whose own World Cup efforts have met with conspicuous, and, some would say, rather inglorious failure, had been awarded the Order of the British Empire for his "services to football". The OBE is a notch up from the MBE, which was recently described by a leading civil servant as something which tends to be awarded "for something achieved locally".

Beckham's award caused little surprise – and still less consternation – in the Ball, Cohen, Hunt, Stiles and the Wilson households. Wilson, who works as an undertaker in West Yorkshire, said: "It's hardly a shock is it? The lad is in the papers every day. He doesn't seem a bad lad, but personally I couldn't do with all that publicity. It was something that I avoided when I was a player. It made me uneasy.

"People often ask me how I feel about the rewards of the players today, and how they compare to when I was playing. I tell them it doesn't cause me to bat an eyelid. I know what I got from my career and I don't blame David Beckham for the fact that the world has changed so much.

"I still consider myself the luckiest man alive to have played in that World Cup final and shared it with the other lads. We were a real team and that feeling has carried on down the years. What you have to remember is that I grew up in a mining village and that there wasn't a day when I didn't want to wake up early and do what I loved so much. If young Beckham gets that satisfaction from his life, I'm just happy for him."

Roger Hunt, who in the opinion of many of his team-mates was the unsung hero of the World Cup win, a prodigious worker whose ceaseless running helped unlock the door for the hat-trick scorer in the final against West Germany, Sir Geoff Hurst, echoed Wilson's feelings.

"There is no doubt," he said yesterday, "that sometimes you wonder about the attention somebody like David Beckham gets. But I've no complaints if he behaves himself well, as he seems to, and gets on with his game. As for him getting his OBE now, while we had to wait 34 years for our MBEs, well, it's not his fault that things are so different. Not one of us can re-make the world, and failing that, there doesn't seem much point in complaining too much. What do you do? You live your life and are grateful for what you get. Anything else is a waste of time."

None of the "Forgotten Five" are inclined to make a point which for some others may have been hard to suppress with the first news that Beckham had skipped over them in the honours' pecking order.

It is that while Ball, Cohen, Hunt, Stiles and Wilson were vital elements in a team performance which created – it was said at the time – national celebrations unrivalled since the night of Victory in Europe in 1945, Beckham's own World Cup experiences are marked by spectacular failure.

In 1998 he was sent off in the vital quarter-final match against Argentina for a petulant, schoolboyish offence. He was 23 at the time – two years older than Ball when he was, by wide agreement, the outstanding player of the 1966 final as he ran the celebrated German full-back Karl-Heinz Schnellinger to the point of breakdown. In his recently published autobiography, Cohen, while writing of Hurst's final goal, said: "Schulz, the last line of German defence, was terribly compromised by Bally's last killing run in a game he had filled with his passion and unbreakable stamina."

Still Ball had to wait 34 years for his MBE. Beckham's superior OBE comes less than a year after England's miserable exit from the last World Cup in Japan, when the equalising goal which turned the quarter-final in favour of Brazil came directly from Beckham's decision to leap out of a tackle and grant his opponents free possession. They promptly translated their gift into a shattering goal by Rivaldo.

George Cohen was in his Kent garden when his wife Daphne heard the news of Beckham's honour on the radio. She went to the kitchen door and said: "George, you'll never guess, David Beckham's been given the OBE."

Yesterday Mrs Cohen confessed to a degree of irony. "I also said," she reported, "the only surprise is that he hasn't been given a knighthood, I suppose that will come next year. Really, he seems a nice enough lad, but you have to feel a little sorry for the boys who had to wait so long for a little recognition. They, after all, did win the World Cup."

George Cohen concluded his autobiography like this: "When the civil servant called to offer the MBE and I told Daphne, she smiled and said: 'Are you kidding?' The prize, such as it was, had come to us down through all the years that separated us from the gilded day at Wembley when our lives stood still. The phone call had come from Downing Street but as we embraced we did not need to say that really it might have been from another world."

Rather like the latest news of David Beckham.

BOYCOTT THREAT SHAMED THE HEROES OF '66

Published: 09 October 2003

Shortly before England's players last night stepped back from a decision to strike that would have clouded the rest of their careers, and made any future statement of patriotism from them no more valuable than a bent penny, their behaviour was appraised from another planet.

It was one inhabited by a compatriot, George Cohen, who had once helped to win the World Cup – and who would not have contemplated rejecting the England shirt at the point of a bayonet.

Aggrieved, but proud and vindicated in their own minds, the England team presented themselves as martyrs to a cause. Of what cause? It was hard to say beyond defence of their team-mate Rio Ferdinand, who was the only one to walk away from a drug test and go to a shopping mall.

When these England players returned from Japan last summer, Cohen was invited to join the campaign to lay on a triumphant return for the team which had reached the quarter-finals of the World Cup. The proposal was for a parade through the streets of London and a reception at Downing Street. Cohen remained silent for some time, long enough for his caller to check if he was still on the line. "Yes, I'm still here," said Cohen.

The ensuing conversation was quite brief. It went like this: "Well, what about it George, don't you think the lads deserve a parade?"

"No, not really."

"Why not?"

"Because in my time we didn't get any prizes for finishing eighth."

Cohen, who has three times resisted the advances of cancer since winning the World Cup in 1966, received £1,000 along with the rest of his team-mates and squad members after his captain, Bobby Moore, had suggested those who had played the majority of games waive the appearance-money bonus.

Back then, on a night described as the most blissful in England since Victory in Europe, players' wives and girlfriends were banished to a side-room when the team and officials celebrated the greatest achievement in the history of English sport. Last summer, Cohen noted that the squad had negotiated a deal which would have paid each of them around £250,000 if a second World

Cup was won. The wives and girlfriends of last night's potential strikers joined their menfolk in a luxury hotel in Dubai before the England party flew off for the tournament.

Last night Cohen was again taciturn when told that the England team were threatening not to get on the plane for Saturday's European Championship qualifier in Istanbul unless their team-mate Rio Ferdinand – dropped because he had failed to respond to a request for a routine drug test, a serious offence which in other sports could bring a two-year ban – was restored to the team.

There was, at first, another long pause – Cohen was a whippet of a full-back, a master of his trade, but nobody does the pregnant pause better. Then he said, quite softly: "This is simply beyond my comprehension. It is surely beyond belief and imagination that a group of English professional players, in any circumstances, would consider not playing for their country. And the reason! They are supporting a team-mate who has made a very serious mistake, broken an important rule.

"What do they think of the England shirt? What does it mean to them if they can even consider risking England's place in a major championship? What will the country think of this? What will the world think of this? I know the world has changed, but it will take a little time for this to sink in."

For those of us obliged to try to keep pace with the philosophical development of English football, who have been obliged to think of the Cohens and the Bobby Moores and the Geoff Hursts and the Nobby Stiles as the glorious fossils of another age, it was perhaps a little easier to absorb the day-long crisis of yesterday, when FA officials issued periodic statements that they were working towards "a solution".

We could handle it more easily, perhaps, because we didn't blast our way to World Cup glory and know that however the style of life changed in the next 30 or 40 years there would be an achievement, and a pride, which could never be broken. Where was the pride of England players yesterday in their schoolboyish bonding?

Who did they think they were helping? Rio Ferdinand? Did they really think the FA could re-instate him yesterday and still have a scrap of credibility? What kind of intelligent understanding of the situation was that?

They might have called Ferdinand and given him all their support on a personal level. They may have pointed out he had a made serious mistake but that he was still their friend and, hopefully, would soon be restored as their team-mate. But not playing for England? Not understanding the pressure on the FA against playing in an important international someone who had broken one of the fundamental rules governing the professional life of a top player?

The behaviour of Manchester United and the Professional Footballers' Association could only accentuate the sense of a game that had lost all grasp of its priorities and responsibilities. United say Ferdinand has been treated appallingly. They say the FA have ridden over his rights. At no point do they appear to have considered the seriousness of Ferdinand's offence. Perhaps they don't understand it, and that all the claims by Ferdinand that he doesn't take drugs do not deflect us from the fact that he walked away from a test it was his duty to take. He was clean 36 hours later. Of course he may have been clean when he should have been taking the test, but drug testing doesn't work like this. United say Ferdinand should have remained innocent until proven guilty. But his guilt has already been established. The rule has been broken.

And last night, Ferdinand's team-mates, led by their lauded captain, David Beckham, were, after finally agreeing to get on the plane, saying that they and their manager had been let down down by the ruling body. But they preened themselves on displaying great team spirit. They had been one for all and all for one. It all sounded quite pretty, even noble. But it didn't impress George Cohen, who knows about team spirit and winning the greatest prize of all in an England shirt. He was still on that other planet where playing for your country is not a matter of negotiation. Or foot stamping.

TIME FOR FERGUSON TO LEARN FROM ARSENAL NOT TO DEFEND THE INDEFENSIBLE

Published: 01 November 2003

Sir Alex Ferguson is right about one old thing. Just because you're paranoid doesn't mean the world isn't involved in some elaborate conspiracy to get you. At the very least, he is right to think that the Football Association punishment handed out to Arsenal players for their disgraceful behaviour at Old Trafford erred on the side of leniency.

Right to think it, but wrong to say it, especially in such terms of controlled venom. It will only the confirm the impression, one not restricted solely to Highbury, that he is about as dispassionately analytical as an inflamed wolverine.

Ferguson should have been big enough to see the positive result of the sentences handed down. The biggest dividend was the grovelling apology of his fiercest rivals, and their admission that the kind of outrageous conduct seen at Old Trafford could no longer be tolerated. But that would have required a wider view, a willingness to see that Manchester United and Arsenal were part of a wider – and embattled – football world and not the only self-obsessed players in some dismal points-scoring game. It needed a wider, more generous view, one that acknowledged some nodding acquaintance with the meaning of the word "league".

Of course, Arsenal and the FA made a deal. Of course, the club's reward for finally challenging the disciplinary myopia of their manager, Arsène Wenger, and accepting the charges against the club and the players, was insignificant fines and skimpy suspensions landing at a time of minimum embarrassment. But Fergie should ask himself a few important questions.

The first of them is about what he was doing when Arsenal were making their accommodation with football authority – and, not insignificantly, admitting that it was time to kick Wenger's appalling failure to control his players into touch. He was blustering his way into the middle of the Rio Ferdinand affair, at one point making the absurd statement that he was pleased with the unity displayed by Manchester United's England players, who had united behind the brainless advocacy of strike action by Gary Neville. That was a gratuitous challenge to the authority of the FA – and an insult to the country in which he has operated so long and so profitably.

Of course, a session on the rack would be no guarantee that the United manager could possibly be persuaded to see things that way. Nor is it likely that in his early sixties he will be converted to the value of diplomacy – or even a more subtle prosecution of self-interest.

One of the reasons why Ferguson is a great football manager is his inability to see through more than one red-tinted lens, but in a matter as delicate – and as profoundly important to the game's image – as the Ferdinand case, partisanship is not a help but a severe hindrance. The more he refused to accept certain realities, the more onus he was putting on the FA to take a firm line.

Arsenal's approach, after a short period of reflection, was precisely opposite. Unlike their manager, or Ferguson in the Ferdinand case, they looked up and measured the mood beyond the terraces of their own club. They saw that it was impossible to defend the indefensible.

So they held their hands up. The Arsenal chairman, Peter Hill-Wood, said that the offending players had behaved stupidly, and that punishment was required. Ferguson took the opposite view. Whereas stupidity was plainly a key element in Ferdinand's problems – as opposed to the poisonous display of malice produced by the Arsenal players who clustered around Ruud van Nistelrooy – Ferguson contented himself with rage that Ferdinand had not been presumed innocent until proved guilty. Unfortunately, Ferdinand was demonstrably guilty the moment he walked away from the drugs test.

Yesterday Ferguson was relentless of his criticism of the relationship between Arsenal and the FA. He said the leniency displayed towards Arsenal over a long period was a scandal, and he was quite right. He was also right that losing players against teams like Leicester and Portsmouth further minimised the damage to the offending club, and certainly he finds no argument here when he says that the suspensions were on the light side. Ashley Cole's escape from suspension was particularly grating on the spirit of an unbiased observer.

But where will the sniping end? Football in this country needs more than anything some sense of renewed values – and a willingness of heavyweight clubs like United and Arsenal to see that they have a duty to set some standards. However unwillingly, Arsenal have been dragged to this position by a show of strength from the FA. Without the threat of serious action, would Arsenal have sued for peace so briskly, and so soon after giving the green light to Sol Campbell's absurd claims that he was the victim of a conspiracy rather than the illegality of his own actions? It has to be extremely doubtful.

Equally questionable is the likelihood of Ferguson accepting that in all their success, and all their power, United ultimately will also be a victim if the credibility of English football continues to crumble. Yesterday he certainly didn't encourage any belief that he will ever see the good name of the game in terms other than of his own advantage.

NEVILLE SHOWS THE DANGERS OF PLAYER POWER

Published: 17 February 2004

Today it is the Eternal City in the wake of Clive Woodward's conquering legion. Tomorrow night it is Faro, Portugal, and something rather more passing: Sven-Goran Eriksson's under-achieving, over-pampered version of what a national team should be about.

Though you wouldn't wish injury on any professional sportsman, it is hard not to see the current one preventing the increasingly insufferable Gary Neville from travelling as something of a convenience. If ever a team needed to get hold of itself and impose a few standards, it is surely one that in its last competitive situation meandered to the edge of a strike.

The instigator of that bizarre possibility was, of course, Neville, who in his column in *The Times* yesterday delivered a staggeringly complacent assessment of the behaviour at the weekend which led to his dismissal from Manchester United's Cup tie with Manchester City after he dived for a penalty and head-butted City's Steve McManaman.

This was the key passage in Neville's version of the "Little Sparrow" Edith Piaf's *"Non, je ne regrette rien"*: "I am annoyed with myself because I will be suspended for some important matches but that is the only reason to regret what happened. It was out of character and I'm convinced that it was a one-off." The "Little Sparrow" pulled at your heartstrings. Neville, if you care anything about the level of thought and character to be expected from one of the nation's leading sportsmen, is more likely to make you feel as bilious as the proverbial parrot.

You have to be in a certain mindset not to feel even a touch sheepish about the travesty of professionalism which Neville produced. You have to believe you are beyond the judgement of ordinary men and women. You have to feel that in the normal course of events you simply cannot do wrong. The mindset can be identified easily enough. It is one that passes for thinking in most corners of English football.

Somewhere along the line Neville picked up some illusions about his potential as one of the game's statesmen. One of the first manifestations of this came after Euro 2000 when, before a World Cup qualifying game with Albania in Tirana, he announced that the England dressing-room was benefiting hugely from being in the control of a new generation of pros.

This was a thinly disguised reference to the end of the dominating influence of Alan Shearer. One of the fruits of this came last October in Istanbul when Neville was the chief spokesman for the faction arguing for strike action in protest over the dropping of Rio Ferdinand, another lion of the New England who, a few weeks earlier, had failed to take a drugs test because he had gone off to do some shopping. Shearer was in Istanbul as a spectator, which was just as well for Neville and his crew. The old pro's influence might have been exerted at the point of his boot.

The difference between Woodward's team in Rome and what we have come to fear from Eriksson's England is, there cannot any longer be much doubt, fashioned by a wholly contrasting set of expectations.

While the Football Association do not see any inherent problem in flying off to Madrid to "discuss" disciplinary procedures and team selection with David Beckham, Woodward makes it clear that Lawrence Dallaglio, an inspiring battle commander at the Stadio Flaminio on Sunday, is only as good as his last piece of leadership ... and 80 minutes of play.

Eriksson talks endlessly of his core of world-class players. Woodward drops Neil Back and Matt Dawson less than three months after they played key roles in winning the World Cup, Dawson's last-minute contribution to the drive which allowed Jonny Wilkinson to land the decisive drop goal already having entered the legends of the game.

England's football team, having trailed out of their World Cup so miserably, having lost to Australia at West Ham, and laboured with bone-chilling mediocrity against the likes of Macedonia and Slovakia, and, finally, having discussed seriously strike action on the eve of that vital European Championship qualifying game in Turkey, have no such underpinning. Their achievements lodge most persuasively in their own minds and Neville, it seems, is the most passionate of the converted.

A competent, much-capped international, he has been around the top of football for a long time now, but you have to wonder about how much professional wisdom he has accumulated. Certainly it is impossible to imagine, say, the great Paolo Maldini considering the rejection of the shirt of the Azzurri because one of his team-mates had behaved as unprofessionally as Ferdinand, or dismissing all criticism after an episode as shoddy as the one at Old Trafford.

Some talk of Neville's suitability as a long-term successor to the

Professional Footballers' Association chief executive, Gordon Taylor. On recent evidence the possibility is quite dismaying, though it is long odds that we will hear a whisper of criticism over Neville's latest performance from Taylor. Though quite prepared to tear into the embattled Eddie Gray over his dispute with his Leeds player David Batty, the PFA leader is not much inclined to chastise his own high-profile members.

Neville's lack of contrition for events at the weekend is just one example of a leading football professional making his own rules without a hint of censure from his own union. Consider the contempt with which Louis Saha, Jermain Defoe and Scott Parker held their contracts with Fulham, West Ham and Charlton respectively, note the lack of criticism from their professional body, and then compare that silence to Taylor's voluble attack on Gray's decision to exclude Batty from the Leeds team – a decision which did nothing to reduce the player's wage packet and certainly came within the manager's professional remit.

Gray has also run a gauntlet of criticism from the League Managers' Association over his lack of a Uefa coaching licence. A hugely talented and entirely professional player in his own time, Gray has now spent 40 years in the game. Disgusted with the self-enhancing growth of the game's bureaucracy, Gray has announced he will not be running off to some coaching course if he just happens to preserve, against all odds, Leeds' Premiership life.

Meanwhile, Gary Neville trumpets to the world: "I made a mistake on Saturday but I'm not going to beat myself up about it. After 500-odd senior games, my red card was only the second dismissal of my career, and the first, against Tottenham Hotspur, five years ago was for two bookable offences. Hardly a crimesheet for a defender to fret about." As things go in football, no doubt this is true, but perhaps a little moment of reflection was due after a flagrant dive and head-butting posturing that even drew criticism from his own manager, Sir Alex Ferguson.

What, you have to ask, would provoke a little fretting in Gary Neville? Not his uncritical support of a team-mate who had behaved as stupidly as Rio Ferdinand. Not the possibility that he might have provoked England's concession of the world's second most important international tournament.

Self-analysis just doesn't flourish in Eriksson's England, and perhaps the most telling evidence of all was when David Beckham was allowed to give a pep talk to errant fans before the game with Slovakia in Middlesbrough last spring – a match for which he was suspended after drawing an utterly gratuitous yellow card in the previous game against Turkey, and then, after scoring a penalty, running into a crowd well in the process of threatening their team's place in the competition.

Such unchallenged player power would not be countenanced in Woodward's England. When the coach faced his own insurrection a few years ago – created by the well founded suspicion of the players that they were being short-changed by their bosses at Twickenham – he said that if the strike happened he would scour the land for replacements.

In similar circumstances Eriksson allowed himself to be summoned from his dinner table by Beckham following a players' meeting and then insisted that he would make no public comment on the crisis that could so easily have eliminated his team and wiped away more than a year's work.

In Rome, another England left rather different imprints yesterday. *La Gazzetta dello Sport* ran the headline: "So much to admire about England – the world champions. They gave us a lesson." It is one also available much closer to home, but Gary Neville, we can be sure, is not about to enrol. He has no regrets. But then in English football, who has?

ARSENAL'S FLAWS STOP THEM REACHING TRUE LEVELS OF GREATNESS

Published: 09 March 2004

How good are Arsenal? Alan Hansen says that they are the most fluid, devastating team the British Isles has ever seen, and you can see easily enough why he might.

Certainly it is hard to recall any rivals to Hansen's mythic crown – the Spurs of Bill Nicholson, the Uniteds of [Sir Matt] Busby and [Sir Alex] Ferguson, the various Liverpools, Brian Clough's double-European Cup winners Nottingham Forest, Don Revie's Leeds at their most eviscerating and Jock Stein's Celtic – ever making the scoring of a goal seem quite so inevitable as do the men of Highbury.

At their best Arsenal not so much humiliate their opponents as bypass them. Their passing is acute to the point of incandescence. Their running is sublime. Henry, Vieira, Pires and Bergkamp achieve extraordinarily dynamic beauty, and those fortunate to share their canvas are inevitably enhanced. Arsène Wenger is utterly entitled to cluck his pleasure at such levels of technical perfection. It is a quality which in all his years of success in England he has never before been able to call upon with such certainty.

So maybe we should ask another question, one that invites a less fawning answer. Let's ask how great are Arsenal? What will all the fluidity and the devastation add up to in the end?

Liverpool's four European Cups? United's two? Forest's brace or even the ones of Aston Villa and Celtic, which was Britain's first and involved the unforgettable disrobing of Helenio Herrera's iron-clad defensive machine of Internazionale in Lisbon in 1967?

Indeed, can we assume they will beat Manchester United in the FA Cup semi-final and go on to match their greatest rivals' treble feat of 1999?

We may get a little more of a clue tomorrow night at Highbury when Arsenal have the opportunity to finish off their work against Celta Vigo, whom they lead 3-2, and pass into the final eight of the European Cup for the first time. The point here is that however much we swoon over the kind of football which ransacked Portsmouth in FA Cup action on Sunday, Arsenal do still have quite a few questions to resolve.

These have nothing to do with mere ability. Already this season Arsenal have deepened our sense of their sublime touch. I do not expect to see anything better than the Bergkamp-Vieira strike that brought Chelsea crashing back to earth at Highbury a few weeks ago, and no doubt aficionados could offer a dozen alternatives as Arsenal's goal of a thus far spectacularly triumphant season. But if the quest is indeed for greatness, then it surely cannot be denied that Wenger's men have some way to go.

What we have at the moment is an exaggerated version of Arsenal's past glory. We still have to be carried beyond the boundaries of great achievement. A whole Premiership season going undefeated would be an impressive mark, no doubt, but perhaps not quite enough to justify the hyperbole of Portsmouth manager Harry Redknapp, who declared: "Arsenal are the team of the future; athletes with lightning pace, power, ability and work-rate. They are very similar to the Ajax of the Seventies. They have such movement. They pop up everywhere."

Arsenal have great movement, indeed, but maybe not enough to win three European Cups on the reel, as the Ajax of Johan Cruyff did, at one point beating Bill Shankly's Liverpool 5-1 and earning the growling rebuke: "The most defensive team we've ever played." Arsenal have also been compared to the Milan of Marco Van Basten, Ruud Gullit and Frank Rijkaard. It is too much, too soon. Milan won European Cups. They also had the phenomenal defender Franco Baresi and the young Paolo Maldini. They had gone to the peaks of football at a time when the Italian club game represented an ultimate level of competition. Here indeed was a body of work Arsenal are some considerable way from emulating.

Of course they have been encouraged to believe that it is possible and perhaps the levels of performance, and consistency, they are achieving now have sources which are not so mysterious.

Perhaps Arsenal have indeed grown up competitively. Maybe they did take a serious look in the mirror last season after giving up the title race they seemed to be engulfing. Heaven knows, there was due cause. Anyone at Bolton, when Arsenal effectively conceded the title, knows that. It was an ultimate example of both the strength and the weakness of Wenger's team. They moved into a 2-0 lead quite imperiously, Henry creating a goal with a run down the left that told Bolton that conventional defence was futile. And then Arsenal went and threw it all away. No-one was more culpable than the great Henry. He fiddled on the ball. He was awash with hubris.

Then there was the affair at Old Trafford, the gut-wretching lapse into the manners of an unruly street. There was Martin Keown leaping vengefully above Ruud van Nistelrooy, and a pack of his colleagues pushing and sneering. You couldn't much believe in a team that was capable of such pettiness and distorting angst, and the doubts were only underlined when Wenger mounted one of his classic holding actions in the face of the indefensible.

But the Arsenal directors finally reined Wenger in from the one flaw in his football make-up. They issued a grovelling apology. It was, on reflection, as though something deep and disordered in the Arsenal psyche had been expelled – as though at last they had been stopped and ordered to think.

What fruits this will bear is still far from as certain as some believe. Yes, Hansen is right about the fluidity and the devastation, but to what level will it be stretched? Arsenal, unquestionably, are dazzlingly good. But great? Not yet.

RIO, EASTENDERS AND THE 'MENTAL ANGUISH' CAUSED BY FA BAN

Published: 23 March 2004

Readers of Britain's largest-selling newspaper have been given another riveting account of the human tragedy of Rio Ferdinand. However, the feeling here is that all those fair-minded people appalled at the behaviour of that jack-booted disciplinary committee towards this brilliant, sensitive young man will agree that an even wider audience should be acquainted with all the most poignant facts.

You know the basic outline of this grievous assault on all our freedoms. Rio was banned from football for eight months simply because he chose to buy new bed linen for his new mansion – a vital chore, everyone will surely agree – rather than submit to a boring old drugs test.

In a few deft literary touches Rio tells us how it is journeying all the way to hell and back.

For one thing it made him cry – "I'm big enough to admit that," says the victim of football fascism. There is worse. Rio lay awake at nights, for whole hours sometimes, wishing he had taken the test. And far worse still. He says – and brace yourself for this – "I can't put a number on how many occasions I have thought: 'How could I have done that?' I can even be there watching *EastEnders* and thinking about it." Imagine a problem so deep, and so unjustly imposed, that it can draw you away from the mesmerising rhythm of life in Albert Square. There you are speculating on the next diabolic move of someone like Dirty Den, or being lulled soothingly into the light badinage of the saloon bar at the Queen Vic and, bang, the horror of your existence is suddenly with you again like a stab of toothache.

What can you do apart from murmur a thousand regrets and mourn the sheer ingratitude of the Football Association, for whom you have played many international football games at various levels? "I've worked hard for the FA in various tournaments all over the world and to be treated this way was very disheartening," writes Ferdinand. "Usually, I'm always smiling, but this has left a bad taste."

Still, there are a few positives. Rio will still be earning £50,000-or-so a week, and he says that he will be immersing himself in charity work for the NSPCC and the Prince's Trust, adding: "When you are playing you aren't able to spend as much time on these things as you would like [what, we have to guess, with shopping and discos and all those other oppressive duties of big-name football stars]. Now I can do that, so at least some good will come out of all this." There is another benefit, and Rio has dropped upon it with the sharpness of a hawk. He covers the point that football will ultimately benefit from his missed test so profoundly that a mere snippet of a quote will no longer do.

Here, for the benefit of those who do not subscribe to the *Sun*, is what he says: "Rules are being put in place which will never allow my situation to happen again. The drug-testing procedures will be the same whether you are at training or a match. After games the testers follow you everywhere until you have provided a sample and that will now happen at training. There is no one more against drug-taking than me and it hurts when my name is associated with it."

In view of all his suffering, perhaps the FA might have the decency to call this new formula the Rio Procedure, and in this way have it as a permanent monument to his contribution to football reform. For who else deserves credit for making the point so dramatically that some footballers are so stupid, or irresponsible, that they need to have testers adhere to them like hound-dogs right up to the dramatic moment when, in one heart-stirring flow of co-ordinated action, they unfasten their flies and pee into a bottle?

It is also apparently true that Andy Cole, whose salary is not too unadjacent to Ferdinand's, complained to his professional body, the Professional Footballers' Association, because his manager at Blackburn, Graeme Souness, reacted angrily to his plan to fly home early from the team's "bonding" trip to Marbella. Why did Cole want to come home two days before his team-mates? Because he promised his wife he would babysit while she went on a shopping spree.

Sometimes you have to wonder how all this sort of thing plays with hard-working men and women who pay exorbitant amounts to take their children to football ... and for cheaply made souvenir team-shirts bearing names like Ferdinand and Cole. Maybe they choose not to think about it. Maybe they manage something beyond the persecuted Rio. Perhaps they are able to tune out with the *EastEnders*.

TIMES HAVE CHANGED QUICKER THAN ATKINSON

Published: 23 April 2004

Ron Atkinson is not a racist. Or maybe it should be said that until his moment of self-destruction as a TV football analyst and columnist, he had given no indication of that to me in countless conversations across the football world.

Killing time in a Japanese coffee lounge, sharing a nightcap after a big game in Brussels or Madrid or Milan, Big Ron did many blood-curdling things with the English language, but none of them included even a hint that he attached any undue significance to the colour of a man's skin.

He was lionised in some quarters of Fleet Street for the pungency of his TV analysis; others enjoyed the fact that the broadsheet which once published the fastidious words of Alistair Cooke took on the weekly challenge of smoothing his exuberant assaults on the mother tongue.

Maybe the greatest irony of all, though, is that the increasingly celebrity-conscious world of showbiz sports TV broadcasting so briskly cut down an exaggerated character they had done so much to create.

Atkinson recognised quickly enough that he had to offer his resignation. The words he applied to Chelsea's Marcel Desailly, while he thought he was off the air, gave him no option but to fall on his microphone.

The fact that Muhammad Ali employed exhaustively the word that was so offensive on the lips of Atkinson, or that it is impossible to listen to a rap record without hearing its constant use, is of course quite beside the point.

Atkinson crossed a line that was unacceptable, and he had to go. But for his sake, it perhaps needs to be said that he was as much as anything ambushed by changing times; also, that at the lowest point of his public life since leaving the maelstrom of football management, in which his record was more moderate than his reputation, his behaviour in the Monaco broadcasting booth was foolish rather than sinister.

On Ron Atkinson you can take your pick: amiable buffoon, self-publicist. But nothing in his professional life suggests racism.

Though some of the detail of his encouragement of black players has been faulty – his predecessor at West Bromwich Albion, John Giles, signed the brilliant Laurie Cunningham from Leyton Orient for £100,000, and the powerful and accomplished Cyrille Regis from Hayes – there is no doubt about the thrust of his record in this area.

When he signed another black player, Brendan Batson, for Albion and boasted that he was fielding the Three Degrees no members of a minority could take exception. Atkinson was drawing attention to the potential of the black player as a vital element in English football, a proposition that had languished until then, and if he flourished a questionable soundbite it was then far from a hanging offence.

When he went to Old Trafford one of his first moves was to sign the gifted Remi Moses, a deal that said that black players could at last gain entrance to the highest levels of the game. If this sounds odd, it should be remembered that it was a time of rampant racism on the terraces. John Barnes for a while had to run a gauntlet in Merseyside derby games. As Liverpool's first black player, he was greeted with bananas from Everton followers when he ran on to the field. Mark Walters suffered a similar fate when he appeared for Glasgow Rangers.

However, if Big Ron's signing policy was admirably ahead of its time, his language and humour was slow to adjust to new levels of sensitivity.

In 1989, when he signed Dalian Atkinson for Sheffield Wednesday, a general news reporter from a local radio station asked him if he had recruited a relative. Atkinson's reply: "Well, you may think I've got a good suntan, but Dalian's is even better."

Atkinson meant no offence, but it was dangerous levity and this week it rose up and, inevitably, took him down.

Ian St John, one of the most experienced former footballer broadcasters and noted for his acerbic wit, reacted sadly to the news of his friend's downfall. "No doubt Ron crossed a line," said St John, "but I know him well enough to say that he is by no means a racist. His record in the game totally contradicts that idea. He just seems to have forgotten for a desperate moment that the times, and what it is not acceptable to say, have moved on."

One truth is that part of Atkinson's appeal has been his non-intellectual approach to both life and football. If he was a media darling, it was as its rather large piece of rough. One football insider observes wryly: "Ron is a great character, but maybe we shouldn't forget that as a young man he went to Oxford to play for the local football club – not the university."

SHEPHERD UNFIT TO BE JUDGE OF SIR BOBBY

Published: 15 May 2004

It's long past the time to praise or bury Sir Bobby Robson. He is what he is and those of us who had the temerity to tell him to be somebody else nearly five years ago – namely, an amiable old pensioner sniffing the roses and amusing the grandkids – should be suitably cautioned. However, somebody at Newcastle United, ideally the incorrigibly opinionated and generally unloved chairman, Freddy Shepherd, should stop for a second and speculate on what might have happened to the club if Robson had been misguided enough to follow our advice.

If Shepherd has such power of reflection – and judging by the frequency of his intervention in strictly football affairs at St James' Park, and the relentless stream of comments with which he bombards the local press and match programme, the evidence is not encouraging – he might question the value of bringing down a managerial regime which, overall, has been nothing less than brilliant.

Yes, notwithstanding the possible failure at Anfield today to ensure any kind of European football at Newcastle for the first time in three years, brilliant.

Brilliant in its feeling for the sweep of the game and the kind of football Newcastle United should represent. Brilliant in the way it so surely rebuilt the foundations of a club which were in danger of being shattered for all time by waste and stupidity and a quite craven alienation of some of the nation's most passionate fans.

Of course, even the greatest of managers are the prisoners of their results and this, perversely, is particularly so when you have lifted expectations as high as Robson has done over the last few years.

Remember his legacy from Ruud – "I'll give you sexy football" – Gullit in September 1999? He inherited a club who had gleaned one point from their first seven matches, had managed to lose at home to Sunderland after dropping Alan Shearer for an obscure teenager who said that Roker Park rather than Tyneside was his spiritual home, and whose chairman – the same Mr Shepherd – had been tape-recorded with his friend and fellow director

Douglas Hall in a girlie bar in Marbella slagging off, in no particular order, Shearer – "old Mary Poppins" – the womenfolk of the North-east, and all those mugs who paid rip-off prices for souvenir shirts.

Now Shepherd is given to homilies about the need for personal discipline among Newcastle's overpaid stars, a position which may have some merit but is not exactly copper-bottomed by his own record or the fact, as reported by my colleague David Conn last weekend, that he and Hall took for themselves no less than a staggering £2.7m in directors' dividends from the club's annual profit of £4.4m.

The word from St James' Park is that Robson is almost certainly a goner, at least in terms of exerting full control over football affairs, and one of the more risible suggestions is that this is partly because Robson has spent more, for example, than Arsène Wenger at Arsenal without quite the same level of success. Here the mind begins to whirl. Apart from all his own talent, Wenger had the advantage of taking over a well run club, whose chairman, Peter Hill-Wood, had long been mindful of family tradition and the old truth that chairmen who preside over truly successful clubs never intrude into the operating space of the manager, and are still less given to fatuous comments at every ebb and flow of a season.

Let us, briefly, consider the transfer record of Robson. Inevitably, he has made his stumbles. Who hasn't? If Titus Bramble is currently proving a disaster, how much worse of an investment was this than Sir Alex Ferguson's splurge on Juan Sebastian Veron or, ultimately, Fabien Barthez? Did Wenger pick out a jewel in Pascal Cygan? Perhaps not. Hugo Viana is disappointing, no doubt, but he is still young and may yet flower. Laurent Robert causes great exasperation, but for a while he was a brilliant extension of Newcastle's football wide on the left, and if Robson had been warned about his personality, so was Ferguson when he picked up Eric Cantona, over whom hands had been widely and thoroughly washed in his native France. Some hunches come off, some don't, ask anybody in football.

Robson has spent £47m, less than half the outlay of Gérard Houllier, who is claiming a "massive achievement" today in possibly finishing no more than one point ahead of Newcastle, and more than half of that expenditure has been largely neutralised in a season of horrendous injury. Robson's key signings, Craig Bellamy, Jermaine Jenas and Jonathan Woodgate – and Gullit's acquisition Kieron Dyer – have appeared together no more than five times this season. These players are the spine and the potency of the team.

One other important factor should not be forgotten. Newcastle have a desperate yearning to win something, which, given the level of support they have received down all the aching years, is understandable enough. Their last title win was in 1927, their last Cup win 1955, and their last trophy, the Fairs Cup, came under Joe Harvey in 1969. Under Robson, Newcastle were one game away from competing in the final of the Uefa Cup until the recent defeat in Marseille – two stages later than when Liverpool, whose manager receives so much unswerving support from his boardroom, were knocked out by the same team.

When Houllier talks of "massive achievement" he seems to forget that his immediate predecessor, Roy Evans, would, under present qualification rules, not have missed a place in the Champions League. Another forerunner, Bob Paisley, once repelled congratulations over a trophy win by saying: "Don't forget, it hasn't been all glory. I remember we finished second one year." Paisley had just won the first of his three European Cups.

If Liverpool have become somewhat easily pleased, the opposite is true of Newcastle. It is a perspective that will be nowhere more valuable than at Anfield today if men in football whose power so far exceeds their knowledge should be tempted to decide between winners and losers. Into the latter category only a fool would place Sir Bobby Robson. But of course, and as usual, this is the worry.

REALITY BITES AS HOULLIER BIDS FAREWELL TO ANFIELD

Published: 25 May 2004

Gérard Houllier, like his countrywoman Edith Piaf, had no regrets yesterday when he was removed from the Liverpool challenge that he insisted ran way beyond the healing powers of a "quick fix". The trouble was that six years in the life of Liverpool Football Club, with ever declining evidence that you have what it takes to be at least in contention as one of the best teams in England, were not some brief, jarring interlude. It had begun to look like the end of life as it had always been known at Anfield, and to suggest otherwise was pure Houllier.

He has many admirable qualities, and not least physical courage, but a willingness to face up to the realities of failure is not one of them. Indeed, there have been times over the last few years when as a spin artist he might have forced even Alastair Campbell to bend the knee.

The problem with spin, as Abraham Lincoln pointed out all those years ago when he said that you can't fool all of the people all of the time, is that it can take you only so far. This is particularly true of football. Once a week, sometimes twice, you are obliged to send out your team to show what you have got them to do. On far too many occasions it was embarrassingly clear that the answer was not very much at all beyond developing a herd instinct to get behind the ball.

There are some places where you can get away with talking endlessly about the potential of your team. Liverpool is not one of them, and when Houllier talked of winning six titles in six years that old Lincoln principle kicked in with some force.

What Houllier's Liverpool won was four trophies – and two knick-knacks, the Charity Shield and the Super Cup. You might get away with such blurring of the facts in some football outpost, where winning is not claiming your due but something close to fantasy.

From Bill Shankly taking over Anfield at the start of the Sixties until Houllier's reign, Liverpool won the old First Division title 13 times and the European Cup four times. This wasn't a run of success, it was a right of conquest – and the brilliant adherence to a winning tradition which was built unerringly on certain basic principles.

The most fundamental of these was the signing of good players who were introduced into a system of play that was unwavering in its belief in the importance of form and shape and a capacity to attack with the ball. When Shankly's successor, Bob Paisley, signed Kenny Dalglish and Graeme Souness he didn't oblige them to treat the ball as though it was a hand grenade with the pin removed. They were asked to do what they did best: use it with craft and imagination.

Souness had a deserved reputation as one of the ultimate hardmen ball-winners, but in possession he was equally effective. Dalglish and Souness, among other things, were masters of subtle movement. Asking them to scamper behind the ball at every opportunity would have been like handing Picasso a paint-by-numbers set.

Yesterday even Houllier was obliged to face the fact that the patience of the club and the city had run out when his close friend and the Liverpool chairman, David Moores, finally acknowledged that this was a Liverpool team, for all the bravura form of Steve Gerrard and the scoring talent of Michael Owen, that was plainly going nowhere.

Some Houllier apologists have asked why Liverpool have some divine right to a place at the top of the mountain. Other football empires have passed. Across the park at Goodison, Everton are a shell of the old force. Tottenham have made a parody of the old fighting cock worn on the shirts of such titans as Dave Mackay, John White, Danny Blanchflower and Cliff Jones. European Cup-winners Nottingham Forest and Aston Villa have had many lean days. Leeds United have defined how not to run a top club. So what is so cataclysmic about Liverpool spending a few years in the shadows? The special problem is that Liverpool are a football club who have continued to do more or less everything right.

It's true they had the aberration of appointing joint managers when Houllier and Roy Evans were put in charge of the team, but the absurdity of the move was noted and acted upon within a few months. Either side of that folly, Liverpool have been demonstrably Liverpool, supporting their manager – Houllier's is the first sacking since Don Welsh fell in 1956 – and ploughing money into the team at regular intervals.

More money than, for example, Arsenal in some recent years, which brings us to the nub of the issue. Houllier wasn't sacked for a failure to fulfil some crazed desire for overnight success. What he didn't deliver, unlike his countryman Arsène Wenger, was a clear sense of a developing team. It was not so much that Liverpool didn't get better. They got worse. Fans, especially those at Anfield, are not always idiots raging down a phone-in line. Houllier lost the fans, beyond a few flurries of sentiment, some time ago.

It happened for the most basic reason of all. It was because of the way his team played. He did some excellent work, especially in the early going. He imposed genuine discipline and competitive pride. He reminded the dressing room of what had gone before. He even won three trophies in one season, but some – including quite a number of the players who in their time had been cornerstones of the old empire – refused to be swept away. Liverpool had played hard and with some good fortune but they had not unveiled a way to play football that might just take them back to the top of the English game.

That was always the ultimate test of Gérard Houllier. The harsh but unavoidable truth is that he failed it. However, the new man will be required to sit the same exam and that it is essentially a fair one was confirmed recently by one of Europe's hottest coaches, José Mourinho, who made it clear that in many ways he was more tempted by the standards of decency at Liverpool than by the vast but crudely applied wealth of Chelsea.

Mourinho has every chance of winning the European Cup for Porto tomorrow night. Who knows, he might just consider Liverpool a suitable case for his attention. With six years and a big budget to play with, he might see it as rather more than an invitation to work a quick fix.

BLUSTER REVEALS BECKHAM'S REFUSAL TO FACE OWN LIMITATIONS

Published: 26 June 2004

Sven backs David. David backs Sven. The nation mourns. A majority think England were robbed. David says: "We want Mr Eriksson to continue because we respect him as a person and a manager – he takes a lot of responsibility off the players."

Sven says David has done very well in the tournament, and why wouldn't he be his captain right up to the World Cup in Germany in two years time? Mark Palios, hard-driving boss of the Football Association, says that Mr Eriksson is utterly bomb-proof and would have survived even defeat by B-list Croatia the other night. As always, everything is fine with England, masters of high-profile potential and second-class performance.

Meanwhile, this Championship rolls on seeking out a team worthy to call themselves champions of Europe. If you love English football, if you believe that the young Wayne Rooney in the last week or so has recalled a time when the nation's footballers were judged on their performance and not their image, when they went out to compete properly with the world, you are entitled to weep.

Not to weep for one defeat against the superior skills of a Portuguese team much more conversant with the demands of international football – a defeat that, after all, came in a penalty shoot-out and after a controversial decision by the referee to disallow a late England goal – but for the culture of self-enhancement that has grown around the national team, where double-talk and denial are always the first response to failure.

Remember Japan two years ago? Then it was the freak kick of the brilliant Brazilian Ronaldinho that did down England in the World Cup; nothing to do with England's palsied tactics and performance in the second half. Here at the Estadio da Luz on Thursday night it was the error of Swiss referee Urs Meier. England lost because of unkind fate not, apparently, because after Michael Owen's early strike they didn't display a clue about how to control the game and conserve the ball because two of England's most celebrated players, the pillar of the team Beckham and his most touted lieutenant Steven Gerrard, reached new lows in ineffective performance.

Yesterday Beckham responded angrily to claims by a television interviewer that many England fans had lost belief in his power to inspire his team – or produce inspirational performance. "What do you think?" snapped Beckham. The hapless man replied: "I'm telling you what the fans told me." But Beckham persisted: "No, no, what do you think?" he asked again. "I don't have an opinion," said the questioner.

If denial has become a religion in the English dressing room, Beckham is surely its high priest. Yesterday he brushed aside his second missed penalty of the tournament and insisted that he had played well.

He said: "I've handled a lot more emotional things than this in my life, I'm a strong person and I'll come back fighting. That's me. We can take a lot away from this competition. No, no regrets... I think after the game you can always look back at things like that, but all the players were saying before every game we have no regrets and you just can't look back and say we could have done this differently and that differently... of course we could have kept the ball better, we could have attacked more, could have defended well, got a bit of luck and won 1-0. But that's football."

No, that's not football, it's escapism and a hard dose of reality is surely on the horizon for the player who for years has been lauded to the skies while operating at a level which in the course of just a few games young Rooney has utterly exposed.

Beckham is no longer the great inspiration of England, the miracle worker, growl the critics, but whenever was he that?

One interrogator, looking to put as kind a face on things as possible, asked Beckham what had happened to the great uplifting performances of the past, like...well, the free-kick against Greece and the goal against Finland?

There in one awful moment was the reality which has been so vividly highlighted by the match-winning efforts of the 18-year-old Rooney here. Beckham's vast body of work is, when you break it down, slight indeed. A beautiful striker of a dead ball, no doubt, the crosser of perfect balls when given time and space on the right, no doubt, but the field general of his own and Eriksson's imagination? The myth is on the floor and lying in pieces.

Here Beckham, after his dreadful form at Real Madrid and the slide in performance which provoked Sir Alex Ferguson into approving his controversial dispatch from Old Trafford, was supposed to re-state his credentials. He was supposed to lead England with verve and style. He talked a wonderful game, and his friend Gary Neville was telling us that this was the best, most talented England squad he had ever seen.

But Beckham's England has beaten Switzerland and Croatia on the back of Rooney, lost to France and failed to exploit the early advantage of Owen's goal against Portugal. England, it should be said, are not a bad team. They have points of considerable merit. While David James is a cause of considerable apprehension among goalkeeping specialists, he has averted disaster in this tournament. The defence has generally played well in all but set-pieces, and from Ashley Cole, whose reputation has been built on attacking flair rather than defensive security, there was an outstanding performance against the rampaging Cristiano Ronaldo on Thursday night.

Rooney has been in a class of his own, the star of the tournament by some margin thus far, and but for injury in the 26th minute it is entirely reasonable to believe he might have found a way to win – especially in view of the fact that his strike partner Michael Owen had applied such splendid application to his own crisis in form.

But that leaves the midfield, Beckham and Gerrard's patch, and it is there where England are still rooted in the abyss of that World Cup quarter-final two years ago.

Then, it was said that Beckham's dubious fitness and the absence of Gerrard were killer blows to England's chances of getting past the Brazilians. Two years down the road, they were apparently ready and able but mostly their performances were wretched. Beckham did play well in the first game against France, holding the ball in a way that might have brought escape from the relentless pressure of Zidane and company. But since then he has crumbled and yesterday it was rather staggering to notice his reluctance to look into the real world rather than the one that he has had created for him.

Here is more Beckham in the wake of another question about his failure to inflict himself on a fourth successive major tournament: "You'll go and write what you want to write, whether it is fair criticism. I don't believe it is. I can only give my best and I believe I have given my best in every game... whether it's not good enough for some people, so be it. I believe in my own ability and I'll carry on doing this. As far as I'm concerned, I want to stay as captain of England – I want to stay as an England player and as long as the manager and the players want me it doesn't matter what anyone else says. You'll have to ask the other players if they want me to be captain. I'm proud to be England captain – and I will be until I'm relieved of the duty."

There was not much more sense to be had out of Eriksson yesterday, or more reflection. He said that Beckham had played well. All the players had played well and speaking for himself, what had he done wrong? He couldn't think of anything. Of course not. England wind along their happy road, talking themselves up – and then going down.

Maybe Eriksson's task is impossible. Maybe the way the Premiership is played makes the fashioning of a genuine winning force on the international stage too much of a challenge. Perhaps Gerrard and Frank Lampard, who despite his goals has also been an unpersuasive figure on the ball here, need to be among midfielders who know how to craft their way to a winning performance. If Eriksson believes this, he should say so, and return to the rich rewards of club football for which the evidence suggests he still pines.

What we are left with is an England coach and a team who believe they can re-write their own performance as they go along. However, this happy, insulated world has finally been punctured... not by the character and the football instincts of Portugal, but from within. Rooney was England's most potent weapon in the European Championship, but he was also the team's most searing reproach. He showed what a real world-class footballer can do when given a big stage. While he was around, England looked as if they could win any game. When he left, we were left with the old reality: big, even huge names – and, when it mattered most, pygmy performance.

MEN OF PRINCIPLE MUST RESCUE NATIONAL GAME FROM DISGRACE

Published: 02 August 2004

The deal was so squalid and crude it might have been conjured by the lower orders of the Mafia. Instead it was proffered by the men who were supposed to be the guardians of our national game, the leading FA officials who in their failed attempt to betray Sven-Goran Eriksson have made a mess that can be cleaned up only with the help of fumigation.

What is needed, the affair cried out last night as Mark Palios found out he had no option but to resign as chief executive, is new men and new principles. Principles like honesty and honour and a sense of responsibility that goes beyond a gutter instinct for survival.

A start would be a real football man who hasn't sold out to a culture of celebrity and profit, and who believes that the game is not some freewheeling vehicle for personal advancement, but something to be cherished and honoured.

This, after all, is the game of men such as Bobby Moore and Sir Bobby Charlton and Sir Tom Finney – men unequivocal about what is important in the game we play. Trevor Brooking, whose honest report on the disastrous European championship shone like a great beacon amid all the excuses and the prevarications, and was perhaps a reflection of the administrative experience he gained through dedicated work on behalf of the Sports Council, might be the man to turn to through the current crisis.

His work, we know, would be at the very least knowledgeable and true. It is necessary to speak in these terms because what we have here is not some fleeting episode of bringing the game into disrepute, a charge that from time to time is placed against decent football men who are guilty, ironically enough, only of speaking what they deem to be right.

What it is, is a scandal that has carried the Football Association beyond the scorn and disrepute that exploded after the initial disbelief that men of authority could behave so wretchedly while attempting to save their skins. It has taken the FA to the point where anything they say has to be automatically referred to a lie detector. They simply cannot be trusted with the truth.

The details are shockingly basic. They concern an attempt to subvert the facts. Colin Gibson, the FA's director of communications, is the central figure, though it remains unclear whether he acted by himself or whether posterity will reveal him to be the hapless messenger boy. He offered the *News of the World* the head of Eriksson. It was a wonderful gift to the nation's biggest-selling Sunday newspaper. It had everything that peddlers of bedroom secrets and celebrity could ever want. Unusually, the cost was negligible: a mere 30 pieces of silver. But then that is the oldest going rate for betrayal.

All that was asked of the newspaper was that it didn't finger Gibson's boss, Palios, who like the Lothario head coach also had an affair with the same junior member of staff. Eriksson, the darling of the Football Association for so long before he became an embarrassing and grotesquely expensive failure, was simply consigned to the fishes. And Gibson did the consigning.

It may hardly need saying, even given the FA's traditionally palsied version of decision-making, that certain consequences were quite inevitable. Palios and Gibson surely had to be told to clear their desks at the Soho Square headquarters where the sickening – and pathetically naïve – plot was hatched. After these formalities, however, a broader question has to be addressed – and not by an organisation that is no longer so much a national institution as a national disgrace.

The Government, if it cares anything for the place of football in the regard and the morale of the nation, has to intervene and say that before we hype up a forlorn attempt to invite the world to a London Olympics we must cleanse the nation's most popular sport; one that so recently had flags flying from millions of cars in the misplaced belief that England's inadequately prepared team might win the first major tournament since Alf Ramsey's men delivered the World Cup in 1966 – and received a bonus of £1,000, less tax.

It has to be said that the tawdry circus has gone beyond mere incompetence. Of course, we have known for decades of the buffoonery and the misadventures of the FA. We know that the organisation's power and influence have been relentlessly reduced by the merchants of greed otherwise known as the Premiership. We know that the salary of the under-achieving Eriksson is a numbing reward for acts of disloyalty. We know that the fiasco of rebuilding Wembley Stadium was another blow to the idea that we can reasonably describe ourselves as a front-rank football nation. We know that only an institution as half-baked as the FA could seriously suggest that the likes of David Beckham and Gary Neville should have any say in the selection of the new coach who will surely be required to step into the void now opening up between Eriksson and his employers.

What we didn't know, at least for sure, is that the FA had simply turned rotten from the top.

Now we know it, we have to act. We have to say that the organisation has proved itself incapable of trust. We have to re-examine the gut-wrenching statements of Palios when he took over from his predecessor, Adam Crozier. We have to hold up to the light his declaration that the FA was going to at last face up to the challenge of discipline. He gave an exclusive interview to, guess who – yes, of course, the *News of the World* – and said the FA was going to fight aggressively for the image of the game.

At least we know now how the FA could have reached its appalling decision to reward Eriksson with a £1m-a-year rise after being caught out secretly negotiating with the Chelsea owner Roman Abramovich. Such thinking could only emerge in a place where loyalty is plainly an alien concept.

What needs to be said most vitally is that this affair is about so much more than one grubby attempt to conceal the truth. It is to do with a profound collapse in values. Gibson's message was breathtaking in its cynicism. It can be quite brutally summarised: slaughter Eriksson, but protect the boss. That the proposal should be carried by the former sports editor of a national newspaper, who is paid to understand the workings of the media, is bewildering but scarcely the issue. We are not talking about strategy here. We are discussing, quite simply, the corruption of truth.

We are talking about a cheap and vicious conspiracy. We are speaking of a refusal to make tough and honest decisions and, let us be sure about this, the absence of a scrap of moral fibre.

Eriksson, it can be argued, would have been sacked in the wake of the European Championships by a football authority which understood what it saw in Portugal. The sheer cost of paying up Eriksson's absurdly inflated contract was, we now know, the main reason it didn't happen.

But then maybe there were ways and means. One of them was to drag the coach through the pages of a Sunday newspaper. That it failed is at least one matter for celebration. The other is that no one now can doubt the need to clean up the offices of the Football Association – with the help of a hosepipe, perhaps.

ANATOMY OF A FOOTBALLING GENIUS: LOVED, HATED, FEARED AND REVERED

Published: 21 September 2004

A thousand tributes poured over the fallen head of Brian Clough yesterday but none of them carried the impact of the one that exploded in the corridors of Derby County Football Club 31 years ago.

It was delivered by a group of his players angry that his relations with the directors had deteriorated to the point of his resignation. They couldn't stand the idea of losing their messiah, the Mercedes-driving, champagne-quaffing socialist who had arrived at the top of English football with a raw but brilliant force.

"We're going to doing something about this," announced the goalkeeper Colin Boulton. It was a statement that was utterly compelling not because of the obvious strength of his emotion but the fact that he was carrying a large axe at the time.

The axe was to smash down the door of the boardroom, where the directors had gathered after refusing to meet the deputation of players. Clough moved on and no blood was spilled, but you saw so much of the effect of him in that tumultuous incident. You saw the fierce loyalty he engendered in one group, his players, and the resistance of the establishment, represented by the boardroom. There was little in between hate and love in response to Brian Clough. He was bitter and brilliant, outrageous and tender, self-destructive and inspiring, and that could be in the time it took to down a couple of brandies.

Clough was a genius in the matter of driving certain football teams into levels of over-achievement so staggering it defied logical analysis. One of his finest players, Archie Gemmill, the Scottish midfielder, once said: "Don't ask me how he does it, I can't tell you why we play for him as we do. It is not always affection, I can tell you. Maybe it's a bit of fear and a lot of admiration for the way he can produce the right mood in a dressing-room. The fact is it happens – and it's phenomenal."

The outline of Clough's career is enshrined in football history – promotion and titles for Derby County, promotion and European Cups for Nottingham

Forest, clubs now anchored in the have-not anonymity of life outside the Premiership – but the nuances of his character will probably always remain a mystery, and perhaps in some ways as much to his beloved wife, Barbara, who from time to time was obliged to pick up bottles littering his Derbyshire garden when it seemed that he was committed to drinking himself to death, as those who tried to chart the erratic course of his life in and out of football.

When I first spoke to him I was on the routine chore of a football reporter. I wanted to know if his fast-rising Derby team was clear of a rash of injuries before an important match. "Aye, lad," he said, "but get your notebook open and take down this. I've just had Dave Mackay [the legend of the game he had signed from Tottenham Hotspur] in my office and told him he's a bloody disgrace. I told him I signed him because he was supposed to represent all that is best in a great professional and he would give a lead to my young lads. Well, in last night's match he didn't do that. He let me down, and I've just told him that if he does it again he's on his bike." Soon enough such a rebuke to one of the greatest players ever to grace the fields of English football would seem relatively mild.

In his 44-day implosion at Leeds United, where he inherited the reigning champions after Don Revie moved to take over the England job, he notoriously told the superb but injury-hampered winger Eddie Gray: "If you'd been a horse you would have been shot long ago." He said that as far he was concerned the Leeds players could throw all their medals in the nearest bin. He said they were cheats.

Earlier he had told a dinner thrown by Yorkshire TV to present the Leeds player Peter Lorimer with an award, that he had no respect for Leeds and, if they would excuse him, he needed to "take a piss".

What made Clough the astonishing force he was before he submitted to the ravages of drink which eventually led, two years ago and some considerable time after he had put away the bottle, to a liver transplant? Those who know him best say there was a substantial element of anger. He never quite forgave the fate that brought his brilliant career as a striker for his home-town club Middlesbrough, and then Sunderland, to end through injury at the age of 29. He felt he should have played for England more than twice and much later he was incensed that the Football Association never saw him as a potential manager of the national team.

"Brian was right to feel that way, though it probably never did him any good," said one of his fiercest rivals in the Sixties and Seventies, the

Manchester City coach, Malcolm Allison. "He was a superb player – I remember when I was West Ham centre-half going out against this scrawny kid from Middlesbrough. He was playing one of his first games and I told my team-mates: 'Don't worry, I'll put the kid in my pocket.' In the first minute he left me for dead and cracked the ball against the bar. Brian Clough was an original, and when it came to getting a team to play he was amazing."

Amazing, troubled, quirkish, he was all of those things. He was suspended for slapping around young fans who ran on to the City Ground at Nottingham. He fined players for the most minor infractions of the club dress code while at the same time pouring drinks down their throats before important games. In the hiatus between Derby County and Nottingham Forest, and the madness of Leeds, he had a brief stint at Brighton. He treated the project with supreme indifference.

In the middle of negotiations with a bright young player and his parents he said there wasn't a lot of money in the club kitty, but did they not like sprouts? He produced a bag of the vegetables and invited them to consider them a signing-on bonus. He said that sprouts were wonderful for youth health.

Less so, hard spirits of course, and by the end of his time at Nottingham Forest his face was a latticework of fiery blotches. In 1998 when the Football Association had vowed to clean up the game in the wake of the George Graham bung affair, they came up empty but for one convenient scapegoat.

Clough was charged with misconduct for allegedly accepting an unauthorised payment in the course of a player transfer. There was an an almost exquisite irony here. They had rejected the best of Clough, the roaring genius that saw him deploy the tubby Scottish winger John Robertson deep on the left and confuse both domestic and European football for years, and then singled him out for disrepute long after his time had gone.

Maybe it was no surprise that for several years he was close to his idol Geoff Boycott, the great batsman-curmudgeon of Yorkshire and England. Egocentric Yorkshiremen, they lived lives entirely on their own terms. They broke rules of convention, and basic politeness, in the belief that the world would perhaps never quite understand what they had to offer.

Clough signed England's first million-pound player, the teenaged Trevor Francis, and he was first to recognise the potential of Roy Keane. He conquered England and Europe. He was a raging anarchist who believed in discipline. He was a football man who understood, most of the time, how to make players give their best, yet in half of his time he was hell-bent to destroy that in himself.

He was a huge presence in the game and in the life of the country and for those who knew him, loved him, even endured him, yesterday's news was like the turning-off of a light. In the gloom they were required to drink a toast. A pretty stiff one.

WHY ROONEY CAN BECOME THE GREATEST PLAYER OF ALL TIME

Published: 09 October 2004

An astonishing claim accompanies Wayne Rooney at Old Trafford against Wales today. It is that he may be the greatest football talent we have ever seen, more gifted than Pelé, more devastating than Maradona and, equally amazingly, more visionary than Cruyff.

This is not, it needs to be said very quickly, the legend on the calling card of a galactico's agent or publicist. It is the gut reaction of a man who in his years as a player and a critic acquired the reputation of the pro's pro, the midfield general who was always known to be as hard as he was cerebral... John Giles, of Leeds United, Manchester United and the Republic of Ireland.

"You don't make an assessment like this lightly," said Giles this week. "You think of all the great players you have seen or played with and against, from Di Stefano through Pelé to Zidane, and you remind yourself of all that they had, what made them unique in their time, and then you look at this kid Rooney, who at first glance doesn't even look like a player. And when you do that over a certain length of time you don't see some lumpy prodigy who might for one reason or another burn out very quickly. You see a beautiful flower of a talent, perfectly formed.

"Then, inevitably, you worry how it might be blown away, and you would be mad if you didn't do that because there is one great problem that none of the greatest players you can think of, Pelé, Maradona, Bobby Charlton and Best, even Zidane when he first started in a slum in Marseilles, ever confronted. At the age of 20, which for Rooney will be in two years' time, none of them could wake up one morning with, say, £10m in the bank and think: 'Do I really need football now? Do I really want to be a player?'"

Giles' fears about the short-to-mid-term effects of the winds of circumstance blowing around Rooney were crystallised this week in the reports that the teenager's fiancée had flown off to New York for a £15,000 shopping spree. "You might say there's nothing wrong in a working class girl enjoying a fantasy," says Giles, "but you have to consider what it suggests in terms of Rooney's future, the kind of basis on which he will conduct his professional life.

"When Bobby Charlton, the purest young talent I ever saw, signed pro he was on £8 a week in winter, £7 in summer. The professional's life was clearly signposted, and you know what that life is if you're going to develop all your potential as a great player. Well, the truth is, it is quite boring, it is doing your training, getting yourself home in the afternoon, getting plenty of sleep, having maybe one good night out a week. This is perhaps not so easily done when you arrive home to find that your wife hasn't put the dinner in the oven but popped over to Bloomingdales for a little bit of shopping.

"Of course, the world has changed. Of course, we cannot take Rooney back to the days of the young Bobby Charlton. There was never a time in the lives of all the great players who preceded Rooney when they had it all made for them. Pelé had to finish his career in New York, drawn by a million dollars and the chance to secure his life after the game.

"All that we can hope is that somewhere within Rooney's nature is some basic instinct to get the best out of himself on the field. Maybe he can make some sense of the circumstances of today's game. If he doesn't, the loss to football will be tragic. Yes, it is true, I don't believe I have ever seen a better equipped, more naturally gifted footballer than Wayne Rooney. He has everything you would ever want in a great player."

Giles, like so many professional observers, was no less than enchanted by the teenager's debut for Manchester United in the Champions League against Fenerbahce, and the euphoria was not notably checked by the subsequent blank against Middlesbrough in the Premiership. "Some said that tighter marking in the Premiership will restrict him, and Middlesbrough was the evidence; nonsense. A talent like Rooney's doesn't do restriction. It might not shoot out the lights every game – Pelé and Maradona and Cruyff didn't erupt in every match they played, but their presence was always huge – and in fact against Middlesbrough, Rooney played well. United could easily have scored three or four in the closing minutes. No one has ever blazed through every game he has played. The game doesn't permit that."

Certainly, Wales are unlikely to draw too much comfort from a relatively quiet showing. In whatever way the England coach, Sven-Goran Eriksson, arranges his team around the player who in his last two full appearances for the national team in the European Championship was nothing less than unplayable for the defences of Switzerland and Croatia, if Eriksson does indeed go with Michael Owen and Jermain Defoe as the front men with Rooney in the "hole" and at the head of a revived "diamond", it will simply be for the convenience of soft-edged decision-making.

The fact is that Rooney and Owen dovetailed superbly at times in the European finals and the real issue before today's game was whether the brilliant performance of Defoe in Poland last month had done enough to supplant the currently struggling Owen – and allow Eriksson the basic shape of a much improved effort after the disaster in Vienna. All of this is, however, likely to prove academic if Rooney's talent continues to unfurl at its recent rate.

Paradoxically, it has to be said that Giles was somewhat appalled when a poll of Manchester United supporters had Rooney shooting to second place in the all-time list of Old Trafford stars after his break-out against Fenerbahce. "What I'm saying," Giles insists, "is that Rooney may well be the best talent I have ever seen. He may have the best balance, the best combination of strength and speed, and the sharpest intelligence of a player of his age at the highest level. But whether in the end he can be ranked above Pelé or Maradona and the rest of the accepted galaxy of the game is something that will be decided by a lot of factors and the most vital one is performance over the long term.

"At this moment Rooney is a great player, no question. But can he become the greatest of all time? It depends on so many things. They include his friends, his girlfriend... or girlfriends, his agents, and, most of all, himself."

On one famous occasion Giles harangued George Best during an FA Cup semi-final between Leeds United and his old club, United. It was a few hours after Best had been discovered in a hotel room with a girl and been dressed down bitterly by the Old Trafford manager, Wilf McGuinness. "Call yourself a professional?" Giles asked Best after one clattering tackle. "You're a disgrace." In fact, Giles had huge respect and a degree of affection for his fellow Irishman. He saw the breathtaking scale of his talent, and admired his courage. But he also saw that the celebrity that had come to him was destroying him, ending his years of genius at least half a decade too soon.

Giles also saw early evidence that the brilliance of Paul Gascoigne could not be sustained. "I saw him receiving a prize at a national newspaper awards ceremony when he was just a kid and it seemed to me that he had fallen in love with the idea of being a celebrity. A few years later I met him again and asked him whether he was controlling his drinking, as he had publicly vowed to do. He said he was drinking just a little wine but it was early in the evening and it was clear he was already well on the way. Gazza was a great talent... but also a tragedy. He mistook football for showbiz and he didn't seem to realise that in football there are no rehearsals. Reading his autobiography, it is is clear that he never had much chance of making the most of his ability."

Most astounding in Rooney, maybe, is that in less than two full seasons he has persuaded a man of Giles' often harsh conservatism that, for all the hazards of today's football culture, the game is still capable of producing arguably its ultimate player. While so much less overwhelming than today, that culture destroyed Best, seduced Gascoigne and turned Maradona into a drug addict. So far, at full tilt, it has failed to wipe out the possibility that Wayne Rooney may be the greatest footballer of all time. Indeed, some time this afternoon Old Trafford could well be not so much a battleground as a shrine.

ERIKSSON'S EMPIRE OF INCOHERENCE IN NEED OF STRAIGHT TALKING FROM FA

Published: 11 February 2005

If Sven-Goran Eriksson was a US President he would be impeached. If he was a film director, shooting would be stopped and Steven Spielberg would be flown in. If he was a cardinal he would be ordered back to Rome: to a Vatican dungeon, that is, not his old club, Lazio.

But he is head coach of England so it appears he can lurch from one disaster to another without any hint of censure, still less any suggestion that he might have forfeited his right to office and a £4.5m a year salary that seems a little more grotesquely inflated with each new piece of evidence that his England team are bereft of leadership or plan. This week's friendly fiasco against the Netherlands was an example of new depths of futility.

Once before, when the "Socceroos" of Australia beat another Eriksson chorus line at Upton Park almost precisely two years ago, the overwhelming instinct was to say that the end of the road had surely been reached. That was after the ultimate failure and incoherence of England in the World Cup of 2002 – and before a similar exit from last summer's European Championship.

Now, here is a challenge that should be presented to the FA's new chief executive, Brian Barwick, and his colleagues who purport to shape the English international game: try to find one point of encouragement in this week's dismal, infuriating and ultimately dishonest shambles, one reason to believe that England's fate in the World Cup of Germany next year will differ in any way to the ones that overtook them in Japan and Portugal.

The charge sheet against Eriksson was critically lengthened in the game with Marco van Basten's makeshift but skilful and scarcely troubled Dutch team. Here are the fresh cases to be taken into consideration when Eriksson's reign is judged...

Case No 1: Appalling negligence in the handling of Shaun Wright-Phillips, a player of thrilling promise, who, when he finally got his starting chance – as opposed to an ordeal by racism as a substitute at the Bernabeu – was played out of position for much of the time, then, after missing two chances but generally displaying more menace than any other England player on the field, yanked off after an hour. Did Eriksson know, or still more importantly care, how the youngster felt when dragging himself off the field with his great chance in ashes?

Case No 2: Having Andy Johnson, an exciting sharpshooter, toil as a workhorse, deep-lying wide player. Result: sickening waste of the opportunity to give an overachieving young player a chance to make a real case for himself.

Case No 3: Granting just half an hour to Stewart Downing, a natural left winger who all season has been suggesting that he might just be England's missing link along the left.

Case No 4: Still another shift in formation after four years on the job, this one, you are to bound to suspect, to justify the selection of his captain, David Beckham.

The wider indictment is that Eriksson, whatever his talent for manipulating the resources of a money-laden Lazio – they are now, like so much of Italian football, virtually on their uppers – hasn't a clue in the vital matter of developing an international team, of building certainties and smoothly dovetailing differing but complementary talents.

It was Eriksson's mind-numbing use of substitutes, which reached a peak around the time of the Upton Park débâcle, that provoked Fifa into imposing a limit of six for friendly games. Showing amazing restraint, Eriksson merely used five on Wednesday night, against Van Basten's two, but if they lacked the usual volume they were as incomprehensible as ever.

Perhaps the FA might prick up its ears now that a few voices of dissent are being joined by a great tide of criticism from the television paymasters. Gary Lineker could scarcely have been more dismissive of Eriksson's usual post-game bromides, Alan Hansen worked himself into a mood of high indignation, and both Graeme Le Saux and Jamie Redknapp were persistently critical.

Some might say that Le Saux and Redknapp were speaking from their own agendas as older and maybe embittered pros never granted even a peek inside Eriksson's England club. But then nothing they said diverted from the central, basic point that here was another night of potential opportunity, of enquiry and development, thrown utterly into the wind.

Almost too much was the self-serving verdict of Beckham. He thought it was good to try different systems and he felt England could take something from the game. What precisely? Another bunch of cheapened English caps, another night of going through some excruciatingly wearisome motions. On the field Beckham had some more than useful moments, one or two beautifully flighted passes, but does his England captaincy truly amount to anything more than a long series of advertisements for himself? Maybe the football nation will one day sit down and sift through the evidence.

Even more urgently, this should be done in the case of Eriksson. It was astonishing that he should be given that £1m pay rise after being caught in negotiation with Chelsea in the build-up to the European Championship. Less surprising in view of the now higher cost of ending his contract, but still regrettable, was the fact that the final chaos of England's failure in Portugal did not provoke any questions about his future at the FA.

It is as though Eriksson and his favourite son, Beckham, have been given the England team as their personal empire. Beckham explains improved form – he seems to be most convinced of this improvement – by the fact that he is much fitter now than when he made such a parody of himself in Portugal last summer. Should this not enrage his patron? How was it that he came to lead England in such admittedly poor condition? He explained that it was because of the training regime at Real Madrid, not his own failure to meet the demands of his position. That was a scandal. So, too, is what happened on Wednesday night.

If English football was properly run, the impeachment would already be under way.

BITTER SUGAR GNAWS AT HAND THAT FED HIM

Published: 15 February 2005

You might think Sir Alan Sugar, mustering all that ineffable charm which it seems he can draw upon so effortlessly, is breaking new analytical ground when he writes off footballers as "scum, total scum."

Not so. Once, while so selflessly fighting to save the life of Tottenham Hotspur, he gave us a vivid idea of what it was like trying to meet the wage demands of "layabouts" who, if they were not kicking footballs around, would mostly be guests of Her Majesty. "It's like," reported the sweet-talking knight who was, he may not now recall, more or less unheard of outside the dreary corridors of business before he set up his stall, so to speak, in the national game, "drinking prune juice while eating figs." Geddit? Yes, he was suggesting it was a bit like suffering financial diarrhoea.

But is this quite right? Could the saviour of White Hart Lane truly not venture too far from home during his stewardship without risking an embarrassing mishap?

The record says that this is not really true. The great patron of Tottenham was never popular on the terraces – a source of some mystification to him apparently and especially when he compared his rating to that of the Terry Venables he despised so much. But when Sir Alan eventually sold off an £8m investment for a nice little earner of £22m, while retaining a 13 per cent shareholding, valued today at around £4.5m, most people thought he had done well enough. It was not even by his own standards of business success a bad return from a pool of "total scum".

This, by the way, is before any rough accountancy is done on the profits of Sugar's firm Amstrad made from the perfectly proper sale of satellite dishes after football's television rights were sold to Sky, a decision which was crucially shaped by his vote, one which he was able to make after declaring a conflict of interest – which, to his astonishment, the football bosses allowed (we should remember, they are not known to swoop on such conflicts in the fashion of screaming eagles).

In these circumstances why would Sir Alan gnaw so venomously at the hand which fed him so generously? Well, it could just be that he is not averse to a bit more attention, and long-due reparation for all those anonymous days when he toiled from the birth of his ambition – starting his selling career in his north-east London schoolyard while putative scumballs were yelling such pathetic cries as "I'm Cliff Jones, I'm Dave Mackay" – to become one of the greatest money-makers in the land. Possibly his television show – modelled on that soaring prototype fronted by a titan of modern life, Donald Trump, in which desperate young wannabe captains of industry and commerce are relentlessly humiliated – could do with the publicity.

This, frankly, is a matter of some indifference here. What does chill the blood somewhat, however, is the sweeping denouncement of an entire section of humanity in such a crude way.

The holier-than-thou attitude is hard to fathom from a man from the ruthless world of business which is perhaps not entirely recognised for its altruism.

Most remarkable of all, of course, is that this unforgiving assessment of footballers should come from a man, who for all their imperfections, bought so profitably into the excitement they often bring to the marketplace. To be fair, he was honest enough about his vision for the great Tottenham. He once told his then manager Gerry Francis that the model should be Wimbledon, who of course now trade as Milton Keynes Dons without offering a prospective young Sugar a ghost of a chance of making five bob, let alone the best part of £20m.

No, Francis could not go careering around the place spending the Sky dish money. He had to do what Wimbledon did, buy low, sell high. Not exactly the old glory game when you come to think of it. Better this, though, he insisted, than the bizarre approach of the late Sir Jack Walker, who, at the age Sir Alan was flogging his sweeties, was sharing his own dream of making business success – he did it in steel – with that of his beloved Blackburn Rovers.

Sir Alan could not understand the style of Sir Jack, which is perhaps not an overwhelming surprise.

Now he talks of football dressing-rooms brimming with grab-all, total scum.

Where does he draw his demarcation line? Does he just limit it to the gang who were so inconvenient when he attempted to sell football as he might any other piece of merchandise? Or does he throw in the men who left him a legacy of such easy profit? Men like the push-and-run heroes of Arthur Rowe's days, or Bill Nicholson's luminaries, or a goalkeeper like Pat Jennings, or such a grafting pro as Steve Perryman, a genius like Jimmy Greaves, an Ossie Ardiles, who won a World Cup and said he was also so proud to play for "Tottingham", or Gary Lineker, who finished one off Sir Bobby Charlton's scoring mark for England and never drew a yellow card?

Speaking of today, does he include a kid like Ledley King, who plays where he is asked and with great heart, and maybe the young arrival Andy Reid, striding into an international career with the impressively organised Irish team?

He did not say. He just said that footballers were total scum. When you think about it it is amazing he spent so long in their midst. But then maybe not when you look at the figures.

ALL SIGNS SAY CHELSEA BUT ARE LIVERPOOL ON THE ROAD TO DESTINY?

Published: 27 April 2005

It's a nagging suspicion that should probably shuffle off into the ether, but, sorry, it will not. It says Liverpool cannot only frustrate the power brokers of Chelsea tonight but pass through to the final of the Champions League – and then, convinced of their destiny, win it.

According to Gary Lineker, Chelsea have unanswerable claims, at least on this penultimate stage of the competition, and no doubt few sound judges would argue with his ratings of the two teams, which gave an avalanche of a points advantage to José Mourinho's men. Certainly the evidence accumulated in their favour is formidable.

Apart from all their other accomplishments, including the spectacular ransacking of Barcelona, they have three straight wins over Rafael Benítez's team, who on Saturday were almost as fragile at Crystal Palace as in defeat at Southampton – a loss Lineker's television colleague Alan Hansen rated the worst performance he had seen from his old club.

But then that collapse came shortly before an almost equally abject display at Newcastle, a team against whom it is not so easy to lose. A few days later Liverpool confounded Juventus, attacking them at Anfield and then producing epic containment in Turin. There is something about Liverpool, something mysterious, unfathomable. Defenders like Jamie Carragher and Sami Hyypia touched sublime levels of resistance against Juve. They were shot through with belief.

The most relevant point about Liverpool and their hopes tonight is that there is simply no correlation between their performance in the Premiership and the Champions League. In the Premiership, Benítez, under the weight of sickening injuries and the limitations of his squad, has tried to eke his way to fourth place and Champions League qualification while holding back major players for the European action. It has been a compromise that appears to have failed in its first objective. However, in the Champions League we have seen a masterpiece of tactical acumen and practicality.

It is because of this, plus the huge factor of Xabi Alonso, that genuine hope can be extended at Stamford Bridge tonight.

Alonso, according to Liverpool icon Ian St John, is now the club's most important player. "This is no disrespect to Steven Gerrard. We know the impact he can have," says The Saint. "But Alonso is a genuine midfielder, who can use the ball so brilliantly, and can keep the team ticking over. At Stamford Bridge the value of this is potentially huge."

Yes, Alonso, the man who was stretching Chelsea to their seams at Anfield on New Year's Day when he was cut down by a sliding tackle from Frank Lampard, is both a key element tactically... and a talisman. With his ankle broken, he was ruled out of the season by a heartbroken Benítez. But against Juventus earlier this month, with just 45 minutes of action behind him, he was superb, as much in his spirit as his accomplishment. Tonight Alonso has to seize Stamford Bridge, show that he is indeed a throwback to the old days of creative midfielders who stitched together a team performance.

Gerrard, surely, will be seen by Benítez as his principal shock troop, a man whose strength and potential to explode will be a permanent caution on Chelsea.

Another encouragement for Liverpool, with Luis Garcia recently showing that his waspish presence can generate moments of authentic devastation, is that at no point in their trail of three defeats by Chelsea did they appear to be over-matched. Indeed, on the day that Alonso was struck down, Chelsea also benefited from one of the season's worst refereeing decisions when Tiago plainly handled the ball in the penalty area. Liverpool had been playing with patience and considerable touch.

In the Carling Cup final Mourinho's team were clearly the better but would they have prospered but for Gerrard's own goal? In football such patterns are always waiting to be broken, and the belief here is that Liverpool have the means to do it. Chelsea have so much, of course, strength, superb application, fine talent – the return of Arjen Robben is a huge injection of menace – and behind the virtue of three contenders for player of the year, winner John Terry, Frank Lampard and Petr Cech, is the will of Mourinho. Of course, they are favourites, but when you say all of that, the suspicion that whispers Liverpool still refuses to go away.

LIVERPOOL'S DREAMERS BREATHE LIFE BACK INTO GAME WITH A FANTASY FINAL

Published: 27 May 2005

In the grey dawn here yesterday it was hardly surprising that Liverpool still groped to grasp fully the extent of their achievement a few hours earlier. It is, after all, not every night that you grovel in the dirt and then touch the stars.

Steven Gerrard, fingering for reassurance the winners' medal hanging from around his neck, was in a place he had never been before, somewhere between bliss and disbelief. But then weren't we all?

Gerrard admitted to night-long chilling flashbacks to that moment when he thought the most dramatic recovery in the history of the European Cup and its successor the Champions League had been broken.

Andrei Shevchenko, the coldest finisher on the football planet, bore down on Jerzy Dudek. Gerrard thought like the rest of us. He believed the lights, along with the fantasy, were about to switched off.

It is history now, astonishing, unforgettable history, that the Polish keeper who was also fighting for his professional life at the top of the game made his stupendous double save.

But it is also history that has still to be understood fully by the football authorities, those men who know the price of everything in the game but apparently so little about its most precious values.

If they persist in their belief that Liverpool should be denied the right to defend the title – the club's fifth – they won here in such an unprecedented dramatic way, they will be guilty of a lot more than the failure of common sense charged by the winning coach, Rafael Benítez.

They will be airbrushing away the most glorious reaffirmation of the mystery and the brilliance of the world's most popular game. They will be saying to all those who scan the lists of next season's contenders, that Liverpool's three-goal fightback against Milan simply didn't happen. They will be asserting that it is a story that, however noble and incredible, cannot be absorbed comfortably by the money-led imperatives of the Champions League.

So it has to be shredded? If such a view is maintained, it will be more than another football scandal heaped on top of all the others. It will be sacrilege.

More than anything, it will be to reject the bone-deep pleasure that accompanied 30,000 Liverpool fans as they wound their way back down through the hills surrounding the gaunt Ataturk stadium. They knew precisely what they were celebrating. It was a new dimension to the most important club game played in Europe each year.

We should be very sure about the meaning of this Liverpool victory on the 50th anniversary of a tournament that was once such an uncomplicated quest for the best team in Europe.

It was not about the power of wealth, because if it was, Chelsea and their oligarch owner and trend-setting coach would have won it. It wasn't about a deep education in the often black art of caution and tactical sophistication. In that case Carlo Ancelotti's Milan would have eased their way home, and the more easily after driving Liverpool to the point of despair with the authority of their football – and their three goals – in the first half. No, it was to do with the unchartable impulse of a collective spirit, a transforming belief that if you play honestly enough, if you refuse to accept the idea of defeat, anything can happen.

What happened on Wednesday night generated emotion that was as sustained – and as pure – as anyone who has been around for roughly the length of the competition can ever have experienced.

No, it wasn't as spellbinding as Real Madrid's slaughter of Eintracht Frankfurt in Hampden Park 45 years ago, when a fine German side were engulfed by the legendary men in white and the peerless Alfredo di Stefano moved so majestically downfield to score a goal that some still claim to be the best ever seen in a European Cup final.

It didn't have such a blinding moment of perfect technique as the one Zinedine Zidane produced when Real beat Bayer Leverkusen three years ago. Liverpool's triumph in the penalty shoot-out didn't represent the brilliant planning and deep strength of their predecessors when four titles were won in the late Seventies and early Eighties. Benítez's Liverpool certainly had none of the hauteur of the Milan of Gullit, Van Basten, Baresi and the young Paolo Maldini, who at 36 here this week provoked the first outrageous drama with a goal inside the first minute.

The hard truth is that when you looked closely at Liverpool this week they didn't have very much at all, not when you analysed individual performances – and detached them from the improbable glory of their earlier victories over Juventus and Chelsea. They didn't have a master-plan, by no means.

The one devised by Benítez was an embarrassing wreckage when his gamble on Harry Kewell – so shocking in the first-half absence of Dietmar Hamann – was abandoned early and Milan had picked their way to an apparently impregnable lead. They didn't have a single outstanding performance if you took away the heroics of Dudek and the magnificent impact of Hamann in the second half.

But they did have that unlikely, even illogical belief in themselves inspired by Benítez in his first year in English football.

Before Wednesday night, Manchester United held the English franchise on the breathing of life back into a dead cause in a European Cup final. In 1999 they too had been outplayed, by Bayern Munich. They too had made failed tactical lunges, with David Beckham adrift in the centre of midfield and Bayern squandering chances to build on their lead. But United merely rescued their destiny with two goals in the last minutes. Liverpool had to pick up their beds and walk.

They did it for the entire second half and 30 minutes of extra time. They undoubtedly went beyond the limits of their talent.

Now Benítez has to make a new Liverpool team, one that can compete properly in the Premiership, and as he does it he knows that he is not blessed with so many certainties. Gerrard, if he does what he is now so strongly suggesting, and takes root in his native soil, is one, no doubt. So is Xabi Alonso, who when he fully adjusts to the frenzies of English football will surely give Liverpool a thread of coherence, and passing brilliance that has been absent at Anfield for so many years. John Arne Riise, despite his shoot-out miss, is now an authentic hero after his contributions in the European games. Jamie Carragher is the heart and the sinew of the club. But elsewhere there have to be severe doubts, even with the Ataturk fantasy still so vivid.

Luis Garcia is a waspish presence, a scorer of dramatic goals, certainly, but a man to rely on in all seasons? He is too often an accident in the making, as we saw when Kaka, the elegant Brazilian who threatened to control the game quite masterfully in the first half, robbed him deep in the Milan half for the chance to send Shevchenko away. Djimi Traoré performed heroics but some of his antics are guaranteed to bring a dryness to his coach's mouth. Neither Milan Baros, for all his industry, or Djbril Cissé seem likely to meet the highest demands, and much will be expected of Fernando Morientes next season.

Benítez says that there will be signings and that those men who have been touched by what has happened here, and who survive the reshaping of the team, will carry with them new levels of confidence.

One day Benítez may admit to the scale of his mistake when he left Hamann out of the initial action, but in the meantime you have to believe that he will continue to draw benefit from his passion and his cultivation of the spirit of his players. No, he said, he did not expect to be addressed as the Special One. He would continue to believe that he was nothing without the support – and the hearts – of his players.

That conviction has made Liverpool the champions of Europe once again. Maybe it has also changed the way we look at football.

PITIFUL PUNISHMENTS PROVE THE GAME HAS NO ORDER OR SHAME

Published: 02 June 2005

Several times the Premier League spokesman said that his bosses hoped that the deterrent value of their action would bite into those who had been found guilty of flaunting their belief that the rules of football are not worth the paper they are written on.

It was a breathtaking performance. It made a mockery of the idea that football has governance. It does not – it has a gang of businessmen who, by their actions yesterday, suggested they would not know a sporting value, a point of principle, if it mugged them in a West End street – or a luxurious hotel.

That is, of course, precisely what happened when Arsenal's Ashley Cole went to the meeting where his agent Jonathan Barnett and Chelsea's key adviser Pini Zahavi had arranged for him to meet José Mourinho and the Stamford Bridge chief executive Peter Kenyon.

Yes, everybody knows that tapping-up is part of football. It has gone on down the decades – one famous manager once invaded the Cup final banquet of a rival club to make a move for their star player – but never before had we seen something so blatant, so arrogant.

It was so shameless in its implication that only money counted, that a key player like Cole, developed down the years by Chelsea's rivals Arsenal, had merely to run into a hitch in contract negotiations, had merely to pick up the phone for his agent to deliver him to the moneybags across town.

What did this say about respect for rivals in a league which is supposed to be the envy of the world game?

It said that it did not exist. It said the devil could take the hindmost – and all the fans who are lured into the belief that the players who represent them, and receive fabulous rewards, at least share a little of their own passions and loyalties.

But of course this did not prevent the Premier League dressing up its feeble stab at authority.

Deterrent? Action? What a truly pitiful organisation this is. It runs a league which cannot foster genuine competition beyond three or four clubs and then when it has a chance to remind its most powerful member, and reigning champions, that they are part of a league, and that this involves certain decencies of appearance, if not behaviour, what does it do?

It fines Cole less than a month's wages, which while not putting anything like a stop to his life of luxury is enough for his lawyer to launch an appeal, while talking about the enduring slave-master relationship in football. This slave, of course, made his run for freedom because Arsenal apparently reneged on an agreement to up his wages to £60,000 a week. In a misguided show of power which does not exist, the Arsenal directors tried to peg him to a mere £55,000.

Cole's lawyer will argue that his client would not risk such sanction in the real world for talking to a prospective employer – but then when was football a part of the real world? Not, certainly, when it was pinning the men who filled the stadiums to groaning capacity to a maximum wage of £20 a week – and not now when Rio Ferdinand demands £120,000 a week and Cole shows his contempt for all those who have cheered him at Highbury.

The fines of £300,000 on Chelsea and £200,000 on José Mourinho are pitiful.

There was only one meaningful penalty for Chelsea. It was to handicap them for next season's campaign – a six-point deduction would have carried the force of natural justice, given their cynical willingness to so damage the campaign of one of their two legitimate challengers. Instead we had the palsied compromise: a suspended three-point deduction, to be enforced only if Chelsea committed a similar offence in 2005-06.

This means, of course, that any future meeting between Kenyon and Mourinho and a putative Chelsea star might have to occur in a rather more secluded place, though not maybe Kenyon's apartment, where Sven-Goran Eriksson was photographed in the process of being tempted away from the national team.

In the post-Bosman world there is a limit on the disciplinary powers of the football authority. It knows how easy it is to make work for the lawyers in the European court, but where is the will to impose values; a code of conduct which might just suggest a desire, if not the capacity, to make the word league not seem so out of place at the top of English football?

League implies awareness of the need for co-operation – a sense that a truly competitive football competition needs to be conscious that ultimately it will always only be as strong as its weakest link.

Yes, of course it is true that Chelsea were not breaking any ignominious ground when they went with their largesse to the hotel to see Cole. They were reinforced by a long and ruthless tradition. But just as in the cases of Eriksson, and Mourinho's shocking intrusion in the life of the Swedish referee Anders Frisk, they did it with a gut-wrenching belief that whatever was good for Chelsea carried its own validity.

Yesterday the Premier League had the chance to strike back at such a philosophy of sporting Doomsday. It could have deducted points. It could have said that even for this organisation a line had to be drawn.

But it rolled over. It said that the lack of leadership in football was just about total.

CANTWELL DREAM CONTRASTS SHARPLY WITH REALITY OF TODAY'S IMPLODING DISCIPLINE

Published: 20 September 2005

A great football man was buried in Peterborough yesterday. It is not one of the power bases of football, but it is where the big man from Cork chose to end his career and for his admirers this is maybe distinction enough for the little town on the edge of the Fens.

Noel Cantwell, 73, was never festooned with honours, but he had a few: he won a Second Division championship medal with West Ham United and he led Manchester United on their first step to post-Munich glory with victory in the 1963 FA Cup final. He gained 36 Republic of Ireland caps in various positions, but his specialist role was full-back: he was one of the first of his breed to grasp that diving into tackles on a Tom Finney or a Cliff Jones was one of the last words in human folly. What you had to do was jockey and make sure of support.

His glory, though, was not in his trophy cabinet but in his vision of what football could be and in his impatience with what he saw as the great malaise of the English game. He wanted football to grow up here as it had across Europe and South America. This was recognised in the church yesterday when the pews were filled by men like Sir Bobby Charlton and Denis Law, Ian St John and Paddy Crerand, Martin Peters, John Giles and Tommy Docherty.

The funeral of Noel Cantwell had a double poignancy yesterday. There was pain at the passing of a brave, generous and handsome man who had a passion for life as well as football.

Cantwell had a dream. It was of a game where everyone fought for improved training techniques in a drive to enhance performance, where footballers behaved like professional men and were given the respect, and the rewards, that were their due. The sadness in his story is the reality of so much of today's football, the game of agents and spiralling rewards and imploding personal and collective discipline.

Many, including the great man himself, saw Cantwell as the natural successor to Sir Matt Busby, but though the Irishman deeply admired the meaning of Busby's career, he was shocked by the Old Trafford regime when he arrived in 1960.

Perhaps fatally for his long- term prospects, he said so. Eamon Dunphy, a young pro at that time, recalled in his acclaimed biography of Busby, *A Strange Kind of Glory*, one Cantwell outburst. He announced that the place "was a joke" and he railed against one pre-game talk by Busby which had as its central point the instruction, "keep it simple, find a red shirt".

Cantwell exploded: "Find a fucking red shirt? You don't need a manager for that. How do you find a red shirt if you haven't worked on it, talked about it."

He knew that Busby's genius lay in other areas, most dramatically in his ability to recognise individual talent that could be embraced in a beautiful style of play and the building of a winning aura, but he wanted a new approach to the factory floor of football. He wanted thinking, working pros receiving the benefit of all the wisdom that had revolutionised football in places like Eastern Europe, Italy and Spain.

The "English revolution" had started at Upton Park when men like Cantwell, Malcolm Allison, Frank O'Farrell, John Bond and Malcolm Musgrove had looked around the English game and been appalled by what they saw.

Allison was the most vociferous. On national service in Austria in the late Forties, one morning he had spied on the Soviet army team training in the Viennese woods. It carried the force of revelation. The Soviets had very little equipment, and were playing in big old army boots, but their training and practice was full of innovation. When he returned to Charlton Athletic, the players were still running endless circles of The Valley. The veteran Jimmy Seed was underwhelmed, despite the impact of Moscow Dynamo, on a post-war tour. When Allison moved to West Ham he did so as a prophet and Cantwell stood by his side when the talk in the dressing-room, and around the corner in an Italian greasy spoon cafe, was of a new football.

Eventually, Allison put his ideas into practice when he inspired Manchester City to the League title, the FA Cup, the Cup-winners Cup and the League Cup in a spell-binding burst of thrilling football between 1968 and 1970. Cantwell, who also served as chairman of the Professional Footballers' Association, didn't find such fulfilment as a coach and manager, but here, too, was a story that defined both the feel that Cantwell had for the game and the often fiendishly fine line between overwhelming success and something so many club chairmen would see as failure.

Instead of waiting on his chances of succeeding Busby, the challenge eventually going to Wilf McGuiness and then, quickly, O'Farrell, Cantwell went to Coventry City to succeed Jimmy Hill, who had carried the club into the First

Division. It is always a perilous situation when a newly promoted club fights to establish itself in the top flight but for four years Cantwell did so superbly. However, he had a season of struggle in 1972 and the chairman of the club, Derrick Robbins, a controversial figure, had an Easter time panic. He relieved Cantwell of his duties and, successively, invited staff members Ian St John and former England goalkeeper Tony Waiters to take over the job. Both refused, out of loyalty to their boss and shock at the injustice.

St John gives a telling account of the firing of Noel Cantwell. He went out to the chairman's house with his boss and waited in the hallway while Cantwell went into the lounge and argued for his future at a club which was brimming with fast-developing talent. St John heard Cantwell tell Robbins that this was a classic situation in football, a time when a strong chairman would be looking to the future and seeing all the progress that had occurred. He cited examples of the success of this policy, starting with the faith the Manchester United board had always shown in Busby. But the argument did not go well. Cantwell came out of the room and said to St John: "I'm finished."

How good were Cantwell's Coventry? Far too good to go down, as they proved in the closing weeks of the season. All of Cantwell's discoveries went on to have fine careers. Dennis Mortimer was an outstanding young midfielder: quick, bright and skilful. Willie Carr was one of the last of the Scottish craftsmen, clever and creative and hugely popular with the fans. Ernie Hunt was one of the game's most colourful characters. The line was led by the strong young striker Billy Rafferty and a fortress was developing in defence with Jeff Blockley, a potential England stopper and the formidable Scot, Roy Barry, and in goal Bill Glazier was a paragon of reliability. But a chairman panicked and Noel Cantwell, a man of great strength and intelligence was gone.

So much of the history of English football is encapsulated in that last forlorn sentence. Cantwell had stints with the New England/Jacksonville Tea Men, he had a year in charge of the Irish team, was manager, then general manager of Peterborough United. But he knew that the tide of his ambition had run its course. He had his hurts, not least the loss of a beloved son, and serious illness which he fought with great courage. You would occasionally see him at a big match and he was always the same, a smile on his fine face and with no cargo of bitterness. Whatever he thought of how things had turned out, he didn't rant about betrayal. He got on with the business of living his life, and from time to time he would rejoice about so many of his experiences in football.

He wanted it to be so much better, as it was and how it turned out to be, and that he was unable, in the end, to make as much difference as he craved, never touched his affection for football. He always cared. One of the mourners, Giles, recalled his own arrival in the Irish squad as a nervous teenager. "Noel was a god but when I reported in the Gresham Hotel on O'Connell Street in Dublin he took me aside, put an arm round my shoulder and told me how I should approach the game. He took away the fear. He always did that."

That is no mean memorial to any football man – and it will be so as long as the game is played.

ENGLAND'S PERFORMANCE: A QUALIFIED FAILURE

Published: 10 October 2005

England may have reached the finals of the World Cup with the help of the Netherlands, but for how much longer can they tolerate the coaching of Sven-Goran Eriksson and the captaincy of David Beckham?

The Football Association will surely be avoiding its responsibilities if it does not question seriously, while there is still time to do something about it, the quality of England's leadership both on and off the field.

After the run of mediocrity, and worse, to a desperately disquieting 1-0 victory at Old Trafford over an Austrian team so far from the heart of football power, Eriksson's claim that some of England's play was "brilliant" was almost as dismaying as the incoherence of so much of their work.

It had to provoke those biting questions. Question one: can Eriksson be expected to draw from arguably the most talented collection of England players since Sir Alf Ramsey led his 1970 team to Mexico any more than he did in the ultimately hapless campaigns of World Cup 2002 and the European Championship of last summer? Question two: can there any longer be any serious doubt about David Beckham's temperamental failure as a captain?

All current evidence says that in both cases the answer is no.

This is the reality amid the optimistic talk that because of the talent of such as Wayne Rooney, Steven Gerrard, Frank Lampard, Michael Owen, and Beckham himself, England must be among the favourites to win the great prize in Germany next summer.

It is a contention mocked both by England's current form, including pulverising defeats by Denmark and Northern Ireland, and any serious charting of Eriksson's efforts in the two major tournaments qualified for under his command.

That Eriksson has the knack of gaining entrance to the big football parties, however raggedly, understandably created much initial gratitude in an FA headquarters desperately conscious of the financial penalty that accompanies any failure in this limited ambition. But at £4m-plus-a-year, Eriksson is plainly failing in the prime purpose of his job: it looks quite beyond him to make England look like serious runners for the prize they last won 39 years ago.

What, it has to be asked, is the point of crashing the party if you make a fool of yourself once the band strikes up?

Any move to pre-empt another crushing anticlimax when serious football nations like Brazil and hosts Germany dispute the outcome of another World Cup, will no doubt be resisted by talk of the extreme cost of ending Eriksson's contract, which runs to 2008, and the difficulty of replacing him. But then what is the alternative? The evidence from here could not be less muted: it is another march to futility. Better surely to airlift in a trouble-shooting man of the football world, someone like the Dutch veteran Guus Hiddink, who did such a magnificent job with South Korea three years ago, or Terry Venables – yes, Terry Venables, the best England coach since Ramsey – or even the FA's director of football, Trevor Brooking.

Brooking is not a career coach but he understands the international game and would be guaranteed to produce a more pro-active performance than Eriksson, who was so bizarrely praised for his leadership at the weekend when he bowed to the overwhelming dictate of form and made Rio Ferdinand the first of his "untouchables" to be dropped. Some might say we are too near to the finals to disrupt the rhythm of the team, but then where is the rhythm or even a vague upsurge of assurance?

The scandal is that while such as Rooney, Lampard and Gerrard, and again Beckham in his last few matches for Real Madrid, can look giants of club football, they invariably shrivel when they find themselves decorated by three lions.

Nor is an explanation at all difficult to find. Eriksson has utterly abandoned the concept of team-building. His feckless approach to friendlies, in which Ramsey built a world-beating force, reached an appalling denouement in Copenhagen last month – one which had its precursor several years earlier on the psychologically shocking night the Australian "Socceroos" won at Upton Park. Now the harvest is repeated in one competitive match after another.

The breakdown against Denmark was harrowing. A poor Welsh side exposed a poverty of creativity and force in Cardiff. Northern Ireland provoked both despair and anarchy in the English team. Against no-hopers Austria, in the penultimate game of one of the softest groups in European World Cup qualifying, the margins were gut-wrenchingly fine, especially when Roland Linz lobbed the ball against England's crossbar.

In the World Cup quarter-final Eriksson and his staff stood mesmerised as 10-man Brazil went by them after Beckham jumped out a tackle and then watched Rivaldo equalise. At the same stage of the European Championship, after the cruelly injured Rooney had promised to carry England all the way on the back of his superbly emerging talent, Eriksson was again becalmed as his opposite number, Luiz Felipe Scolari, showed the nerve to replace the great Luis Figo and revamp his side. Does anyone, in or out of the FA, not see enough evidence to fear a similar fate in Germany?

The doubts about Beckham as captain should not be softened by the legitimate argument that at least one of his yellow cards was harsh. His crime, and in a captain it was unforgivable, was to yet again lose his head in a critical situation.

A born captain, a Bobby Moore or a John Terry, never loses his sense of team and responsibility. In Beckham's case it appears to be an unbreakable habit. The fact that he is now the only England player to be twice sent off is less important, given the pettiness and the petulance of his offences, than the reality that this Wednesday's final qualifying game against Poland, which but for the Dutch could have been so hugely important, will be the third he has missed in as many years.

It is not the track record of a leader, no more than the countless times England have looked unsuccessfully for persuasive leadership from the man wearing the armband.

On Saturday Eriksson agreed that Beckham had been "angry" after the first booking, that a lack of composure was indeed evident, but this, he said, was no reason to reconsider his captain's role. Beckham, Eriksson added mysteriously, wanted to win. So what does disqualify a captain? Eriksson wouldn't say. But then what disqualifies a coach? Here on Saturday making the list was the bleakest of chores. World Cup euphoria? It is a bad joke only the FA can now possibly avert.

TERRY FITS IDENTIKIT OF CRUYFF'S WARRIOR

Published: 12 October 2005

When English international football was suffering an earlier crisis of confidence, one that foretold the kind of doubts which assail the team tonight against Poland at Old Trafford, some words of powerful reassurance came from an impeccable source.

Johan Cruyff, who once destroyed England at Wembley while rarely crossing the halfway line, said: "You know I don't think there will ever be a time when the English player is not respected, and feared, across the world of football.

"There is a good reason for this. The English footballer is very brave and strong and committed and there are always enough high-class players in his team to cause concern in any opponent. This is not a passing thing. I have found it always to be the same. It is a national characteristic and it is one you should be proud of."

Cruyff's days as the glory of Dutch football were over then. He was coaching Barcelona and his views were a welcome antidote to a growing despair in this country. Sir Alf Ramsey's reign had collapsed after the failure to qualify for the 1974 finals and, four years later, Don Revie found it impossible to duplicate his success with Leeds United when he took over the national team.

There was a certain poignancy to Cruyff's tribute to the English, who on the face of it had been utterly eclipsed by the "total football" of the Netherlands. Twice, the Dutch had played brilliantly to reach World Cup finals, those of '74 and '78. Twice they lost in the most haunting circumstances, and when Cruyff spoke of the English players' warrior quality there was perhaps a hint of regret about a missing element in his own nation's football.

No such yearnings would have besieged Cruyff in the last month or so – as England's displays against four non-World Cup qualifiers, Denmark, Wales, Northern Ireland and Austria have lurched from one bout of incoherence to another – and this is especially so given the assistance provided by the promising Dutch team in England's qualification. But this still leaves an intriguing question: does the old theory of Cruyff still hold good, is it merely waiting for proper leadership, on and off the field?

It is a question which carries us to the heart of what should be the most intensely debatable aspect of tonight's match. Why, we have to ask, is it Michael Owen rather than John Terry who is leading out the team in place of the suspended David Beckham? Who, of contemporary English footballers, most fits Cruyff's Identikit drawn on that sunny day at the Nou Camp? Terry, no doubt, heads the candidates.

This is no disrespect to Owen. He is what he is, and this is another kind of glory of the English game: a born goalscorer of deep professionalism whose instinct is to do his job as well as he can and if he has a role of leadership it is one of example. But Terry is surely the Cruyff prototype of the best of the English competitive nature, a man of action and natural leadership. Terry plays with an intensity that cannot fail to brush against, and lift, his team-mates' psyche and spirit.

He is supposed to lack pace, and to a degree this is true, but not cripplingly so. It was said of Bobby Moore that he wasn't exactly the West Ham express. Nor was he, but he saw most things before they happened and had a seek-and-destroy mechanism that was no less acute because it was housed so stylishly.

Comparing Terry and Moore doesn't take us to the real point, however. Terry may never touch the distinction of Moore, who, even in the most compelling action, the kind provoked by somebody like Pelé so memorably in Guadalajara in 1970, was much the more cerebral. A little part of him always stayed detached, no doubt the better to read and respond to the game's flow.

The cynical may have their theories about why the England coach, Sven-Goran Eriksson, was so emphatic that the armband surrendered so petulantly by Beckham would pass, as a formality, to Owen, and they have nothing to do with the fact that when the latter twice took over in similar circumstances he scored on both difficult occasions. They may say that the potentially galvanising effect of Terry's leadership might cast in an even more questioning light the coach's faith in the erratic course of Beckham's captaincy.

Whatever the truth, one reality is self-evident. José Mourinho's faith in Terry has been devout and magnificently rewarded. This most unforgiving of coaches has seen in Terry the unquenchable force of the English footballer, one that Cruyff recognised so long ago. Perhaps Eriksson will see it one day; who knows, maybe, the next time Beckham is suspended.

THE WARRIOR WHO SHAPED FERGUSON'S EMPIRE

Published: 19 November 2005

In the sudden wake of the Roy Keane era there is a single imperative, one that his patron Sir Alex Ferguson accepted as long as he could after the tumultuous good years turned into a time of pain and anger. From a critical distance we can only follow suit, and say as we do of the careers of most great figures: you take the best and live with the rest.

You live with the arrogance and the insults; the intolerance of all who do not fit into one man's fierce picture of what is right in a professional footballer and the organisation that surrounds him. You forgive the old bouts of drunkenness and the violence on the field that sometimes it was hard to separate from thuggery.

You do not compare this rough style – and Ferguson's need to bail him out of a police cell and defend him against charges that he had run out of control – with the grace and the statesmanship of a Sir Bobby Charlton, or the engaging manner of his immediate, warrior-like predecessor Bryan Robson.

No, if you do that you lose sight of the essential truth. It is that Keane was not only the heart and the soul of Ferguson's United. He was also the most dominant player in the history of the Premiership. This carried him as far as it could in a relationship always so potentially explosive. Yesterday time simply ran out on Keane and Fergie.

Plainly, the point of breakdown had been coming for several years. It had kept pace with the ebbing of the physical powers of a player who had been more than a leader.

He was no less than the guardian of the team's conscience. Ferguson didn't lightly give him the power of his master's voice, a privilege which turned horribly destructive recently when, like some disenchanted wolf, he snarled, so damagingly to the embattled leader of the pack. Ferguson gave Keane his huge leeway not out of affection but debt and the deepest of professional respect, because if Keane couldn't keep a dressing-room honest, nobody could.

Any review of Keane's performance, for both United and the Republic of Ireland, is inevitably clouded with ambivalence... and paradox.

Nowhere was this better exemplified than in the ferocity of his rebellion in

Saipan. Then, on the eve of the 2002 World Cup, he gave Ireland's coach Mick McCarthy no choice but to send him home.

Keane, far from the first time in his life, had given way to excess, this time in his judgement of the world around him. He wanted it to be not as it was but how he believed it should be, right down to the last detail.

For him it was impossible that Ireland's preparations should be less professional than those he had grown used to at Old Trafford, and if making the point involved a grievous blow to his nation's World Cup hopes, and the distribution of terrible insult to his coach and his team-mates, if it meant that his position as an icon of Irish sport would be perhaps permanently compromised, he made it clear that he could scarcely care less.

There was the ultimate contradiction because no one could have done more to carry the Irish team beyond their collective talent and into those World Cup finals at the expense of the Netherlands, a major football nation. On a leg that was becoming an ever-increasing challenge to medical science, Keane played the star-spangled Dutch to a standstill. He was, as always, the core of the Irish effort and the Dutch were just another team astounded by the depth of his will.

It is not easy to like a man who cares so little for the feelings of those around him. Once at an airport he was introduced to one of his greatest predecessors in the green shirt of Ireland; he grunted, and didn't look up. He lived in his own world, and nothing that had gone before or would follow could intrude upon that.

John Giles, as it happened, shrugged away the insult, saying: "There is a lot more about Roy Keane that I like than I dislike. Why? Because he was the most influential player of his age. He was the ultimate competitor and as United are finding now, he was utterly irreplaceable in what he represented." What was that, precisely? It was a competitive passion that rarely comes more than once a generation.

In polling of United fans, Roy Keane regularly runs second to the talismanic Frenchman Eric Cantona when the question of the best Old Trafford player of the Ferguson epoch is raised, just as he came off worst with David Beckham in lists of voting for the World and European Player of the Year awards.

But then ask Ferguson over a single malt who was the man who most shaped his empire, not for a day or a season, not in a burst of virtuosity, not in some Gallic flourish or mesmerising free-kick, but match by match, effort by effort, and the strong suspicion must be that he would nominate his turbulent Irishman.

Cantona unlocked the future and Beckham gave it skill and decoration. Keane was its warrior leader and, in a boisterous form of law and order, its policeman.

He didn't do it on his own, of course. Paul Scholes and Peter Schmeichel, Ryan Giggs and the Neville Boys, Denis Irwin ... the depth of United's drive was formidable, always, but when it mattered most, who was it who dug deepest, who threw his fist most defiantly to the heavens? Invariably it was Keane.

He did it in a way that makes a nonsense of all the tactical musings about diamonds and holding players, the man who sits and the man who goes. Keane was a holding player when he needed to be but did anyone ever go more wholeheartedly for the jugular? Did any of his generation ever read the game more acutely, or were any less likely to allow confusion if he had ever been put in the company of a Steve Gerrard or a Frank Lampard? No, Keane's way would have been the option, and for the best of reasons. It would be the classic way of the midfield general.

There have been more graceful midfield operators. He didn't pass the ball like Glenn Hoddle, or create the brief wizardry of a Paul Gascoigne. But what he did, and all the essentials were incorporated into his game, was with ultimate conviction and efficiency. The most unforgettable example of Keane's commitment surely came at the Stadio Delle Alpi in Turin in 1999, when United slipped two goals down in the opening exchanges of the second leg of the Champions League semi-final against Juventus. United had been ambushed but Juve's timing was reckless. It gave Keane too long to rally his team and his blood. He scored the goal that carried United to the Nou Camp for the final and United's second trophy with a wonderfully arching header – and the fact that he had picked up the yellow card that would keep him out of the game proved utterly immaterial.

In similar circumstances in a World Cup semi-final, Gascoigne burst into tears. Keane merely clenched his teeth – and his fists.

Sooner or later the sinew of all men wilts, but in some cases not the spirit. We saw that well enough at Highbury last February, when United were required to make something of a last stand.

Keane faced down Patrick Vieira, for so long his one serious rival as the most influential player in the Premiership, both in the tunnel and on the field. Vieira had dared to throw around his weight in the presence of Keane, a dangerous thing to do at any time but suicidal at such a point of competitive tension. The Frenchman may have guessed that the fire had finally flickered down. He will probably always carry the burn marks that came from his miscalculation.

After Keane, what at Old Trafford? There is talk of Michael Ballack, hopes for Alan Smith and Darren Fletcher, and much scouring, no doubt, of the world market. But you cannot replace a Roy Keane. You can get various versions.

A Ballack would give you bold strikes from an advanced position in midfield. One day Smith's natural aggression might mature into significant value. Fletcher might overcome doubts about his pace and his force.

But a new Keane, a new roaring boyo from the streets of Cork City, a boozing, bar-clearing tearaway who knew quite how well he could play the game of football, and had the nerve to write to his first big-time manager, Brian Clough, to prove it? It is not likely.

Ferguson knows this better than any football man alive. Indeed, he took the best and he lived with the rest. It was, by some distance, his most decisive pact with glory.

BLESSED WITH GIFTS FROM GODS, BUT CURSED BY HIS OWN NATURE

Published: 25 November 2005

George Best's fight for life was ebbing away yesterday in London's Cromwell hospital at the age of 59 but, if that is the record, it is maybe not the truth, not all of it anyway.

Something inside him died long ago and, even in his last hours, there was a forlorn echo of that when his doctor, Professor Roger Williams, clearly moved, reported he had told the family of the great, fallen football icon that all hope of his recovery had gone. He might live another 24 hours but, in effect, the story of George Best was over.

Some, and they included his deepest admirers, might have said that, in one way, that was true even before his final few years of pain and controversy, when some questioned even his right to what was left of his life. Others will see a terrible irony in that the end of Best's losing battle against alcoholism coincided with the arrival of 24-hour drinking licences.

What had died in Best somewhere along the uncharted days was something that once burnt so fiercely that the chances of it surviving to a wise and mellow age were probably always remote.

It was the fire of his conviction that he could do something he loved maybe better than anyone else on earth, a view that was mirrored later in his droll, maybe unconsciously sad reflection that, had he been born ugly, the world might not have settled on the Brazilian Pelé as the greatest player in the history of the game. That doesn't make the jolt of Best's passing any less intense, at least for those – and they still number in their millions – who will never forget the magical promise and so much of the dazzling fulfilment of his youth.

It is so because even if you cannot join the righteous indignation of those who complain he threw away the gift of a transplanted liver that might have been more rewardingly placed, at least in the sober preservation of an individual life, as he did so many of the other advantages that were heaped upon him, there is nothing so tragic as a wasted life.

Wasted? Maybe it is a matter of degree when you consider the density of the brilliance he produced in the brief years he allowed for a full expression of his talent. However, the fact that cannot be avoided, even by those who loved him dearly, at the end of Best's booze-washed journey is that in his world of football perhaps no one had wasted quite so much, quite so quickly.

This will no doubt offend the romantic view of Best's impact on the game to which he brought such unique and mesmerising gifts.

Even in the final months of his desperately sad existence, some still gloried in the wildness of his ways, as though they were some inevitable consequence of genius. They weren't. They were the long played-out results of his own weakness in the face of unprecedented celebrity – and also the failure of football in the Sixties to adequately protect such a luminous young star from the rush of fame.

No one in football had a greater reputation for wisdom, on both sides of the touchline, than Best's manager at Manchester United, Sir Matt Busby. But in the end even he was forced to wash his hands of the prodigal son, though any suggestion of abdication by the great manager has to be tempered by the fact that football, and indeed few aspects of English life, had ever seen a young man so besieged as this essentially shy Irishman.

One of Busby's successors, Frank O'Farrell, delivered a haunting prophecy when Best, still in his mid-twenties, ran away from Old Trafford and told a media pack in the Spanish holiday resort of Marbella that he was putting back a bottle of vodka a day.

Said O'Farrell: "The worry is not so much for George today, he is still young, he has his looks and his celebrity and no doubt he will be able to make some sort of living outside of football. But I worry about him in the future, when he has lost those looks, when he cannot be fit again, and then I wonder how he will feel."

We will never quite know because, somewhere along the line, George Best reinvented himself. He became a pundit, a sage of the game and in the process he seemed to lose sight of the fact that when he should have been in the prime of his talent, someone standing alongside the likes of Pelé and Cruyff and his United clubmate, Bobby Charlton, he was drifting into an irreversible descent.

He was playing for Second Division Fulham, for Dunstable, for the Los Angeles Aztecs, the San José Earthquakes, for Hibs and Stockport County, for the Toronto Indoor Soccer School, Cork Celtic and the Jewish Guild FC, South Africa; he was getting arrested for drunk-driving, he was meandering from one failed marriage or liaison to another, he was falling on his face. When he was taken down from the dock on his way to prison, he cracked to a bystander: "I suppose that's blown the knighthood," but only he was laughing, and not with his eyes.

No doubt it is the right of any man to live his own life, though some of his fiercest critics will probably say that ceased, morally, to be true when he took possession of someone else's liver, but then George Best carried an extra burden. The world took a proprietary view of the gifts he had displayed so unforgettably and this, in the end, was where he most exhausted forgiveness.

He left Old Trafford, finally, in 1974. He was 26 years old. Now it seems impossible that he did so much so quickly, that his football remains so vivid for all those who witnessed it.

Before he was 20 he played like a man but no ordinary one: he did everything you could do on a football field with astonishing grace and courage and power, and that he had the looks of a film star, and was christened the "Fifth Beatle" by the Portuguese press after he had eviscerated Benfica, one of the greatest teams in Europe in their own stronghold, ensured attention unprecedented in football. He was a magnet for young actresses and assorted celebrity-seekers.

Everything he had was used up so quickly, as much by an adoring world as himself. He left his landlady in a house nominated as suitable by Manchester United for a young footballer who had grown up on a council estate in Belfast and moved to one he built in a leafy, up-market Cheshire suburb. He was proud of its modern design, hurt when he read in one newspaper that it resembled a public lavatory. The attention was relentless and overwhelming and soon enough it began to douse the exquisite flame of his football.

Not so long ago he told one of his ghostwriters: "I recall moments which most fans wouldn't remember, but which meant a lot to me, like scoring twice against West Bromwich in the dying minutes to win a game we were losing 2-1. West Brom will always have a special place in my memory because it was against them that I walked out of the Old Trafford tunnel for the first time and experienced that feeling of the hairs standing up on the back of my neck. They still stand up sometimes when my mind reels back to that day, and others like it.

"All the bad days cannot wipe away those memories. And despite all the ups and downs, when I look back at my life as a whole it is impossible not to feel blessed."

Blessed, no doubt, with gifts from the gods but also cursed with the fault line of his own nature, and perhaps also the timing of his days in the sun.

If he was incapable of protecting his talent beyond that first rush of glory which brought bewitching performances in places such as Benfica's Estado da Luz, when he was still a teenager, and Wembley, when he helped Manchester United to their first European Cup at the age of 22, then so was his great club and the wider football world.

Twenty years later a young star at Old Trafford, Ryan Giggs, was described as the second George Best. It was a wild assertion, and a heavy burden for an intelligent and talented player but it provoked a fierce reaction from Busby's great successor, Sir Alex Ferguson. He threw up a protective screen that was never damagingly breached. By comparison, Best drove a Rolls-Royce while living in a council house.

He was haunted by the prospects of fame even as he flashed a beautiful smile for the cameras. There was the pain of his mother's death as a result of alcoholism. Part of Best's reinvention of himself and the nature of his life, was that he had all that the world could offer. The reality was that the more he had, the more he lost.

Soon enough, the greatest of his assets was gone. It was the ability to play breathtaking football, to display courage and timing and skills that brought a tear to the eye.

There is now a particular desolation if you happened to be at Old Trafford that day he walked out for the first time.

He was 17, and though he did not instantly light up the grey sky, there was a beguiling maturity about everything he did out on the field. Out on the street he was the quietest of boys, one who two years earlier had run home to Belfast because he was homesick.

In one way, George Best, brilliant and doomed, never stopped running. But from what? Sometimes it seemed that it was from the white heat of his own talent. In the premature end, he destroyed that talent, but not the meaning or the memory of it.

Yesterday his tearful friend and agent Phil Hughes said that one of George Best's last wishes was to be an organ donor. Another terrible irony, some would say, but then it is also true that the last thing to fail him was his heart, as it was his first unforgettable gift to those who now mourn not only a departing superstar but some of the magic of their own lives.

GEORGE BEST WAS A TIMELESS GENIUS. BUT BOBBY CHARLTON WAS THE BETTER FOOTBALLER

Published: 29 November 2005

In all the sadness of George Best's departure, and so much of the glory it recalled, perspective was always likely to be listed as a casualty – and so it was with the assertion that he was the greatest football player produced in these islands.

Saying that he was the greatest talent is quite another matter. It is one sustained quite spectacularly in a barrage of film for those who never had the privilege of seeing him in the shining flesh.

His virtuosity has been demonstrated so many times in the past few days. But the greatest player? It has been a claim allegedly supported by such giants of the game as Pelé and Diego Maradona and Johan Cruyff, but when you closely examine their remarks, and review the very meaning of the term, we see that an understandable generosity has been in the air. George might have been due that ultimate accolade of being Britain's all-time No 1, and maybe the world's, had he gone the full course; had he in his playing maturity – one that generally comes around the age George, 27, was turning his back on the best of himself – brought a new degree of discipline to the outpourings of his native genius. But he didn't, and no amount of revisionism or sentimentality can alter this.

It means that in honouring the beloved dead we may have done something of a disservice to the living, and that among their number is one of George's most public mourners, Sir Bobby Charlton.

No doubt this naturally retiring man would discourage speculation of this kind at such a time, as would other contenders for the title of greatest British player like Sir Tom Finney and the late Sir Stanley Matthews and John Charles.

But their work, too, is on the record and it glows no less intensely because their lives outside of football accumulated so much celebrity – or because they never argued for their place in a game to which they always extended the greatest of respect. When George left Manchester United in 1974 he had been a first-teamer for 11 years. He had played 474 times and scored 181 goals, an astonishing ratio by any standard, but then it is also true that in his final days at the club he had become a sad parody of himself, and it was a decline which became sharply progressive just a few years after his European Cup final triumph in 1968 as a 22-year-old.

Charlton played 766 games and scored 253 goals, which meant that from midfield and for several frustrating years from the left wing he scored a goal every 3.027 matches. George, who marauded at will and hogged the ball often to the torment of Charlton and Denis Law, did it at the ratio of 2.619. Law, the third member of the blessed trinity, scored 239 in 409 games at a strike rate of 1.71. Statistics will always be only part of a football story, but when they accompany performance of great beauty, as was the fact in different ways in all three cases, they probably have added relevance.

In the end the obligation is probably to detach yourself from all the recent emotion and ask a simple question: whose performance and talent was most satisfying for the longest time, who seemed to understand most implicitly the demands of a great player, whose underlying, supreme loyalty, was to the team? Was it Best, Law or Charlton? The opinion here is that it was Charlton, spraying passes of magnificent range and insight, moving through the midfield like a great galleon with the wind in its sails, scoring goals of bewildering power and authority like the one he scored against Mexico to set England rolling towards World Cup victory in 1966. Because of circumstances, Best never had the chance to display himself in a World Cup, and Law only when the best of his talent had flown, but then if Charlton got the opportunity no one could have exploited it so masterfully.

With his United team-mate Nobby Stiles, Charlton is the only British player to have won both a European Cup and a World Cup winner's medal, and if this was to exploit favourable circumstances his presence was undoubtedly part of their creation. In the European Cup final Best scored a goal of unforgettable enterprise, but the record reminds us that Charlton scored two. Two years earlier England had triumphed over West Germany in the World Cup final, and one of the most significant reasons was that West Germany's player of genius, Franz Beckenbauer, was deputed to mark Charlton. Four years later in Mexico, England were again dominating West Germany – right up to the moment which broke Sir Alf Ramsey's career, when Charlton was withdrawn, to preserve his sharpness for what seemed like a certain semi-final, and Beckenbauer was suddenly emboldened to go forward.

Charlton played his first game for United in 1956, a few days short of his 19th birthday, and scored twice; 18 months later, after surviving the Munich air crash, he was the hope of the ravaged club and a new star for England. He played his final game 17 years after his debut in, most appropriately, Shakespeare's city of gentlemen, Verona.

After the game, at the age of 35, he fought back tears in the little restaurant where he said farewell. He raised a glass of red wine to the good days. It had been a career marked by both humility and the deepest understanding of the needs of a team. That last quality has been displayed an encouraging number of times, not least in the European Championship of 2004, by Wayne Rooney, the young man who sometimes seems to be carrying on his shoulders the full weight of a great tradition.

These past few days Rooney might be excused the belief that the star he must follow once belonged exclusively to George Best. That one shone a beautiful light, no question, but it was not so constant; the one guiding Bobby Charlton was never obscured. In giving to the young, dark Caesar all that he is due, it is maybe something that should not be forgotten. Not, this is, just for the morale of a great, ageing footballer, but to remember how it was all those glorious, understated years.

George Best was a timeless genius. But Bobby Charlton was the better footballer

DEAR JOSÉ, YOUR DESIRE FOR REFLECTED GLORY HAS LOST YOU A CHANCE TO ILLUMINATE GAME

An open letter to José Mourinho

Published: 20 December 2005

Dear José,

Not so long ago, when you were a figure of hope rather than darkness, you said you were a star in your own movie. We could all enjoy that; it implied fun and celebration of outstanding deeds. It even added a little to the gaiety of the football nation. But now we have a better idea of the kind of movie you had in mind.

From where you are sitting, in the penthouse of your mind, you may not have noticed that it is turning into a grotesque mix of *Sweet Smell of Success* and *Citizen Kane*.

You have blown it, José; not in terms of column inches or television exposure or advertising spin-offs or security at the heart of your oil-rouble empire, but in the regard of all those who long for new messiahs of the game, men like Busby and Stein who gloried in their teams and their achievements and didn't scramble in such unseemly fashion to be at the heart of the reflected glory.

To tell you the truth, José, your current performance would look bad enough on reality TV.

You have jettisoned style for some chintzy version of celebrity for its own sake. Some woolly-minded observers say that your antics provide a valuable service to the team, that it deflects attention from them, allows them to go about their relentless work. Well, here's a fact: I never saw a great football man, and this includes Ferguson and Wenger, who willingly tried to grab the attention from their players, not on occasion but as a matter of carefully calculated course.

You know why? Because they are football men to their bones and they know that their great glory will always be the performance of their players. That's why they are so excitable and natural on the touchline. Wenger can be a cold fish at times, God knows, and he has that reputation among rival managers, but he doesn't pose, he bares his hopes and his fears and he doesn't turn everything into his own glory – and if Ferguson was not ready to salute his team, and express his gratitude, why would he run along the touchline like some demented schoolboy in the tuck shop when United achieve something extraordinary?

The harsh view of your own self-absorbed act must be that it can only be explained by your own lack of a significant playing career.

You never knew the cheers from the terraces, and now it is presumably not enough for you to shape great achievement through your talent for coaching and plotting a set of winning tactics. Now you have to plunder the glory of your players while it is white-hot.

The last time I wrote to you it was, believe it or not, in a spirit of avuncular concern. I thought, like so many others weary of the back-biting and self-interest of Ferguson and Wenger, you were a star on the cusp of shining a brilliant light on English football and that all you needed to do was rein in the cockiness, not entirely but to a certain pleasing degree, and then march on to only the heavens knew where along the peaks of achievement.

It was in that phase when you were still capable of wit rather than appalling bombast, but a lot of people know better now. It has become apparent you don't know the difference between a feisty stance and sickening control freakery. We could not know back then you would soon be saying it was all right to ruin the reputation of a referee with an outright lie, and that you were capable of the kind of boorish performance you put in at Highbury on Sunday.

Presumably you thought you were being smart, even masterful, storming off down the tunnel like that without offering a hand to the vanquished Wenger, and then hurling abuse at the Sky TV people for their "crime" of rerunning shots of Michael Essien's disgusting tackle on Dietmar Hamann a few weeks ago.

You said that Barcelona, your next opponents in the Champions League, thanked Sky. Wrong, everybody who cares for the morality of football and who isn't always bowled over by the bite of their analysis of their own flagship product, thanks them. They showed up the bruising cynicism that is growing at the heart of your all-conquering team: the £24m signing whose function is becoming increasingly apparent. Essien has talent, no doubt, but against the frail young things of Arsenal's midfield his essential role was highlighted with gut-wrenching clarity. He was there to bully, and no doubt he should have been sent off for his fouls on Lauren and Robin van Persie.

Your team are becoming dauntingly efficient but with each machine-like victory they are becoming a notch more charmless, and in this they are only keeping pace with you.

To be fair, you are far from the first and certainly will not be the last football manager to develop a siege mentality. It was long a basic plank of Ferguson's success, and Wenger has seen more conspiracies than the command posts at MI5 and the CIA. But if their positions were often absurd, if all grace melted at moments of victory and defeat, let's be honest, they never quite carried the baggage you have had to haul to your position of power in English football.

They didn't have to confront the unease which would have greeted any Chelsea success even if you had displayed endless layers of charm and your boss Roman had come over as a merely well-heeled version of Peter Ustinov. But the fact is whatever Chelsea achieve there will be the worry that success has been underpinned by unprecedented wealth – resources taken from a country where the majority of the population live lives of hardship unimaginable in all parts of this country, let alone the Fulham Road.

So, José, there are unanswerable misgivings about the crowning of Chelsea as the undisputed masters of English football. This doesn't prevent admiration for the strength of your work, and the team ethic you have developed at Stamford Bridge. You have done it with a skill which has been at times awe-inspiring. But admiring is not the same as celebrating, or even liking, and anyone beyond your own support who says this is not so is spinning a line.

What it really means is that there is an obligation on you to perform with a lot more understanding of your highly privileged situation. If you don't, if you carry on in the style you displayed at Highbury, the result will be beyond speculation. Even your victories will not inculcate the envy you imagine, because all football supporters are not fools, and a recent visit to Stamford Bridge – for a grinding victory over unglamorous Middlesbrough – confirmed the suspicion that if Chelsea's fans cannot quite believe their luck, if they are pleased with the power of their club, it does not express itself in the kind of joy which is so tangible in places like Anfield and Old Trafford and, in the not so ancient good days, Arsenal.

You will probably hate this, but there is a model you shouldn't ignore, and his name is Rafael Benítez.

Your scorn for his Liverpool is not so convincing. Admittedly you have a series of victories, but they have outsmarted you in Europe and please, as a matter of urgency, drop the fiction that they didn't score against you in that European Cup semi-final at Anfield. The goal was awarded, it is on the record, and if it hadn't been, Liverpool, the whole world could see, were due a penalty and the sending-off of your invaluable goalkeeper Petr Cech.

That's the kind of reality you have to absorb if you are going to win the respect which your achievements are due. You may not know it, but Benítez is drawing a lot of neutral admiration. He isn't backed by seamless millions, he doesn't sneer at the rest of the football world, he doesn't tell lies about referees, he just gets on with the job of building a football team.

There will be quite a bit of unpatriotic support for Barcelona, too, when you collide with them again in the Champions League.

This isn't pure envy, José. It comes from the feeling that you bent the truth terribly when you last met Barcelona, and that victory came through a most cynical foul by Ricardo Carvalho on their goalkeeper. Your silence on that was noted by those who believe in the old truth that these things have a way of levelling out.

One last point: the Barcelona of Ronaldinho and young Lionel Messi play beautiful football. It has brilliance and charm. It can lay a hand on the hearts of the unattached. It is a sad truth that your current effect is one of repulsion.

Yours in sport,
James Lawton

CAUGHT OUT AGAIN, THE SERIAL OPPORTUNIST WITH A ROVING EYE

Published: 16 January 2006

Even though some would say catching Sven-Goran Eriksson with his trousers down, philosophically or otherwise, is merely to operate the law of averages, the picture of him which emerges from a *News of the World* "sting'"at the weekend could not have been sketched more passionately by his most ferocious critic.

It is a portrait of opportunism that might bring pause to a huckster with an ounce of reflection. But, then, maybe not Eriksson.

For the "Iceman" Swede there seems to be one unyielding priority. It is the best deal, the best terms that might just be out there. No matter that his salary – for what many in his "industry" believe is essentially a part-time job, and certainly in the way he operates – pays a net £3m a year with bonuses on top, the quest for improvement is apparently unending.

The latest account of his style and ambitions certainly reek not of his sparse upbringing in a small town in Sweden but *la dolce vita* he adopted in his years in Rome with Lazio.

One moment he is devouring crab and lobster and drinking vintage wine in a five-star Dubai restaurant while coolly proposing to an undercover reporter, decked out as an oil-rich Sheikh, a £25m takeover of Aston Villa and his own installation – while still under contract to the Football Association – as club manager at a £5m-plus salary which would carry him beyond even the earning power of football's best-rewarded coach, Chelsea's José Mourinho.

Then, flanked by his agent and a lawyer, he is on the top deck of a luxury yacht, swigging back "bottle after bottle" of champagne and white wine and throwing a juicy titbit into his takeover suggestion – the guaranteed signing of his England captain, David Beckham, of Real Madrid.

After confirming that his FA contract runs until 2008, Eriksson is quoted on his responsibilities to the England team, saying: "After five-and-a-half years, it's a long time to be manager. Anyhow, if we win the World Cup I will leave and say goodbye."

Touchingly, much of the nation apparently sees Eriksson – despite his background as a serial chaser of new opportunities of enrichment – as a crusader on behalf of English football, a man in pursuit of the Holy Grail of the World Cup. Yet on his flying, luxury-filled trip to Dubai he resembled nothing so much as a fervent salesman of his own shopworn goods, a man on the prodigious make.

None of this adds much fuel for any fresh assessment of Eriksson as someone quite perfectly fitted to the role of coach and guardian of the nation's most talented young footballers. He is, we surely know well enough by now, a man under-burdened by the sense of duty and sober commitment that marked the style of the only coach in English football history to win the World Cup, Sir Alf Ramsey in 1966.

Ramsey retired to a modest house in Ipswich after being fired by the FA. Eriksson has always made it clear that his own departure would be to a new and even more lucrative horizon. Since his appointment in 2001, he has been three times caught out in negotiations with prospective employers, Chelsea twice and Manchester United. His commitment to his partner, Nancy Dell'Olio, complicated by hugely publicised flings with the television presenter Ulrika Jonsson and the former FA secretary Faria Alam, has similarly been irresolute.

However, are these grounds for firing a man whose job is to deliver results on the football field? Hardly so in an age when results, and the profits which flow from them, have long become all important and it is here that the Swede retains some strength. He has a perfect record in qualifying for major tournaments, the World Cups of 2002 and this coming summer in Germany, and the European Championships of 2004.

Certainly the FA retain gratitude for Eriksson's ability to avoid the disaster of 1994, when England failed to qualify for the World Cup in America under Graham Taylor – and the one that was looming in 2000 when Eriksson's predecessor, Kevin Keegan, walked away with the team in confusion after a World Cup qualifying defeat by Germany in the last competitive game played at the old Wembley stadium.

Eriksson's practical streak – he picks the best players and then makes himself their friend – has always guarded against the worst fate of a football coach, a loss of support in the dressing-room. But then, even here, the weekend "sting" has not exactly helped his position.

The *News of the World* also revealed tittle-tattle from Eriksson on key players like Michael Owen and Rio Ferdinand. He told the undercover reporter that Owen had joined his new club Newcastle United "only for the money" and that at the time of his recent exclusion from the team, Ferdinand was "not in good shape".

Eriksson named Shaun Wright-Phillips – who earlier in the season was shaping up as one of England's most promising young players – as the object of the most extravagant transfer fee paid in English football when Chelsea outlayed £24m. He also talked about the "rough background" of England's best player, Wayne Rooney.

None of these indiscretions are likely to hole Eriksson beneath the waterline. However, his confident declaration that he could deliver the signing of Beckham goes to the heart of the most severe criticism of his regime as England coach. It implicitly supports the idea that he has accorded his captain Beckham a special status within the team.

This impression has always been strong with Eriksson's constant refusal to criticise Beckham for lapses of discipline, which have led to him being dismissed from the field – against Austria in a World Cup qualifying game earlier this season – and missing three important qualifying matches while serving suspensions over the past three years.

When Beckham admitted to deliberately fouling a Wales player in 2004 so that he would be suspended – and serve the ban while injured – Eriksson dismissed it as a trivial matter unworthy of his serious attention.

Yet at the time England's 1966 World Cup hero Sir Geoff Hurst talked about a "national disgrace". He said that his old manager, Ramsey, would not have countenanced such behaviour from his own captain, Bobby Moore. Said Hurst: "Even Bobby wouldn't have lasted a minute if he had owned up to something like that."

More recently, the leadership qualities of Chelsea's centre-half John Terry have glowed in performances for both his club and his country – and during a period when Beckham was dismissed from the field three times – but Eriksson brushed aside suggestions that he had become a legitimate contender for the captaincy on the approach to the World Cup finals.

Beckham, said Eriksson in so many words, was the coach's man. The extent of this reality is perhaps a little clearer now. Certainly it throws up grave questions about Eriksson's approach to selection during the course of the coming World Cup finals. Would Eriksson's interest in Beckham as a viable bargaining tool in his own future affect his thinking about who would best serve England on the right of midfield? Here, inevitably, you are reminded of Beckham's dismal form in England's last major tournament, the European

Championships in Portugal, when Eriksson was emphatic that his captain's place in the team was not in jeopardy.

Also self-evident is the preoccupation of the coach. At no time in his talks with somebody he believed was capable of investing more than £25m into an English football club, did he suggest that his own immediate future was utterly dominated by the challenge of delivering the World Cup to his adopted country. Did he have time to think about – and perhaps get physically involved – in the strategy necessary to pull off a takeover of Aston Villa, and persuade the ageing, ailing chairman Doug Ellis that it was a good course? Plainly he did. It was, after all, his idea.

Meanwhile, Eriksson will lead England to the greatest challenge in world football. At the very least, it is something to pass the time... and who knows, there may just be a nice little bonus.

ROBBEN'S SHAM BETRAYS A GREAT TALENT AND THE GAME WHICH HAS NURTURED IT

Published: 07 February 2006

When Arjen Robben first emerged as a Chelsea superstar he addressed with some patience but admirable firmness the question of whether he was the new Johan Cruyff. To the disappointment of his BBC interrogator, he said the proposition was absurdly premature, and probably just plain absurd.

Cruyff was one of the four or five greatest footballers ever to draw breath. Certainly there wasn't even a hint that the Golden Dutchman was a cheat. It makes it all the more disappointing that with the great goal of getting vaguely close to the achievements of his fabulous predecessor still a thousand miles away, Robben has claimed that shabby territory for himself.

He sounded like a self-elected football statesman in his broadcast to the nation that had become enraptured by his brilliant raiding. Here was a real one. Perhaps not Cruyff, but someone more likely to touch the stars than scuffle in the dirt. He seemed to know where he was – and the meaning of football. Now he has performed a self-immolation and a terrible disservice to the game that has nourished him.

In one way what the Chelsea player did when the Liverpool goalkeeper José Reina put his hand, illegally but without serious menace, to his face, was a routine piece of Premiership diving, but the timing of it and the reaction of his coach, José Mourinho, could hardly have been more depressing.

This was supposed to be the dawning of a fresh age of English football with the old ascendancy of Manchester United and Arsenal put to bed and a decisive Premiership game between the reigning champions, and those of Europe, defining a new order.

New order? New world? New tests of evolutionary football brilliance? Surely no one can be that easily pleased. If Chelsea's 2-0 victory represented the truth that they are by some distance the strongest team in England, if it made their second straight Premiership title more than ever a formality, that was about as much as you could say.

Liverpool have improved, no doubt, since their unlikely Champions League triumph but they are still a long way from being a finished product. The match itself had a deep-set mediocrity of playing ambition. Players like Frank Lampard, Steven Gerrard and Xabi Alonso operated in small areas of limited impact. There were no big, sweeping plays and the goalkeepers saw little action. Then Robben made a sickening statement about the level of his professional integrity, and what did Mourinho say? He preferred to talk about his 50th Premiership win and the fact that Chelsea might have won 4-0. It is a familiar pattern now.

This is a coach known to complain about opposition diving, despite his authorship of a Porto performance in a Uefa Cup final against Celtic which Martin O'Neill's men will always swear was an ultimate exploration of the tawdry business. Mourinho's protégé Deco was said to be the finest exponent of the skill since Greg Louganis performed it legitimately in an Olympic pool. Mourinho's self-regard, his selective morality when discussing football, his gracelessness in both victory and the odd defeat, have already been explored in this quarter, but Sunday represented a new low in his public habit of washing his hands of any responsibility to lay down something more than a winning formula at Stamford Bridge.

Only those who believe, as Mourinho apparently does, that victory, any kind of victory and advantage, justifies itself, could ignore what Robben did so shamelessly.

Apologists will no doubt point out, accurately enough, that both Sir Alex Ferguson and Arsène Wenger showed a similar reluctance to criticise the misdeeds of their own players. But then it is true that neither was affected by the levels of narcissism which so regularly engulf Mourinho. It meant there was little confusion about where their primary passion resided. Plainly it was in the performance of their teams rather than their own images.

That was regularly reflected in the quality of play on the field. Some recent encounters between Arsenal and United have been disfigured by sour, indeed shocking behaviour, but even the most grudging neutral could not deny that their collisions always carried the promise of open and exciting football. Arsenal went a season without defeat and played exquisitely. United represented the certainty of an attacking game enriched by high, freely expressed skill.

We saw little of that at Stamford Bridge. We saw the new order of highly programmed method football. We saw Robben's dive achieve its sickening purpose, the dismissal of a fellow professional.

We saw the new football. Also on view: another betrayal of the game once played by someone like Johan Cruyff.

UGLY CHANTS BORN OF MISPLACED HATRED AND NOT OF PASSION

Published: 20 February 2006

The Liverpool fans who shouted "Munich scum" at the Manchester United supporters who were being marched into Anfield between columns of Merseyside riot police were standing just a few yards from the main gates, where an eternal flame burns on the memorial stone to those who died at Hillsborough.

They seemed oblivious to the hateful irony, and when later some United fans shouted their insults to the memory of the Hillsborough dead there were more shouts of "Munich" from Liverpool ranks.

The left-hand corner of the main stand, from where Liverpool fans traded the most sickening taunts with the United contingent facing the Kop for the 90 minutes of what should have been an absorbing Cup tie, was a place where hatred was expressed in varying degrees of intensity, but its disfiguring presence was never absent.

Liverpool fans celebrated the crash which destroyed the cream of English football who just happened to play for Manchester United. The United riposte was gloating cries over the deaths of innocent Merseysiders. At one point there was a chant from the United fans of "There's only one Michael Shields." Shields is the Liverpool fan held in Bulgaria over an assault on a local barman. He maintains his innocence.

There would, you knew, be other claims at the end of this scabrous afternoon. The principal one was that the incessant hatred is simply a fact of football life; it is out there, it is unshakeable and anyone who still cares about the game, for all its diving and grabbing and general cheating, is obliged to live with it.

This, presumably, included the gut-churning amusement at the disaster that befell United's Alan Smith.

The Liverpool fans wanted to know how their hero John Arne Riise had broken Smith's leg and dislocated his ankle so hideously that some team-mates and opponents could not stand to look as the medics attempted to secure his injuries before lifting him on to a stretcher. In fact, in trying to block Riise's free-kick, Smith had fallen back and inflicted the injuries on himself.

Later someone tried to draw the Liverpool manager, Rafael Benítez, into some reaction to the cries of the fans. His reply was one that sometimes provokes accusations of evasion, even hypocrisy. But when Benítez said his English was not so good that he could quite understand what the Liverpool fans were chanting he was surely beyond criticism.

Benítez is building a team and lurching into ancient hatreds is no part of his brief. However, it did make you think of some of the pre-match comments in defence of the United captain, Gary Neville.

The only acceptable one might have been that Neville, 31 years old and one of the most experienced professionals in England, was utterly oblivious to the filthy undercurrents on the terraces whenever United and Liverpool meet on the field. What did Neville imagine he was brewing when he ran down the Old Trafford pitch a few weeks ago and postured before the Liverpool fans after United's late winner?

On Saturday morning we had been treated to the "overview" of Rio Ferdinand, who declared: "There's no way on earth Gary should have been charged. Do we really want to kill off all the passion in the game and make it like going to the cinema? Why shouldn't he celebrate when his own Manchester United score a goal? I'd rather Gary than a cold fish who just walks off the park or ties his bootlaces on the centre line while everyone else is celebrating."

Ferdinand – no more than Neville – seems not to understand how easy it is to stoke up sickeningly heightened emotion when it is commonplace to gloat over tragic death, when the response to Wayne Rooney touching the ball is a volley of "fat bastard, fat bastard". That was another little formality on Saturday.

Aggravating the spirit still further was that this was a proper Cup tie. United's midfield remained woeful and Liverpool might have added two goals to Peter Crouch's if the otherwise excellent Steve Finnan had pulled the trigger with a little more authority when Steve Gerrard found him alone on the right side of the box. Harry Kewell also snatched at what should have been, for a player of his skill, a comfortable opportunity. However, there was an edge to the contest right until the last kick, one that in another football age would have guaranteed a compelling need for attention on the terraces.

Instead we had the fusillades of grievous, grotesque insult. We had the mockery of sport. We had the need for every high-earning pro to look at his responsibilities, to his employers and those decent supporters who have not been engulfed by the tides of hate.

Hours after the game riot wagons roared down Scotland Road. Mostly preventive action, no doubt, but it still brought more poison to an afternoon that should have been memorable for much better reasons. "Do we really want to kill off passion?" Rio Ferdinand asked. No, not passion, but the hatred borne by malignant lemmings.

The fallen Smith has known his moments of controversy, but he has one overwhelming characteristic. It is to play with every scrap of ability. Once he was despised by United fans for no better reason than he had played for Leeds. Now, at Anfield, the worst moment of his career was a matter for mockery because he played for United. It was especially sad to note he had made his debut in this ground. He came on as a substitute and scored. Now his career might be over and some fans thought it amusing. One shouted: "Get the shite off the field."

Ferdinand warned that we shouldn't kill off football passion. But what did passion have to do with it?

RUTHLESSNESS AND EFFICIENCY GUARANTEE MOURINHO TROPHIES BUT NOT LASTING GLORY

Published: 18 April 2006

Despite all the trails of rancour he has put down this season, the petulance, the lack of any natural sportsmanship and the graceless self-advertising, which has inevitably been included in his latest brittle charm offensive, there is still one unassailable claim to be made on behalf of José Mourinho.

The point flies beyond clear signs of new progress at Arsenal and Liverpool, and yesterday's reaffirmation of the authority Wayne Rooney brings to the stuttering cause of Manchester United. It is that Mourinho has been as good as his belligerent, self-anointed word. He has once again produced the best team in England.

Of course, he has had the means, so much more of them than any of his rivals and there have been times when he has brandished them as repellently as a ruinously spoilt boy.

But then that basic statement about his team's merit, its competitive discipline and consistency, probably needs to be underlined with special force in another week when the primacy of Chelsea in domestic football is again in danger of being overshadowed by Arsenal's brilliant charge for Champions League glory.

So Chelsea were ushered out of Europe by the coruscating if not, ultimately, entirely convincing Barcelona. It doesn't matter. Arsenal may well be overtaken by the same fate, against a Villarreal masterminded by the superb playmaker Juan Roman Riquelme, in the semi-finals, or maybe by Mourinho's nemesis, Barça, in the final, but what can't be disputed is that it is in the Premiership where an English team must prove themselves. It is there that they have to establish they have the character and the talent to go the distance, all the time answering questions about their depth of professionalism and their resolve.

Liverpool's success in the Champions League last season was astonishing, unforgettable, but it persuaded no one, and least of all their redoubtable coach

Rafa Benítez, that they were in position to challenge Chelsea seriously in a new campaign. The same will be true of Arsenal if they upset the European odds this season – and Manchester United if Sir Alex Ferguson finds himself able to strengthen the wasteland of his midfield significantly.

It leaves us with the extreme paradox of Mourinho. He is the reason for both Chelsea's success and their now raging unpopularity.

It is never likely to change. While Chelsea negotiate a mega salary for the German star, Michael Ballack, and Mourinho plainly has the facility to throw another £50m or £60m into the transfer market, maybe with the jettisoning of such as the unfortunate Shaun Wright-Phillips, the coach's policy appears to be set in stone. Categorising it is simple enough: success not through the seamless development of the quality and adventure of their play – as Don Revie's Leeds United, like Chelsea deeply reviled in their formative stages, eventually won the respect of even the most grudging of serious football analysts – but by the accumulation of known strength.

Mourinho's move for Ballack is the perfect example. He is not a player of any kind of football fantasy: he is a strong, functional operator in advanced midfield positions, another Frank Lampard if you like, and if Mourinho did have any serious intention of lightening, even beautifying the product, he would of course be besieging a Riquelme, if not a Ronaldinho or Lionel Messi.

The lack of such an initiative tells you a lot of what you need to know about Mourinho's football persona. He has a trick, and it is an extremely good one, but it is not subject to modification or refinement. If he signed a Ronaldinho, or a Thierry Henry, he would be obliged to surrender some of his mystique at the head of the team; tearing up his game plan, as he did with such toe-curling effect at Fulham recently, would be rendered even more absurd if it was done in the presence of game-changing players of self-evident genius. Mourinho wants to hog the genius department: in this way he can make a virtue of his self-glorification, justify his excesses of ego.

Consider, for a moment, the meaning of paying roughly £72m for Didier Drogba, Michael Essien, and Wright-Phillips. All of them are players of certain talent, but none enters the airspace of an Andrei Shevchenko or a Messi and, still less, a Riquelme. They are controllable players and if Mourinho deserves great credit for the development of such as Lampard, John Terry and, not least, Joe Cole, what can you say of his stewardship of the three mega buys?

Wright-Phillips at times suggests he is midway through a football version of a nervous breakdown, so shorn is he of the old, splendid simplicities of the game he played for Manchester City. Essien is a great physical presence, like Drogba; both of them, however, have been apparently completely unchecked in their portrayal of the ugly face of today's game. The consequence was that, whatever happened yesterday, the inevitability of Mourinho's latest title triumph was bound to be accompanied by a wagonload of ambivalence.

It was, unavoidably, an overwhelming case of giving to the Special One not an ounce more than his due. The coach, and the Stamford Bridge public relations department, will surely have complaints, but their attitudes cannot be seen as conspicuously strange when it seems that whenever he decides to reappear in public, gratuitously sneering at his rivals or jokily philosophising on bird flu and the trophy expectations of his six-year-old son, a blanket of forgiveness in much of the media tends to drop over the cheapness of so much of his preceding public performance. It is a deeply unattractive process but it will be maintained as long as Mourinho fulfils his central function of winning games.

Maybe eventually Mourinho's regime will come under some ultimate judgement but we can be sure that it will not come from those who inhabit the world of football for its possibilities of beauty and artistry and, by way of a rare bonus today, grace under the harshest competitive pressure. That verdict, as we suggested here recently, will have to come from the patron of Mourinho's Chelsea, Roman Abramovich. He will have to decide if he will be content with a future of success guaranteed by Mourinho's strengths as a motivator or an organiser, but a triumph of the kind which can be appreciated, if hardly loved, only by the club's own following.

He has seen the kind of passions which can be released when a team is in the hands of a Frank Rijkaard at Barcelona, or a Ferguson, Arsène Wenger or Benítez. Mourinho doesn't, and you have to suspect he never will, provoke that kind of reaction. His creed is the old one of the gridiron coach Vince Lombardi: winning isn't the important thing, it's the only thing.

How else could he generate such contorted reactions to the reality that Barcelona play a different, much more satisfying football than his own? How could he not speak out against the cheating of Drogba, Essien and Arjen Robben? How else could he so unswervingly proclaim his belief that winning excuses everything, a statement that was implicit even in his smearing of the good name of a referee at the cost of admitting that he had lied? It may have been a fiction that Chelsea kept their pitch in the condition of a ploughed field so long merely to neutralise the superior skills of Barça, but it was significant that the view could be so widely and easily held.

These are not the offshoots of glory and, indeed, Abramovich may well come to wonder if they represent too high a price for his dividend of ruling English football. In the meantime, though, Mourinho cannot be faulted in his central purpose. He has done what he always promised; he has made Chelsea winners of the most formidable kind.

They are a team imbued with self-belief, and if some recent pratfalls encouraged doubts, they have been resolved in a now familiar way. The response to the crisis of going a goal and a man down in the recent game against West Ham, a team who have made impressive strides of their own this season, was quite withering.

It was then, of course, that Mourinho emerged from his brief, smouldering hibernation. He was returning to claim the stage, as he will always do. It is the right of conquest bestowed by the best team in English football, the one he has built and shaped, and no one can dispute the degree of his triumph. This doesn't mean, however, that anyone is obliged to throw flowers in the air.

THE CONTRADICTIONS OF ARSÈNE WENGER: AN EXHILARATING WINNER ...BUT A SOUR LOSER

Published: 25 April 2006

A high wind is tearing at El Madrigal stadium where tonight the football destiny of Arsène Wenger is so finely balanced. It means that, as the palm trees bend this way and that, you are bound to speculate on the turbulence that is going on inside the erudite Frenchman who yet again has let down his guard.

The ugliness of his confrontation with the Tottenham head coach, Martin Jol, is certainly not something easily blown away into the white-capped sea.

It is as tangible as the smell of the salt in the air and the nearby fish cannery and inevitably it deepens the sense of the contradictions and the tension building in one of the most remarkable coaches – and men – the game has ever seen.

For some exhilarating weeks, Wenger, with the help of his bravely reforged young team, had been at the heart of an extraordinary charm offensive. He had never been more philosophical or impassioned. His sophisticated view of football and life seemed to lap effortlessly beyond the borders of his own ambition. As Arsenal cut through Real Madrid and Juventus, he talked of leaving a little bit of his soul at Highbury. Here was a man who might just be overhauling the very roots of his football existence. He even, with huge irony, talked about the need to attack the curse of diving that has so undermined the game.

Then came Robbie Keane's Tottenham goal, which could denude Arsenal of Champions League football in the first season in their new stadium – if things do not go well against the stealthy Villarreal tonight or in Paris in the final next month.

Then we saw the other side of Wenger, the one that whips up as suddenly as the boisterous winds which welcomed him and his team here. We saw the man who hates to lose, the man whose value system can crumble as dramatically as an avalanche if fate is not to his liking.

When the consensus was gathered in yesterday the overwhelming view was that Wenger, so close to what might be his crowning triumph, had let himself down badly when he insulted Jol so profoundly with the charge that he was a liar, and that his team were cheats.

The incident has already been analysed exhaustively, and the dominating professional view is that Spurs did not act unreasonably when Emmanuel Eboué and Gilberto Silva collided and the close-up referee, Mike Riley, indicated plainly that he had no concern for the health of either player. Those are the details, but the significance of Wenger's reaction flies so far beyond the question of who was right and wrong in the split seconds allowed for response on the field.

In his bitter eruption Wenger has doubtlessly complicated any neutral reaction to the possibility of his landing the greatest triumph of his superb career in the next few weeks.

One distinguished old pro, who, like many of his contemporaries, worries that so many fundamental values of the game are being flushed away on a tide of all-consuming self-interest, sums up the dilemma quite briskly. He says: "There is no doubt an Arsenal triumph in the Champions League would be a wonderful gift for English football; it would remind everyone that the beautiful game can also be a winning game. But then I also believe that Wenger, who everyone in football should admire for his knowledge and his ability to recognise greatness in young players, could also have given the English game a gift of equal importance over the last few years. That would have been if he had taken a lead in being honest about what was happening in football, if he had spoken out against all the attacks on the spirit of the game, some of the most notable coming from his own players."

That was the terrible indictment Wenger inflicted on himself when he raged on the Highbury touchline. That was the breathtaking oversight he made when he charged Jol with evasion and lying. It was as though he was pressing a replay button on a long list of his own offences.

Here was the man who thought that the dive of Robert Pires against Portsmouth to win a penalty and preserve Arsenal's brilliant unbeaten run of two years ago was a simple matter of adjudication by a referee. It was not, after the briefest examination of the video, a matter for one of the most influential football men in the game; it was not a situation that screamed for a moral view, for someone to step back and say that we had gone far enough down the road of deceit.

The Pires case will not go away – because it was, ultimately, flagrant. It required the Arsenal player not to overreact to contact, not even to feign contact, but to seek it out and then go down in the most transparent way.

When Wenger upbraided Jol last Saturday he turned away from all that recent glory and charm and hope and took us back to some of the grimiest episodes in modern English football.

Unwittingly, he recalled the time of "Pizzagate", when he saw no evil, heard no evil when Sir Alex Ferguson was splattered by food thrown by Arsenal players, and it was left to the hierarchies of two of the greatest clubs in England to make some kind of feeble accommodation. When Patrick Vieira, in his first highly physical impact on the English game, fell foul of officials Wenger's public position could scarcely have been more partisan. He warned officials that if they were not more careful both Vieira and his team-mate Emmanuel Petit would be packing their bags for home.

When half his team swarmed around Ruud van Nistelrooy, spewing hatred that would have done credit to some street mob, Wenger's response was to name the Dutchman as one of the game's great cheats. It was an opinion that might not have lacked some support, but the problem was it was so arbitrary, so detached from the wider view that you might expect from one of the great men of the game, and, of course, it deflected any need to pass judgement on behaviour that still stands out so depressingly as a prime symbol of eroded respect.

No, maybe these are memories that should not be carried on this high wind as Arsenal strive to deliver one of the great achievements of the English game. But then who put them there? It was Wenger. Not the Wenger of superlative achievement, not the Merlin of the game, but the one-eyed Wenger, the one who made a verdict on his rival Jol so harsh, so intemperately delivered, that the Tottenham manager deserved some kind of reward for forbearance.

None of this, of course, detaches us from the hope that tonight we will see the best of Wenger and his team. There is, after all, no new fault line in the man. The central contradiction has always been there. His vision of how the game should be played, his ability to groom players in that way, has always been accompanied by an unwillingness to look beyond the interests of himself and his players.

The charge can be made with equal force against his great rival Ferguson, and perhaps neither of them are currently in danger of surpassing the boiling self-regard of José Mourinho. However, this is supposed to be Wenger's time, as 1999 was supremely Ferguson's, and the instinct here is as it was up the coast in Barcelona, when Manchester United expressed the will of their manager so extraordinarily in those unforgettable last minutes at the Nou Camp.

The desire is to praise rather than bury Wenger as he strives for the penultimate triumph in a superb campaign. If the searching passes of Juan Roman Riquelme do damage to Arsenal's composure, if the yellow submarine of Manuel Pelligrini stifles the brilliance of Thierry Henry, the regret will not be cheap in all those who value football most for its spirit and its beauty.

You might even say that football owes Wenger one abiding triumph, one supreme statement about the value of playing in a certain way. But then there is another debt, and this is one against the name of the man wading in frustration who called Martin Jol a liar. The hunch here is that tonight he will be a step closer to being confirmed as a champion of the game, but will that quite settle the account? Not if you believe that English football right now needs a single truth as much as any amount of silverware.

O'NEILL FINDS HIMSELF ON THE SIDELINES FOR NOT TELLING THE FA WHAT IT WANTED TO HEAR

Published: 02 May 2006

Surely all mockery has been spent in analysing the Football Association's ultimately cack-handed pursuit of a successor to Sven-Goran Eriksson. Monty Python, Basil Fawlty, Mr Bean can be invoked only so many times. Even so, yesterday morning's odds, which had Steve McClaren installed as the 1-4 favourite, did provoke one last question.

It was simply this: why has Martin O'Neill, widely seen as one of the major managers in British football, indeed a potential successor to Sir Alex Ferguson before his enforced leave of absence because of the serious illness of his wife, slipped so far down in the running he is now 8-1 – four points longer than the eternal self-publicist and guru of the long throw Big Sam Allardyce? This, you may have guessed, is a rhetorical question – as lawyers say, never ask one publicly if you don't know the answer.

We are told that O'Neill interviewed poorly. That's one way of putting it but it depends entirely on your point of view. Those in touch with the realities of the game in which O'Neill has distinguished himself at every level this side of managing an international team would certainly express it differently. They would say that O'Neill simply didn't tell some of the committee men what they wanted to hear. He didn't go along with the moonshine that the coach of England also has to be the overseer of some bureaucratic coaching system, some mythical pyramid that had delivered World Cup success to France in 1998 and in the European Championships of 2000 but did nothing to guard them against complete disaster in 2002 and 2004.

Allardyce, of course, is a big coaching man. He has had the impertinence to say that Eddie Gray and Sir Trevor Brooking, whose backgrounds in the game and whose company they kept in careers of great distinction make that of Allardyce seem so like so much scuffling on the wrong side of the football tracks, were under-qualified as managers or advisers to the Football Association. Allardyce showed up for one of his interviews with the FA armed with a laptop which was filled with coaching plans – a big contrast to the approach of O'Neill, no doubt, but let us briefly examine the difference for what it's worth.

Coaching certificates tell you that the holder knows how to organise a group of players in work sessions. It is not anything that warrants sneers. As a national serviceman Malcolm Allison, one of the most original of post-war English coaches and a spectacular winner, watched a Russian army team training in the Viennese woods with eyes that were opened wide with the force of revelation. He compared what the Russians were doing with the tedious formalities of a training sessions back home at Charlton Athletic. But Big Mal, unlike Big Sam, never made a coaching certificate the proof of a football man's worth. It was a job aid, not a badge of football brilliance.

O'Neill's position, apparently, was that if he took the England job it would be as a manager, not the head of some elaborate system, one no doubt bestowing jobs for the boys who had the right certificates and the right accompanying patter.

O'Neill wanted to do the one job that marks down great football men. He wanted to do with England what Busby did with Manchester United, Stein with Celtic, Shankly with Liverpool, Ramsey with England – all without a set of coaching badges. He wanted to put into force all he had learned in a long and successful career as a player and a manager, someone who had known the force of one of the greatest, and most mysterious, of all football men, Brian Clough.

O'Neill didn't play any games when he made his case to lead England. He certainly stood aghast at the point of questions about how he might handle a celebrity figure like David Beckham – the answer to that could scarcely have made more fundamental sense, he would be treated like any other player, someone as good as his last performance.

There is no apology here for a stated preference for a Guus Hiddink or a Luiz Felipe Scolari, coaches who had the opportunity to operate as international coaches and did so with conspicuous success and with an obvious ability to walk through any amount of chauvinistic drivel.

However, O'Neill's chances, you imagined, could never be easily discounted. Here, no doubt, was a football man of substance and force bright enough to play a game dictated by his available resources.

Yet he languishes, hopelessly, behind McClaren, a man locked into the failures of Eriksson at times of maximum pressure and who, it has been alleged by his senior professional, former England player Gareth Southgate, had reached an untenable position at Middlesbrough some months ago. McClaren is said to have scored some brownie points at the FA for his cool handling of unremarkable tabloid stories about his private life, accounts that in a reasonably adult society would not have been deemed worthy of the newsprint and whose successful countering say little or nothing about a man's potential to motivate the England team. O'Neill also trails Allardyce, who not so long ago embraced his player El Hadji Diouf for outrageously conning a referee and winning a penalty kick, and then said that he would react differently only when rival coaches did so.

Did we say that this whole business has gone beyond mockery? No doubt it has, but more seriously, also beyond reason.

CHANCES OF GLORY IN GERMANY SLIP FROM SLIM TO NONE

Published: 01 June 2006

Whatever you think of his chances, it is no longer possible to avoid the truth about Sven-Goran Eriksson: the more he changes his team, the more he stays the same. Depending on how strongly you feel about what he is doing – or rather not doing – to England, the picture has to be of a straw man blowing in the wind, a flibbertigibbet, or, worst of all, a fraud.

The alternative view? He is a genius, someone who can break every rule that has ever been laid down in the building of a football team and still retain the potential to win the greatest challenge in the game, with or without a miraculously revived Wayne Rooney.

You take the latter view if you believe that football is truly an ultimately funny game. On the other hand, you may want to borrow the line of the boxing promoter Don King when he was asked about a certain long-shot proposition. "It's got two chances," said King. "Slim and none, and Slim just left town."

Either way, for critical opinion it is a time to be counted in these last steps to the World Cup. You can argue the technical details of Jamie Carragher's performance, as yet another candidate for the "holding midfielder" role, against the sadly pallid Hungarians on Tuesday night as long as you like – and apparently the BBC analysts did it *ad nauseam* back in the studio – but surely the need is to address the broader point.

It is not whether Carragher is technically and instinctively equipped to play in midfield – everyone except Eriksson, and not least the player himself, knows that he is not. The real debate is about what Carragher's selection said about Eriksson's state of mind – and preparation.

If the Brazilians lost Ronaldinho, the Argentines Juan Roman Riquelme, the Germans Michael Ballack or the French Thierry Henry, would their coaches now be overhauling their entire tactical approach and personnel? Of course not. So why is it happening with England? It is the Eriksson way, and now it promises to unravel in a third straight major competition.

He makes the classic pattern of team development, of honing players and performance, seem not like a basic ingredient of any recipe for success but something akin to acquiring the Holy Grail.

When the former West Ham and Liverpool full-back Julian Dicks, who wore his hair in the Mohawk style, was signed amid grave misgivings, the manager was asked, by one critic, to "talk us through the haircut". Rather more relevantly, he might now ask Eriksson to talk us through the Walcott decision.

The Carragher "experiment" was bizarre, no doubt, as has been the obsession with Rooney's injury, right up to this week's astonishing resolve to have the player fly to Germany for a couple of days, then return to Old Trafford for his final, decisive scan. But however you question the logic of Eriksson's reaction to the Rooney mishap – and it has plainly offended the basic imperatives of a team game – and his desperate tinkering so near to the off, it is the Walcott business which is impossible to comprehend.

The boy flickered across the Old Trafford stage like a nervous firefly. What else could be expected? Owen, a big-match performer if ever there was one, is plainly far from match sharpness, but if his time is limited his temperament is huge, and plainly he is worth the gamble. But selecting one fit, experienced striker for the squad was astonishing folly, and Peter Crouch's goal underlined the reality of this after Steven Gerrard spent 45 minutes proving that he is no more a forward player than Carragher is a midfielder (as opposed to arguably England's best pure defender.) This was on top of the reminder that Owen's predatory instincts are best served by the company of an authentic target man.

Meanwhile, and with certain honourable exceptions – not least the BBC's pungently opinioned Alan Green – a droning debate is conducted. Can Carragher play the holding role? Can Gerrard play with his back to the goal? Does Theo Walcott represent a thrilling initiative or risible aberration? Should we play 3-5-2, 4-1-4-1, 4-4-2? It is almost beyond belief that such basic questions are being asked so near to the moments of truth.

Eriksson juggles formations and players and invites all of English football to play a fool's game of unfathomable calculation. The witless Ian Wright draws licence-payers' money to join in. He applauds Gerrard's dive against the Hungarians and makes barely decipherable contributions to the Carragher discussion. The hugely influential Alan Hansen chooses not to say the unsayable. It is that England's World Cup bid has become a joke.

Why the vow of silence? Surely it cannot be out of fear of an outrageous punchline? Maybe some of us should check the airports and the railway stations. Just to confirm that Slim has indeed left town.

WITH ERIKSSON ON COURSE FOR DISASTER, WHERE IS THE MUTINY?

Published: 22 June 2006

The potential folly of rushing to appoint Steve McClaren, a man at the heart of this England regime which has broken every rule of intelligent football planning, and under which the requirements of individual responsibility and leadership are handed around like hand grenades after the pins have been removed, has been painted most luridly in the sky above the RheinEnergieStadion in Cologne this week.

If ever a team needed a new man on the bridge, someone untainted by the years of waste, even outright stupidity – how else do you categorise arguably the most brainless squad selection in the nation's competitive football history? – it is this drifting and hopelessly indulged collection of English players who, for some strange reason of their own, believe they are beyond criticism.

Instead England are bequeathed a man who has been party, willing or not, to so many of the ineptitudes which take over England whenever the bar is lifted to world-class standards.

Maybe you think this is harsh, that McClaren has merely been a prisoner of the Eriksson years. In that case, it must be said it has been a well-heeled prison without bars, one from which the head coach-elect of England could have walked out of any time.

He could have railed against the miserable excuse for team-building, the pathetic little cameos granted to players of promise who never got the chance to prove, either way, their true status, the constant changing of tactics and personnel and now, in the middle of a World Cup, the dawning horror that once again Sven-Goran Eriksson, the £5m-a-year man, simply does not have an overriding strategy. But then only McClaren knows precisely the extent of his own input.

Eriksson has become a parody of Mr Micawber, the Dickens character who always believed something would turn up. Could the 18th World Cup turn up for Eriksson? Because football is football, unchartable ultimately, beset often by outrageous fate, it would not be the equivalent of the world shifting on its axis – not quite. But it would be the supreme example of a coach winning the greatest trophy in football in spite of himself and what passed for his policies.

McClaren could have complained, along with a true World Cup hero, Sir Geoff Hurst, when Eriksson refused a word of criticism when the captain David Beckham admitted to fouling an opponent deliberately in order to draw a convenient suspension.

He could have demurred to the point of rebellion when Eriksson delivered his absurd squad selection, when he picked a unit of four specialist forwards: two of them plainly unfit; one of them, a bewildered teenager, utterly untested in the top flight of football, even unseen by the England coach; and Peter Crouch.

He could have said this was unprecedented madness. But of course he didn't. He has a career to protect, a lush appointment to inherit. He could have said that the team needed a new kind of dynamism, new leadership on the field, after the disasters of both Japan in the last World Cup and the European Championship in Portugal. But instead, and possibly because he was so much part of it, McClaren stayed silent, at least publicly. His reward is that now he is the man responsible for the future of English football.

Here right now it is as if the first mate of the Titanic is being handed his own command even as the iceberg looms into view.

This is a team without direction, at times even logical purpose. It is riding the hope that Wayne Rooney can do something to match the stupendous achievement of Diego Maradona in Mexico 20 years ago, when he came closer than any footballer in history to picking up a team and carrying it single-handedly to a World Cup victory.

Whether you think even the brilliantly gifted Rooney deserves to be bracketed in such awesome company is not really the point. This is the expectation placed upon the 20-year-old, who, even as he struggles to become match-fit, and throws one of his trademarked tantrums when he is brought off the field at a point when his aura is beginning to fade and there is a ripple of suspicion that he is beginning to favour his so recently broken foot, has to do nothing less than inspire trust in a team currently incapable of putting together 90 minutes of coherent football.

On Tuesday we had the quintessential England of the Eriksson era. We had 45 minutes of football which made sense, disciplined passing football which was quick and intelligent, spearheaded by Rooney and magnificently supported in the first half by a Joe Cole who, like his virtuoso team-mate, seemed utterly committed to shake off the dead hand which had gripped the team in their appalling performances against two of the weakest teams ever to appear in a World Cup finals, Trinidad & Tobago and a desperately under-performing Paraguay.

Then the system, the belief, collapsed again – this time in defence, purportedly an area of reassuring strength. England defended set pieces with no more proficiency than a rabble assembled at the local park. The pattern is relentless. At the highest point of Eriksson's reign, England were rampant against Germany in Munich. In their next game, at home to Albania, they were rescued by a goal from Robbie Fowler.

On Tuesday, Sweden, a team of modest talent indeed if you took away the subtle Champions League hero Henrik Larsson and Arsenal's indefatigable Freddie Ljungberg, were the side of heart and conviction in the second half when Frank Lampard again disappeared from significant action and Beckham, who has talked so long about the importance of this World Cup to his own view of his career, virtually disappeared from sight.

Again there was the gravest concern about England's ability simply to last the course of 90 minutes of World Cup action. Against Trinidad & Tobago they were revived by the arrival of Rooney and the superb, biting application of young Aaron Lennon. In Cologne, Steven Gerrard came off the bench consumed with the need to make nonsense of his original removal from the action. He did that quickly enough and there was reason for celebration.

In their current condition England could inspire little or no confidence going in against a Germany who will be welcomed as heroic successors to the likes of Franz Beckenbauer and Gerd Müller when they step out in Munich on Saturday. Even Ecuador, who left half their team on the bench in an implicit announcement that they were happy to surrender the chance of winning their group if it meant meeting either England or Sweden, are not without threat.

The aim here is not to pillory McClaren – only to say that England are missing so many of the vital ingredients of a team on the rise, are performing so far below standards that could reasonably be expected of such alleged talent and established celebrity, that the idea of transferring power within rather than to outside becomes a little more bewildering each day.

When Sir Alf Ramsey took over as England manager 40-odd years ago he dismantled everything – selection policies, interference from outside, methods of preparation, levels of discipline – and he demanded levels of personal responsibility and leadership which had never been met before in a brief 12-year participation in World Cup action.

Who could say that such a dramatic statement of new values is not required of England at this point in the 18th World Cup, one which elsewhere is alive with evidence of new and brilliant football, of national teams who have come here to Germany fired with ambition and a willingness to devote a month of mostly hugely rewarded lives to the single goal of beating the world? England assure us that they are as committed as Argentina, Spain, the Netherlands, Germany and Ghana – to mention just five teams who have so far drawn attention to either the quality of their football or the extent of their commitment. So why are we not convinced? We see the erratic levels of performance and the circus of celebrity shopping and social life which the wives and girlfriends of the England team are generating in Baden-Baden.

Like so many aspects of the England approach under Eriksson, the picture is not one of serious intent. Yes, of course, there are possibilities. Rooney might yet catch fire. Gerrard may continue in a vein of supreme confidence. The promise of Tuesday's first half might just be ignited again.

But where are the certainties? Where is the evidence that in the weeks of his parting Eriksson is capable of doing anything more than again throwing the dice? It does not exist. So of course you have to tremble for the present as well as despair of the future. The only antidote is the blindest of hope. Maybe the World Health Organisation will send an emergency supply. No doubt Beckham is guaranteed to pose for the picture.

WILL WE LEARN THIS TIME FROM ERIKSSON'S YEARS OF MISRULE?

Published: 03 July 2006

Blowing forlornly into the gutter here in the morning breeze in the gritty Ruhr town of Gelsenkirchen, so far from the glory and the drama that will engulf Berlin as it stages the final of the 18th World Cup in a few days' time, is once again the question that haunts all those who care about English football.

It asks quite simply: will intelligence and courage ever again be applied to the shaping of our national game on the international stage? Will the lessons of Sven-Goran Eriksson's disgraceful stewardship of England be properly learnt or, under his successor and right-hand man, Steve McClaren, will the old mythologies build again? Will we talk ourselves once more into the preposterous argument that we are in a position to beat the best of the world game? Here, despite the defiance displayed by England's 10 men after Wayne Rooney's natural brilliance was so terribly negated by that fundamental lack of discipline that in the past has been conspicuously ignored by the England coach, it is impossible to provide an encouraging answer.

Eriksson, a broken man but vastly richer than when he arrived as a symbol of knowledge and winning experience five and a half years ago, was not simply a beaten coach on Saturday night.

The charges against him were many and serious, but the greatest of all was that he was a disastrous example of all that follows too many easy choices, when investments are made in such myths that David Beckham was the man to put at the centre of the hopes for a "golden generation", and that you can keep changing your team, as you might your aftershave, and still expect coherence and rhythm and confidence when the big issues have to be settled.

Beckham spilt more tears yesterday when he announced that he was giving up the England captaincy, a decision which guaranteed him another burst of personal publicity at the end of his fifth major tournament – and how much of it would be tempered by the hard truth that in all of his appearances in three World Cups and two European Championships his influence and his impact have been negligible? Probably not much. He was applauded from the room in Baden-Baden despite the unassailable fact that the manner of his resignation summed up all that has been wrong with the Eriksson-Beckham regime.

The captaincy of England is a rare and precious gift and should be received and returned at the bidding of the man in charge – the coach of the team.

Zinedine Zidane was the man of 1998, Ronaldo of 2002, and this time it could be the great Frenchman again. And where has Beckham been? The most celebrated and rewarded player of his generation has never stirred, when it mattered, from the margins. He sobbed in the dug-out after being withdrawn from yet another match in which his captain's armband represented not a natural right of leadership but a privilege granted to him, and unchallenged, in all these years of numbing underachievement.

However, Eriksson, even as he neglected to find solutions to the enduring failure to exploit the talent of Steven Gerrard and Frank Lampard, has always insisted that Beckham was the natural captain of England – and that he never once considered changing that assessment. There, maybe, we have the central problem of Sven-Goran Eriksson, an intransigent ninny.

But if we are bound to catalogue the failures of Eriksson, the relentless decline in belief that he could supply any of the necessary answers to the problem of England's failure to begin to match the standards set by Sir Alf Ramsey 40 years ago, the blame cannot be completely isolated.

A coach, of course, creates the ethos of his team, but it may also be true that Eriksson perhaps believed that slavish loyalty to those players favoured, in the face of all evidence, would inevitably bring at least one dividend. Maybe if he told them they were indeed the golden generation often enough, they would first believe, then prove it. They believed it all right. Even after the final, sickening denouement, the tragi-comic failure in the penalty shoot-out, Lampard, was lambasting the media for its criticisms. It was an astonishing departure from reality.

This, unquestionably, was England's worst World Cup finals campaign since their first in 1950 – when they were ambushed by a team of American part-timers and amateurs. Portugal, though denuded of bite by the absence of their playmaker, Deco, had rarely looked like being breached before the dismissal of Rooney, and this was the first serious team England had faced. They were appalling against Paraguay and Trinidad & Tobago, played one half decently and another catastrophically against Sweden, who were eaten up by Jürgen Klinsmann's Germany, and the victory over Ecuador was a triumph for the lesser of two inept teams.

Yet how could it be otherwise? Apart from chopping his men and his tactics from one match to another, he picked a squad which defied all logic, and in the selection of the untested Theo Walcott stepped on to ground which Pelé, no less, described charitably as "unique". Yes, that was the word – unique. Uniquely misguided, uniquely uncaring for both his squad and the boy, uniquely indicative of a man not serious about his business.

If the "great generation" has once again been revealed as one made not of gold but clay – the likes of Lampard should not complain about such an assessment but simply reflect on their lack of achievement – it is possible only to weep for what might have been if the Football Association had taken the decision that would surely have presented itself as inevitable to any organisation of spirit and nerve after the failures of Japan four years ago and Portugal in 2004.

On both occasions the combination of Eriksson and McClaren was found to be utterly wanting. They had no tactical initiatives. They sat transfixed as Luiz Felipe Scolari guided Brazil and Portugal past them as though he had arrived at the traffic lights at precisely the moment they turned green.

It is reasonable to imagine that if the FA had acted on either of those occasions something of the "golden generation" could have been rescued.

Could we imagine for a second the confusions and meanderings of Eriksson happening under a Guus Hiddink or a Scolari, or the best of the rest of the shortlisted candidates, Martin O'Neill? Could we begin to believe for a second that the stupidity of a Walcott decision might occur, that England would have come here to Germany with a strike force of one player who had both full fitness and a modicum of experience? Would it have been possible that, confronted with the years-long evidence that Gerrard and Lampard simply did not have the natural instincts of true midfielders, any one of those serious candidates for the job would have allowed the situation to drift into the impotence that was displayed on Saturday?

A Hiddink would surely have recognised, as Rafa Benítez did at Liverpool, that Gerrard's remarkable talents did not sit easily in any conventional midfield format. It would have occurred to him, surely, that a solution would have been to play him alongside the right touchline, where he has generated so much power and dynamic intervention for Liverpool, along with his freedom to move into striking positions from various points behind the front line. Beckham would, of course, have had to move. To where? Maybe a place in his life where he had to produce more than a daily forest of headlines.

Eriksson is gone now but then who takes his place? McClaren, the willing assistant or the reluctant ally in decisions which were plainly wrong? Take your pick. Certainly he was the man who was supposed to provide flair and intuition at Eriksson's shoulder. The evidence mounted here that his influence has been either too much or too little. Whatever the reality, it is hardly possible to imagine a man less endowed with the aura of someone who can easily bring in a new mood, a new sense of the possibilities of the future.

The image of England in defeat was tear-stained, but, as we might ask of Beckham, for whom was the crying? For the disappointed nation, for all those flag-waving, "football's coming home" optimists who believed they had a serious chance of competing with the big guns? Or the implosion of their own inflated belief in who they were and what they represented? Could it really be the surreal circus that surrounded their headquarters?

One Brazilian observer, though consumed by despair that his own team had failed to respond to the challenge of winning their sixth World Cup, offered a view painful to English sensibilities. He said: "We know England founded the game, but it it is amazing that every four years they seem to assume that they have a right to win the great trophy. But on what is it based? What have England done since they won at home in 1966? They simply have not been in the big league – they haven't even won a European Championship..."

Such realism surely needs to be applied at home, within and without the game. But then where is the encouragement? One of the runners to succeed Eriksson, Sam Allardyce, yesterday told the readers of the highest-selling Sunday newspaper in the land that the cause of England's demise here on Saturday was a cheating referee.

The mind – and the heart – recoils at such drivel. Rooney, who had carried so many hopes, who remains a young footballer of brilliant talent, stamped on Ricardo Carvalho in the region of his genitals – and inspired an Irish wit to remark that the real question had turned out to be not whether the problematic foot would stand up to a tackle, but whether Carvalho's "tackle" would stand up to Rooney's foot – and anyone who had thought such a flashpoint was not possible had been living deep in the Eriksson land of myth and legend.

Not so long ago in the Bernabeu stadium in Madrid, Rooney lost control of himself in a friendly against Spain and was withdrawn by Eriksson, wisely in that it was clear the referee was on the point of showing a red card. But then later he said, no, there was no long-term problem. Rooney would not be taught a lesson, not dropped for a game or two, as an indicator that merely being a superbly promising talent was not enough to guarantee your place in international football. As we saw so devastatingly here at the week, chickens do have that bothersome habit of coming home to roost.

Of course, Cristiano Ronaldo, who showed some of the less appealing aspects of his nature while performing formidably on the field, and dispatching England with a confidence and authority quite beyond Gerrard and Lampard, is the available scapegoat. Alan Shearer, who is being lined up as a McClaren assistant, and perhaps a man with the prestige to defuse future criticisms of the England operation, suggested that Rooney was entitled to chastise his Manchester United team-mate forcibly when they next meet at the training ground. How easy, how convenient, to forget that it was Rooney who caused his own downfall – and betrayed his team.

But then, also, how typical of the English football psyche, one which has been so easily lulled by the platitudes and the inaction and the sheer futility of the Eriksson years. Yes, he qualified for major tournaments, but who did he beat, what force did he topple, except Germany on that beguiling, deceiving night in Munich nearly five years ago? That he succeeded where Kevin Keegan was plainly failing and Graham Taylor had fallen eight years earlier when the challenge was against Dennis Bergkamp's Netherlands, was an achievement hugely inflated when you considered Eriksson's reputation and rewards – and the level of opposition he faced. In Munich it did seem that the church bells were ringing for the dawn of a new age of English football, but again it was a myth. England struggled desperately in their next game, against Albania, while Germany began to rebuild, all the way to the World Cup final less than a year later.

Once more Germany march on a World Cup, once more their team play with a strength and a conviction well beyond the sum of their individual talents.

Once more England fall well below the mountain top – and yet again England pile up the excuses. But they do not wash; they are beyond the blurring effect of Beckham's self-regarding tears. The truth is indeed blowing along the gutter here. What happened, give or take some passing heroics, is what England deserved. They simply didn't come up to scratch, and they never will until they are given a little leadership – and some basic truth.

ZIDANE'S FALL INTO DARKNESS WAS THE FINAL ACT OF BETRAYAL

Published: 11 July 2006

Few cities on earth are less likely than Berlin to mistake a mishap in sport for the tragedies of real life. Yet even in the bustle of Friedrichstrasse, near where Checkpoint Charlie used to stand, it is impossible to put aside the extent of the damage Zinedine Zidane did to himself and to football in the gaunt Olympiastadion on Sunday night.

He was supposed to leave a light burning in his permanent memory. Instead he brought a peculiar darkness, a fatalism that might have played well here in one of the cabaret clubs of another age.

Yesterday, in the tortured wake of an 18th World Cup that had promised, briefly but gloriously, nothing less than the regeneration of a game dying of greed and deceit, football played its usual trick in the face of a crisis of public belief and respect. It fussed over the details of a disaster. Was Zidane's red-card punishment for his shocking head-butt of Marco Materazzi illegally imposed? Was video evidence, not the eyes of the match officials, the reason why a horrible distortion of football justice – the possibility that Zidane might have stayed on the field and influenced a game he had already mutilated – was avoided? Perhaps these are indeed matters of administration worthy of investigation, but do they carry us within a thousand miles of the real problem? Of course not.

Football's fundamental need is not a review of its rules but a scourging of its spirit. That one of its greatest players, a father of four sons, a man surely aware that every nuance of his performance, even the expression on his face, was being examined in close-up by a television audience of more than a billion, should behave, with such shocking suddenness, like a back-alley thug, is perhaps the ultimate example of how the game of the world so frequently loses not only its head but also its conscience.

No less depressing for some, no doubt, was the overwhelming suspicion that Zidane's victim, Materazzi, now taking the salute of his proud nation, had provoked Zidane with some sickening insult from the gutter, maybe a sexual allusion, after touching his nipples, or perhaps a flash of the racism which is such a relentless problem in the Italian game.

That, for the time being at least, had to be speculation. The reality was that Zidane had produced not a crowning statement of his brilliant career but an act of barbarism. The artist had turned assassin, and, as any civilised law insists, provocation is never a defence.

The resulting extent of disillusionment in those who focused on Germany and its splendidly organised tournament as a point of renewal is surely now impossible to exaggerate.

Even the joy in Italy, where there was justifiable pride in the resolution of a winning squad who might easily have been overwhelmed by the corruption scandal that has caused such dismay among followers of great clubs like Juventus and Milan, was so brittle you had to wonder how close it was to a hysterical statement of denial that the nation had been betrayed, utterly, by *Il Bello Calcio*. The foot soldiers had won, magnificently in the case of heroes like Fabio Cannavaro and Gianluca Zambrotta, but where had they been left by the generals? They had been marooned without certainties the moment the great tournament ended in a barrage of fireworks and silver paper and broken promises.

Yes, broken promises. A few weeks ago football seemed to be following some mystical summons towards redemption. The Germans, so derided in their own land as a potential embarrassment rather than a glory, were playing with magnificent application, Miroslav Klose and Lukas Podolski striking so hard that their status had changed, almost overnight, from derided "Polish rats", to stalwarts of the Fatherland. The Africans of Ivory Coast and Ghana played football of heart-touching honesty and speed – even Didier Drogba, a man derided by his own Chelsea fans as a serial cheat, seemed to find the best of himself, playing with a rousing strength of purpose.

The Spanish were a revelation, the Brazilians, as usual, were in waiting, and then, in Gelsenkirchen, a week into the tournament, something extraordinary and moving happened. Argentina played like gods; they persuaded some of us that their 6-0 dismantling of Serbia & Montenegro, a few days after winning a fine match with Ivory Coast, had set a daunting, even magical standard. If anyone could beat Argentina, and wipe the smile off Diego Maradona's face, they had the right to call themselves great champions of the world.

Whether that was a reality systematically destroyed by the Argentina coach, José Pekerman, who granted hardly a peek at the mesmerising talent of Lionel Messi and was suicidally cautious when he had the Germans at the point of breakdown in their quarter-final, is one of those many football questions that will probably never be resolved. What, sadly, is not in doubt is that the 18th World Cup was already locked into betrayal.

Cheating was the killer, and if England chose to believe that most of it was located in the strategy of the man who rejected them, Luiz Felipe Scolari, and the play of the hugely gifted Cristiano Ronaldo, that was maybe one more way of excusing their own desperate failure to meet the challenge that is placed before every allegedly significant football nation every four years.

The truth was that cheating was everywhere and infecting everybody – even England, as we saw when Peter Crouch yanked the hair of a Trinidad defender as he scored a vital goal on a night of draining ineptitude in Nuremberg. Portugal, no doubt, were wretched, particularly in their semi-final with France, where Ronaldo marred some superb passages of play with a relentless attempt to win a penalty from a referee he believed had been duped by Thierry Henry – the author of the most shameless piece of play-acting in the entire tournament.

All the time you hoped that the early momentum would be rescued, certainly that Brazil would eventually burst into life. But Brazil failed, as did so many players who had been loosely described as great. At the end of it all, the great French artist Michel Platini said that coaches had placed a dead hand on the tournament, insisting on religious observation of tactical plans rather than any genuine freedom of expression. But if Platini was right to assail some coaches – notably the near-paralysed Pekerman – his principal targets should surely have been some of those players with the huge reputations.

Pekerman was assailed for withdrawing his playmaker Juan Roman Riquelme, the choice of many as the player of the tournament in the early going. But the truth was that Riquelme did not grow in the World Cup. In fact, he shrivelled. When he was taken off against Germany he had become virtually anonymous.

It was true of almost all the men who were supposed to write their names across the German sky. The greatest disappointment of all was Ronaldinho, twice elected player of the year and a man who, before the ultimately ill-starred diversion created by Zidane, was supposed to turn the tournament into a personal coronation.

In Brazil's headquarters on the edge of the Black Forest you saw him work beautifully in training; a blue bandana was worn against the fierce sun, and a smile was hardly ever off his face. But sometimes it was an enigmatic smile, and one made more so when he heard that the great legend Tostao, a star of Brazil's most spectacular World Cup triumph in 1970, was asking some harsh questions in his column back home.

The most pertinent one: "When is Ronaldinho going to show up here? Not the one who plays for Brazil – the one who stars for Barcelona. I haven't set eyes on him yet." Nor would he, we knew that, as the life drained out of him and his team in the quarter-final against France.

That was the high-water mark of Zidane. He played well against Spain, less well against Portugal in the semi-final, but against Brazil he changed the tournament, gave it a new core. That was true until the moment he threw so much away, when he turned and walked up to Materazzi welling all that unstoppable venom.

Italy were brilliant when they stopped Germany. They stripped down all the fierce qualities Jürgen Klinsmann had imposed in the face of such disdain. Cannavaro was immense, the player of the tournament beyond any doubt, but as the Italians added one good performance on to another, the value of a strong coach was increasingly obvious. You saw the relentlessness of the Italians, how they compensated seamlessly for the loss of Alessandro Nesta, and when it became obvious that they were serious contenders, despite several players of distinctly ordinary talent, notably Mauro Camoranesi and the plodding strikers, Luca Toni, Alberto Gilardino and Vincenzo Iaquinta, it was impossible not to make comparison with the work of England's Sven-Goran Eriksson. Marcello Lippi plainly had both the respect of his team and vital control over them.

Eriksson's failure is well documented now; his apologists have presumably run to the hills or reinvented their view of a man who was supposed to develop the golden generation. What had to be said, when the World Cup had done the last of its business, was that England's lack of impact was one of the major disappointments.

Sometimes it is easy to exaggerate the foreign view of England's potential – often we are told what we want to hear, especially that we are still a major force in the game despite the fact that it is 40 years since the only success at this rarefied level and that the team are still to appear in the final of a European Championship. But this time there has been little pretence that England were a major force; the failure to strike any kind of rhythm was duly noted, and shrugged away. What does linger, with a still strong force, is the arrogance of Frank Lampard, who when England's misery was over made an impassioned attack on the English media. He had merely missed a few goals, and in view of all he had done for the country was entitled to more respect. There, maybe, we had the most basic problem: a failure to remember that true respect flows only from consistent achievement.

Now, when you look at the broader picture of this World Cup, you see that England were far from alone in their belief that there was not so much to prove.

Brazil's Ronaldo, the star of 2002, made an engaging speech on the eve of the tournament. He said that he still believed he had everything to play for, that the triumph of the last tournament was something for the history books and that now he would redefine himself all over again. He scored two against Japan, and one against the naïve defence of Ghana that took him past Gerd Müller's record, and he was widely acclaimed. But the truth was that mostly he was an embarrassment, so out of match conditioning that he could move only in a small arc that required his team-mates to deliver the ball to his feet, and in striking positions. That was one scandal at the heart of the great tournament; the other one that grew in ever increasing intensity was that level of cheating.

So many games were decided not by skill but a sleight of dubious hand. The dive is no longer an outrage; it is an intrinsic part of the game.

Here was where the 18th World Cup took its greatest defeat. You can change as many laws as you like but you cannot legislate the heart and the conscience of the game. You can only appeal for the decency and spirit that it will take to put matters right. You can only hope that someone like Zinedine Zidane remembers who he is and what he is supposed to represent. No, you wouldn't want to talk about the tragedy of football in the shadow of Checkpoint Charlie. But then maybe you could make a small, sad point. You could say that if Zidane, the fabled Zizou, was supposed to be the best, what on earth can be made of the rest?

BRILLIANT FUTURE AWAITS WARRIOR WITH WISDOM OF PAST MENTORS

Published: 25 August 2006

There is a flaw in the widespread belief that Roy Keane, the prospective new manager of Sunderland, today becomes officially a volcano waiting to erupt.

It lies in the failure to remember that if all managers start off as footballers, with their own set of priorities, it is only the failures who retain that status in their hearts and their minds when they move into the manager's office. The winning managers know, from the start, that they have to change; they have to acquire cunning, if not instant wisdom, but more important than anything they have to understand that what they demanded from themselves was a burden they alone knew they could carry.

Keane, it is reasonable to believe, is too worldly in the ways of the game he dominated for so long not to know that too quickly asking for the standards he imposed upon himself would almost certainly lead to a collective nervous breakdown in the Sunderland dressing-room.

Much has been made of Keane's brisk acquisition of the required coaching certificates. But it is an irrelevance. Long before he sat in a lecture room, Keane had sailed through the biggest test of managerial skills a working pro could face.

He persuaded Sir Alex Ferguson that he could gauge the mood – and the possibilities – of a dressing-room better than any pro the old warhorse had encountered. The result: a one-two combination which ravaged Premiership opposition and delivered the European Cup and, in the process, made Keane so much more than the manager's alter ego. He was also an interpreter of trends, a scout for weakness, a sergeant major of the barrack square and an ultimate warrior in the trenches.

Yes, it ended in tears and an apparently lingering bitterness, but then that is often true of the most passionate of partnerships. The one between Ferguson and Keane was moulded by mutual self-interest and a shared belief in the proper ingredients of a successful football club. That Keane overstepped the mark in Ferguson's view – as he certainly did in his fierce civil war with Ireland's former coach, Mick McCarthy – is often what happens when a little balance is lost, and in Keane's case there was a reason that was perhaps available even to amateur psychology. His decline as a truly great player was accelerating at a pace that assaulted his spirit.

But Keane is about to become a manager now. He has been through the greatest turmoil of his life, the one that came with the dying of his physical power, and now he has to make some sense of the rest of it. How will he fare as a manager? The suspicion here is that ultimately he will be brilliant. Yes, there will be some eruptions, some moments of drama, but Keane understands football with the keenest of eyes for those who are prepared to go to their limits, as he did so consistently, and those whose hearts are perhaps less than resolute. In the meantime, no doubt he has to polish a few communication skills which in the past have not often suggested a career in the diplomatic service.

One old pro was confident enough last night, saying: "As a player Roy Keane was something of a wild man, particularly in his youth, but as his career wore on you could see what a fierce intelligence he brought to his play. He became a consummate professional and I've no doubt that he has the means to be highly successful as a manager. More than anything, he has the desire and the ambition ... just like Ferguson, and just like his first manager, Brian Clough."

Most crucial is his ability to weigh the strengths and weaknesses of the winning managers he played for so successfully, Clough, Ferguson and Big Jack Charlton. They often, close up in the most ferocious competition, gave insights and lessons not available in a coaching course, and now it is his job to separate the good from the bad, a chore invariably undertaken by the most successful football men.

Yes, to a degree he has to change. For the present he has to accept his football life for what it is, which is to say a tight corner, but one with immense possibilities in the matter of proving that he is capable of dynamic leadership. There is no shortage of reasons to say that the Sunderland chairman, and tiro administrator, Niall Quinn, who was sneeringly referred to as Mother Teresa by an angry Keane, has chosen to live dangerously, and many of them have been advanced already with impeccable logic.

Can the man who reacted so violently to the imperfections of his United team-mates really be expected to tolerate the limitations of players who have crashed so dismally to the bottom of the Championship? When his job is on the line, will he walk easily away from the blunders of a referee or the needling questions of a post-match interviewer? Again, the suspicion is that he will. It is because he knows football down to his bones, because he knows what it takes to survive in any situation, and despite the worst of his own weaknesses. And, also, because so often something subtle and profound happens when a footballer has to settle for management, if only because it keeps him in touch with the central driving force of his life, and the thing he knows best.

At the time of his retirement as a Celtic player this summer, Keane was seen walking alone on a street of Puerta Banus, a place of dubious glitter in the Lotus Land of the Costa del Sol. He was without his dog, without a spring in his stride, and, it seemed, without much of a point. A different Keane is about to be unveiled. Different from that least tranquillised of players, and different from the lost soul who walked past the boutiques and designer houses with unseeing eyes. But then it will still be recognisably Roy Keane, a man most unlikely to have forgotten how to win.

COLE'S DEFENCE OF THE INDEFENSIBLE A BITTER REMINDER OF FOOTBALL'S LONG FALL FROM GRACE

Published: 12 September 2006

When the novelist Graham Greene lost patience with the authorities in his adopted town of Nice he wrote a stinging attack entitled *J'Accuse*. Perhaps this was the inspiration for the latest addition to the literary firmament, Ashley Cole, when he felt an irresistible urge to go public with his complaints about the injustices heaped upon him by Arsenal Football Club, the most shocking of which was a proposal to raise his wages from £25,000 a week to a mere £55,000 – or, to put it in its full grotesque perspective, just £2.86m a year.

In language that Mr Greene perhaps might only have envied had he swopped his usual lunch-time Perrier for several vats of absinthe, the author of *My Defence* is spectacularly withering about this outrage.

He says that Arsenal were "taking the piss" and despite the fact that he had given his "heart and soul" to the club they had done "jack-shit" to retain his loyalty.

Some might say this is a heart-rending, important story even if the telling of it may have a few rough edges, and certainly they will find agreement on the editorial board of *The Times*, who on the anniversary of 9/11 chose to flag the book across their front page. Explaining their decision to publish this vital document, *The Times* wrote: "This is no ordinary football book – for once we are taken into the mind of a footballer who is not afraid to speak his mind [sic], to reveal his innermost thoughts and expose the furious rows at one of the world's biggest clubs."

Speaking for oneself, the excavation of an ancient sewer might have been somewhat more uplifting.

Cole is a fine footballer, one whose improvement has been increasingly impressive over the years, especially on the international stage for England, for whom in several recent games he has been the difference between a kind of respectability and desperate humiliation. But as a chronicler of the mores of modern football he carries us to the heart of the ever-deepening disillusionment of so many who have supported the national game for so long.

Consider, for example, the trials of everyday life that afflict ordinary people, some of whom still battle to pay the prices required to gain entry to Stamford Bridge, Cole's new home and the Emirates Stadium, where before his betrayal he was due to continue a career which had been nurtured by Arsenal since he was a boy, and set them against the crisis that came to our hero as he drove to his mother's house in Chigwell.

"It was a good job I was well away from it all," writes Cole, "as my agent and the vice-chairman [David Dein] locked horns in an office in Central London. Somewhere along the North Circular Road [Greene's locales were generally more exotic] one phone call changed everything about how I viewed and felt about Arsenal. 'Ash! Are you listening' said a virtually hyperventilating Jonathan [agent Barnett]. I'm here in the office and David Dein is saying they aren't going to give you £60k a week. They've agreed £55k and this is their best and final offer. Are you happy with that?'

"When I heard the figure of £55k I nearly swerved off the road. I yelled down the phone: 'He's taking the piss, Jonathan'. I was so incensed. I was trembling with anger..."

We know the likes of Cole live in their own bubble, and if football society has allowed its creation, there's not much to be done about it, and so perhaps we shouldn't care less when they dress up in their white wedding-suits and flog off the ceremonials to a celebrity magazine and forget to submit to drug tests and boast about how many bottles of Cristal they can get through of a night and talk about the respect that is their due – win, lose or draw. But the problem does kick in a little more seriously when they apply to themselves the same emotions as working people living rather tougher lives while trying gallantly to look after their families.

There is not much point in recalling how a beautiful old player like Wilf Mannion had to sit on a cardboard case in the corridor of the third-class section of a train taking him home after he had helped fill Hampden Park with 120,000 fans. Or Tom Finney being told by a director of Preston North End that he could forget about the interest of an Italian club and just go on collecting his few quid a week. Or Hughie Gallacher throwing himself off a railway bridge in despair. Or Tommy Lawton, one of the best strikers the English game has ever seen, being splashed by the Rolls-Royce of a Notts County director when he stood at a bus stop and then being prosecuted for passing modestly sized bouncing cheques.

All that's been said and done and it belongs in another age but sometimes you do have to wonder if someone like Ashley Cole ever had the remotest clue about the good luck he enjoys in relation to the men who went before him and built the traditions and the glory from which he now so strikingly benefits.

There is not much of such reflection in the pages of *My Defence*. Only a relentless self-justification and certainly no apology for, not even a sense of its effect on those who follow the club he allegedly once loved, his meeting with the Chelsea hierarchy while he was still under contract at Highbury. He could not help making comparisons between the treatment he received and that given to Thierry Henry. "The club made Thierry Henry feel wanted with their special wooing of him, wining and dining him, speaking in public about how much they wanted him to stay, going on a deliberate charm offensive to win their man. But me? I didn't have one dinner, one meeting or one phone call. The truth is that the Gunners had done jack-shit all season to hold on to me."

There was another title Ashley Cole might have borrowed from Graham Greene. It was *The End of the Affair*. But then that was about fractured love rather than greed, and there is not much evidence that the author of *My Defence* is aware of the difference.

SCHOLES ENJOYS HIS RED-LETTER DAY AS GERRARD IS RUTHLESSLY ECLIPSED

Published: 23 October 2006

England's Steve McClaren has already been rejected once by Paul Scholes, who for several weeks now has been conducting a master-class in the art and the vision required to play in midfield as a consistent match-winning presence rather than an occasional virtuoso contributor. McClaren apparently took up a mildly beseeching posture while making his first request. Now he should go all the way. He should get down on his hands and knees.

The new, desperate entreaty must surely follow Scholes' total eclipse of current England resident Steven Gerrard in this almost embarrassingly comfortable Manchester United defeat of Liverpool... and ascension to the top of the Premiership.

Had it been any easier for the 31-year-old, who walked away from the international stage two years ago in his disgust at the midfield tinkering of Sven-Goran Eriksson, he would have been entitled to light a cigar in celebration of his 500th appearance in a red shirt.

Gerrard's deserts? A long and lingering look in the mirror. Stevie G, as he is referred to by so many fervent admirers, was a quite shocking counterpoint to Scholes.

It was hard to know which was the more dismaying... his almost completely irrelevant performance, a strolling, posturing parody of what might reasonably be expected of a "world-class" midfielder in one of the most vital games of the season for his suddenly embattled club, or body language which spoke of something which was hard to distinguish from outright indifference.

In the early, formative stages of a match in which Liverpool would be ultimately outclassed, Gerrard several times took the time to deliver lectures to his team-mates. He made it clear where he wanted the ball to be delivered. It was to his feet. In the meantime, though, Gerrard's duty to be involved at the heart of matters was blithely ignored. By comparison, Scholes was both the heartbeat and the central force of his team. He pushed United into the lead in the 42nd minute, an advantage which Rafa Benítez's critically misfiring team did not truly threaten on a single occasion. Rio Ferdinand's goal in the second half was taken with exquisite skill. But it was also the last word in formality. Liverpool, once again a quilt weaved by a Benítez apparently increasingly obsessed by the need to rotate his squad, had completely failed to examine United's right to a goal-difference lead over Chelsea at the top of the Premiership.

Xabi Alonso, who at various times has promised to be a bitingly intelligent and technically brilliantly force at the heart of the Anfield midfield, was only marginally more influential than the anonymous Gerrard. It meant that Scholes, with the most significant assistance of Ryan Giggs, ran the game so nonchalantly he might have been doing his regular shop at his local supermarket in Oldham. The least starry of major players, Scholes displayed both absolute authority and an astonishing appetite. He was, as much as anything, a stake aimed at the heart of celebrity football.

Perhaps only second to David Beckham in this department, Gerrard from time to time runs narrowed eyes over the title-winning potential of his club – and issues warnings about their need to show title-winning potential if he is to remain a contented Anfield soldier. But their chances of delivering on promise that seemed to have reached a high watermark coming into this season will inevitably dwindle if a player of such vast reputation cannot contribute more to one of the key games of the season.

There were other Liverpool disaster areas. Luis Garcia, a sporadic scorer of spectacular goals, is notorious for his lack of economy on the ball, but this was a notably wasteful performance even by his own profligate standards. Mark Gonzalez on the left was pacy enough but was utterly lacking in guile.

Given such deficiencies, it was inevitable that United would again persuade their manager Sir Alex Ferguson that they have the potential to end Chelsea's two-year domination of the Premiership. Naturally, he glowed after such easy superiority over a team which not so long ago were being spoken of as Chelsea's likeliest challengers. The reality, though, was different. Liverpool brought no kind of challenge to Old Trafford and if United had some impressive moments in their easy control – not least when a Louis Saha clearly growing in both power and confidence was on the ball – it was never quite enough to dissipate the memory of Chelsea's superb triumph over European champions Barcelona last week.

United, with Wayne Rooney again showing at least hints of the power that deserted him so profoundly after his first game of the season, no doubt have enough reasons to believe they can make a more serious run at the champions this time, but then the depth of their will and the hard edge of their talent was never properly tested on this day.

This was alarming for a Benítez who had hoped for a major contribution from the lionised Gerrard. The manager has coaxed and flattered Gerrard, he has tried to impart tactical discipline by giving him fixed roles, but still he looks for a sustained and winning influence. Yesterday he saw only a Liverpool wasteland. And, of course, Paul Scholes.

SIR ALEX FERGUSON: COURAGE TO BUILD AN EMPIRE

Published: 04 November 2006

Even now, 20 years after he arrived at Manchester United, dressed in a blazer and an attitude that explained all over again the reason for Hadrian's Wall, the theory of some is that Sir Alex Ferguson has yet to provide a truly defining image of himself, a flash of revelation to carry us beyond all the anger and the joy, the obsession and the stored-up vengeance. They hold that the mystery of his competitive will is hidden somewhere between a still boyish love of battle and the angst of the ageing general who looks into the skull's head of his past and wonders if he will ever see another great victory.

The theorists are wrong, however, and anyone who was in the Nou Camp for the European Cup final of 1999, when his team became the running embodiment of his belief that defeat is not so much a thief in the night as an outrageous impostor, can say so with a special edge of conviction.

When Ferguson's eyes swivelled from the gut-wrenching sight of the colours of Bayern Munich being pinned to the trophy which had become his version of the Holy Grail to that of Ole Gunnar Solskjaer conjuring a winning goal something happened to him, at the age of 57, that you see in young boys when they leap ecstatically into the arms of their fathers.

What happened was the wonderment that comes only to those who still harbour in their gnarled old lives, and souls, a little corner of innocence. Seven years on, the force of that moment, its need to be reproduced, remains the magnet drawing out a career that is reaching beyond all precedent.

Innocence in the man who at times has seemed to wish for nothing more than the imposition of a rule of terror on all of English football? A man for whom loyalty has never been fashioned by sentiment but need – ask Roy Keane, ask Gordon Strachan, ask Jaap Stam, and, supremely, a David Beckham who thought he had reached the stage when he could operate at Old Trafford on his own terms? A man who could cry conspiracy at the mere run of the ball? A man who once confessed to not feeling an ounce of compassion when a sworn enemy was diagnosed with cancer because to do so would compromise his idea of his own honesty? A man for whom ferocious partisanship has been not a tendency but a deeply ingrained way of life?

Yes, it is the innocence that all of the great football men have always had and expressed in their belief that they could find an answer to a football problem, that potential would again flower gloriously, all wrapped in a passion that will not die and which one recent night persuaded Ferguson, just a few months short of his 65th birthday – an age at which the men he admired so much in his youth, Jock Stein, Bill Shankly and Sir Matt Busby, had long withdrawn from the front line of the battle – to go to the touchline in the rain and wind of a tricky night at Crewe.

When the moment of glory was ebbing in the Nou Camp, when the sight of him dancing down the touchline with his eyes glistening and his arms outstretched was already frozen in the memory of all who saw it, Ferguson was still stunned. He sat shaking his head and murmuring: "I can't believe it. I can't believe it." And then, a small phrase that radiated from the core of his existence: "Football – bloody hell." If they called Busby, who would have been 90 on the day Ferguson delivered United's second European Cup 31 years after the first, the father of United – and maybe even all of football – how could they describe the man who had picked up his tradition and given it a new and amazingly consistent dimension?

You couldn't call Fergie the father of anything except his burning desire to push back the barriers of his own ambition. He cleared out talented players like Norman Whiteside and Paul McGrath not because he didn't recognise their ability but because he questioned too deeply their will. They might have been money lenders in the temple.

He made mistakes, some of his signings were indifferent at best, but always there were moves that were as bold as they were inspired: Keane and Cantona were not exactly model citizens, but they were the catalysts of change that required the hardest of nerve; when the generation of Scholes, Giggs, Beckham and the Neville boys replaced a winning team, Alan Hansen, drawing on his Liverpool experience, announced that you couldn't win with kids. But you could, as Busby had proved 40 years earlier, if they were the right ones.

When Ferguson made a rare and fundamental mistake in the organisation of his life and his career, and prematurely announced his retirement, it was his wife and sons who saw most clearly that for him an honoured retirement would not be a prize but a sentence.

They wanted the vintage wine-drinking, horse-fancying maker of football empires to stay on the front line because they knew any alternative would be a shell of the man whose intensity – and furies – had shaped their lives. They knew that in the case of Sir Alexander Chapman Ferguson there was an unswerving obligation... you took the best of the zealot and you lived, however turbulent the ride, with the rest.

The conventional path would have been to walk away, as some part of him said, with the glory piled so high: 17 major titles for United, including the unprecedented treble of Premiership, FA Cup and European Cup, and nine for Aberdeen.

But walk away to what? To a sudden hush. Better, he decided, to hear the boos that greeted him, for the first time, when United lost to Blackburn at Old Trafford a few years ago; better still to be cut and to bleed than to have everything settling into place, never again to be disturbed by the irreplaceable surges that come when you are on the line between winning and losing.

We do not yet know the outcome of his decision to walk back – whether it will be seen ultimately as an act of folly, an old man's wish to reinvent himself and the most thrilling days of his life – or a sensationally vindicated belief that there is still more than a little good wine left in the glass.

There is, however, an interim verdict to be delivered. It is that if Ferguson has yet to return to the mountain top of English or European football, he has already achieved something that seemed to be beyond anyone's power with the arrival of Roman Abramovich and José Mourinho at Chelsea.

He has brought a degree of suspense, and one that was brilliantly augmented last weekend when Bolton Wanderers, the anti-football specialists who pride themselves on delivering hammer blows to such aristocrats as United and Arsenal with football as spontaneous as an old May Day march past in Moscow, were played off their own park. Wayne Rooney, who some saw as the old gambler's last throw, re-emerged with a thunderous hat-trick. It meant Ferguson, with his arch-rival Arsène Wenger, could still be seen as an investor in a game that was about more than unabashed cynicism and spite.

Here, in the manner of United's open-hearted and flowing play, was another large hint of the innocence – and the courage behind a face that for some has long been seen as ruthlessly self-serving; a willingness to believe that the great prizes can still be won in a certain, thrilling way, and that he might still be the author of success which made no compromises with the meaning of football.

Sir Bobby Charlton saw it clearly enough when, as a United director, he elected himself to the job of finding a man who would not be dwarfed by the weight of Busby's legacy, a task that had been beyond such formidable football men as Frank O'Farrell, Tommy Docherty, Dave Sexton and Ron Atkinson.

"I saw what Alex had done with Aberdeen," says Charlton. "I saw somebody who had the nerve and the belief to go out and get what he wanted; somebody who would never be overawed by any situation. Somebody who would give the job everything that was required – and someone who also saw it as the biggest challenge in football. I have never doubted any of this since the day of his appointment, and my confidence was not harmed by the fact that I saw the old man [Busby] felt the same way."

Such faith has, of course, been tested. Ferguson's war with the Irish horsemen plutocrats John Magnier and J P McManus was always going to be perilous in the shadow of the Glazer takeover. But Ferguson's imperatives in the matter of Rock Of Gibraltar, the horse he believed he partly owned, were similar to those in so much of the rest of his life. They were dictated by the values of his native Govan, where the tough shipbuilders and stevedores taught him that no time was too soon to fight for your rights.

Ferguson swears that he learnt more in Govan than in any of his football assignments. From his first games with Queen's Park and his hard-won success and subsequent angst with Rangers, his managerial survival ordeals with East Stirlingshire and St Mirren, and then his glory at Aberdeen and at Old Trafford, he carried the tough wharfside with him.

It proved a dimension that was probably best expressed in the wake of a 5-1 defeat by Manchester City, devastation that came when Old Trafford had still not decided whether Ferguson was a messiah or just another lamb at the altar of a squandered dream. Ferguson felt he had let down every United supporter. He felt like a criminal, a betrayer.

This was a bleakness which still comes to him with every defeat. But then when United win, and when he is redeemed, there is the overwhelming desire to run like a boy. In the often jaded world of big-time football no one has done it for so long and with such competitive courage. For so many talented football men one bad season can feel like a lifetime.

The measure of Sir Alex Ferguson, still, is that so often he makes 20 years, with all the good and some of the bad, seem like a single heartbeat.

GAZZA:
A CRY FOR HELP

Published: 09 November 2006

Paul Gascoigne already has a signature tune. It's *Fog on the Tyne* and at the peak of his celebrity, in 1990, it reached No 2 in the charts. But then when yesterday you heard that he had spent the night in the cells at a Chelsea police station, another song came to mind. It was the one which goes: "On the Sunday morning sidewalk I'm wishing Lord that I was stoned, there's something in a Sunday that makes a body feel alone."

Yesterday happened to be Wednesday but for Gazza you have to fear life has long seemed like a desolate Sunday morning, about which Kris Kristofferson also wrote: "There ain't nothing short of dying, half as lonesome as the sound of the sleeping city sidewalks, and Sunday morning coming down."

There is nothing much we don't know about the Gazza story now. It is at least as well documented as that of George Best, but just as it was when the great Georgie meandered into fresh crisis, and futility, and for similar reasons – obsessive behaviour and an inability to see celebrity and many of the friends it brought for the dangerous mirage it was – the sadness remains just as acute.

Calling for the rescue of Gazza is no doubt a little like shining a small torch into that fog he celebrated at a happier time. So many people in and out of football have tried, and the truth, even as he became a household name not for the brilliance of his talent but for his teary breakdown in the semi-final of the 1990 World Cup, was never far from hand. Gascoigne, even at that early stage of the race, was programmed for self-destruction.

But if you knew deep down he was never going to conquer the weakness of his nature, and deliver more than fleeting evidence of a gift that at its best was the most thrilling seen in these isles since the decline of Best and the arrival of Wayne Rooney, it never made the process any less disheartening or painful.

Yesterday, even though it was so soon after his charity mission to Africa had turned into another personal ordeal of an excruciating kind, was no exception. There was the familiar regret about the inevitability of his fate but perhaps also something more, a stabbing question about whether, when it still mattered, when it might, who knows, have been a little more in the balance, something extra could have been done.

Was Gazza delivered a little too easily to his self-elected fate? And if this was so, at least to a small degree, is there anything to learn from his present plight? Does the vigilance that Sir Alex Ferguson successfully applied to the formative stages of Ryan Giggs, say, and his current and thus far largely successful attempts to protect the prodigious Rooney, need to be redoubled with so much player, not to mention managerial, anarchy in the air?

If Gascoigne's psychological profile, and background, was always deeply worrying, it is still true that not everybody sought to impress upon him the reality of his situation – and the inevitable brevity of the time he would have to show that he was indeed one of the most naturally favoured footballers the world had ever seen.

Even mild criticism of his elevation to the status of a great footballer – as opposed to one of immense promise – drew a fierce reaction. His agent, Mel Stein, shortly before launching into a biography of his client that might have been penned, for all its reserve, by a Hollywood press agent, once invited a sportswriter to lunch so that he would have the chance to explain why he had been so wrong to say that Gascoigne was still in the foothills of Best's stature in the game.

A few years later, when Gascoigne was rejected by the England coach, Glenn Hoddle, on the eve of the 1998 World Cup – and the player promptly rampaged tearfully in the team hotel – a small army of celebrities made angry protests, and were joined by quite a sizeable section of the media. The force of showbiz was formidable in the life of the football superstar, and ebbed only to the point of extinction when the prospect of reflected glory had faded beyond recall.

Though he will do it with the backing of a vast fortune fuelled by years of relentless celebrity, and possibly a knighthood, even David Beckham is having to contemplate the challenge of life in the dwindling afterglow of being at the heart of a media circus. His Real Madrid coach, Fabio Capello, was saying this week that the loss of the England captaincy has inflicted a heavy psychological blow, which was a salutary reminder, if we ever had one, that even footballers infinitely more grounded than Gazza, are in danger of believing their more fanciful publicity.

It is no doubt true that Gascoigne could have been deposited in a Trappist monastery between match-days and still found diverting mischief but this does not alter the fact that because of his ability to make headlines, often at the cost of turning football logic on its head, a certain indulgence was granted to even his most errant behaviour.

At the time of his disappointment at the hands of Hoddle, it was pointed out by an old pro that all the support he received from the showbiz fraternity was essentially worthless. In showbiz you have rehearsals. In professional sport you don't. You have to walk a line that can offend all the instincts of an extremely wealthy, red-blooded young man. You have to get the rest. You have to be ready to deliver now, not in some airily projected future.

Of all his mentors, no doubt Terry Venables got the best out of Gascoigne. As Tottenham manager he put aside the stories of poor discipline and bizarre behaviour and in 1988 invested a then British record £2m in what he saw as uniquely creative talent. Gazza largely flourished at White Hart Lane, right up to the point where he went berserk in a Wembley Cup final.

Soon after that denouement Venables expressed his deepest fears, saying: "I had Diego Maradona when he was a kid at Barcelona and sometimes you saw an expression which made you worry about his future. Sometimes I look at Gazza and see the same thing in his face. I don't worry so much for him now but 20 years down the road." Frank O'Farrell, then manager of Manchester United, said almost precisely the same thing when Best defected to Marbella and confided to a mob of reporters that he was getting through a bottle of vodka a day.

In their different ways, Best and Gazza were two of a kind. They had been given inordinate talent and not a lot to protect it. It was their burden and football's problem. As the spotlight gets ever brighter, it is one not likely to go away.

FOOTBALL IN DESPERATE NEED OF TRANSPARENT HONESTY AS THE 'WHITEWASH' STARTS TO PEEL

Published: 23 December 2006

The whitewash Lord Stevens was accused of daubing over football graft is already beginning to peel, a fact which should be uplifting to all those who groaned when they heard his hurried-up, anticlimactic report this week. As the City of London fraud squad, the outfit which has put jockey Kieren Fallon in the dock, yesterday confirmed its now active interest in the football bung culture, the widely assailed old cop was maybe due a little credit.

Given that his role was never that of an independent, judicially empowered investigator but an employee of the Premiership, honest men in football may fairly conclude that in the long run one answer he gave this week might just be worth the near £1m it cost.

Lord Stevens was asked: "Is there corruption in football?" His answer was brief but unequivocal. "Yes," he said.

Stevens may have been kept away from the core of that corruption – and the fact that eight agents refused to have dealings with him will for many tell its own story – but in refusing to sign off 17 transfer deals he considered dodgy, and, at least by implication, inviting police and income tax officials to inspect the evidence he has produced, he did not exactly deliver a ringing endorsement of football morality.

The Premiership may believe it can now draw a line under the allegations made by the Luton manager, Mike Newell, and former England coach, Sven-Goran Eriksson, but they are deluding themselves. When the City's Old Bill announced they were investigating two agents, the issue was taken into another realm.

It is not one where agents can refuse to co-operate. It is one where they can be investigated thoroughly and where their failure to talk would lead directly to an assumption of their guilt – and lead to a rigorous application of the law in the matter of gathering evidence.

George Graham, the only leading football man to be punished for accepting a bung, was not trapped by the force of football's self-policing which, as Stevens has also helpfully pointed out, scarcely exists. He was hunted down by a Danish journalist and British income tax men.

Now, suddenly, the game has widened in the wake of the Stevens report. Under the new terms of reference, dictated by the legally backed investigators, Premiership chairmen can no longer talk airily of statutes of limitation set by themselves or have their chief prosecutor soften the outline of his report; now the piper will be paid not by vested interests but the man in the street.

Some are sceptical about the degree of public support that would gather at the back of a sustained police probe. At least one high-profile commentator has asserted this week that Joe Bloggs doesn't give a damn about the issue. He wants to see his team triumph, and how they do it is utterly beside the point. But then the law is the law, however arbitrarily, or ham-fistedly, applied, and those who do believe that clean sport is rather a good idea will surely be happy that the police appear to have recovered their nerve after a previously disastrous foray into race-fixing allegations.

Fallon, a jockey of consummate brilliance, has had his career severely disrupted by the City of London's fraud squad, the biggest, best-resourced unit of its kind in this country.

Football can only shudder at the idea that agents who have most aroused suspicion will now be invited to help this aggressively proactive unit in its enquiries.

We all know a little of how this works – and how those under investigation can best help both the police and themselves. They can provide hard evidence, something that Lord Stevens and his men plainly found elusive at best. The exceedingly good news for all but the men of graft is that a trail of real investigation has now been laid down. Tough questions are going to be asked. Interview dates can no longer be ignored.

Joe Bloggs may not be thrilled, but maybe the football lover who struggles to meet the costs levied by the modern game will feel a little more enthusiasm. He may just be able to begin to believe that his interests are at last coming under a degree of protection.

At the time of the Graham affair, foreign observers, particularly in North America, were aghast at the lack of official supervision of transfer dealing. They wondered how on earth English football had managed to operate without the kind of checks and balances which underpin any legitimate business in most parts of the developed world. They assumed there would be an automatic tightening of control, at the very least a central clearing office where all transfers were carefully inspected by trained lawyers and accountants. More than a decade on, Stevens is insisting on such reform.

Now the fraud squad is on the job, who knows, the mind of football might just be concentrated on the need for transparent honesty. The hope may still be a little fanciful, but no doubt much less so than when a football bung-buster lacked the ability even to feel a collar.

Maybe, just maybe, this time the whitewash has been spread a little too thinly.

ALAN BALL: GREAT SPIRIT FOR WHOM FOOTBALL REMAINED THE ESSENCE OF LIFE

Published: 26 April 2007

When Bobby Moore knew that he was near the end of his life, he made a series of calls to the players he led to the World Cup in 1966. He wanted to say both goodbye and thank you.

All of them were deeply affected; all of them put down the phone with that terrible sadness that comes with the certainty that you will never again feel quite so whole.

It was not a contest in grief but then if you had played an emotional Geiger counter across the land the most dramatic register might well have come from the house in Hampshire occupied by Alan Ball, who is now, with shocking abruptness, the second of the heroes to step down from the gilded carriage that has borne them from the moment Sir Geoff Hurst completed victory over West Germany.

If there was any reason for the extremity of his reaction, other than that "Bally" was by far the most overtly emotional of the "Boys of 66" – a random memory, a glance at the photograph of someone he knew and loved could be enough to bring tears – it was maybe because what happened in that long-ago summer set for him a level of perfection that, even in a brilliant playing career, could never again be matched.

He felt that acutely when his managerial career meandered and misfired at Blackpool, Portsmouth, Stoke, Exeter, Southampton and Manchester City.

At the age of 21 he was the baby of the team on the mountain top, but for the 41 years that followed the place would never again be accessible. It made him, rather like some dislocated war hero who finds, when the drama is done, that he has to live out the rest of his life on another plane of less heightened experience, a prisoner of both time and old glory.

The best tribute to Alan Ball now is the overwhelming sense of loss that must be felt in English football by all those who have not been quite seduced by the age of instant celebrity which so relentlessly seeks to impose greatness when really, when you look closely, the matter to be celebrated is not that, because it awaits the test of time, but extraordinary promise.

No such ambiguity ever attached itself to Ball, who played 975 competitive games, starting as a teenaged firebrand with Blackpool, and finishing 21 years later, with 17 outings and two goals for Bristol Rovers. Ball was always more than a great midfielder of immense energy and wonderful mental sharpness; he was a great spirit, a passion, a recurring statement that football would always be the essence of his life.

Some of that spilled out one night when he came to my house for dinner when we were both exiled in Vancouver – he was playing out some of the last of his talent for the "Soccer Bowl" winning Whitecaps.

It was a jovial evening, not least for the mock outrage of Ball's late wife, Lesley, when the former Chelsea forward, and Ball's Vancouver team-mate, Steve Kember, played a familiar trick of depositing his dentures in her wineglass. But at one point Ball returned to the table wiping away tears. He had lingered over some pictures hanging on the wall – pictures of men and times he carried around with him like baggage.

He said: "Sometimes I long to be 20 again – when everything seemed to be so easy, when playing football with great players was such a natural thing to do. I miss those days so much – and I suppose it's not going to get any better."

It never did, not deep down, because he could never quite reproduce the splendour of that day at Wembley; the climax of his supremely competitive life came when he was still a boy.

But then he was a boy who, under the driving influence of his beloved father Alan, had already won one huge battle. He was rejected by both Wolves and his local club Bolton because for them he was too small. Yes, he had a brilliant sense of space and time, he could run all day and always with waspish intent, but he was more than anything, in their dull eyes, a firefly, darting in the night, rather than claiming it for his own.

It was epic miscalculation as he played superbly for Blackpool and England – and then Everton beat such as Leeds United, Manchester United and Liverpool to his signing, and then later, Double-winning Arsenal came calling.

Sir Alf Ramsey had no doubts; and nor did John Giles, who was playing so well in midfield for Leeds that Manchester United manager Sir Matt Busby would quickly say that letting him go was the great mistake of his football life and Ramsey said how much he regretted he had not been born an Englishman. Yesterday, Giles said: "People talk about how a player from the past would fare in today's game, well, let me tell you something, Alan Ball would have been a giant in any age. Forget his size; he had a magnificent engine and a tremendous brain.

"Sometimes when you read about how England managers struggle to get the best out of world-class players like [Steven] Gerrard and [Frank] Lampard, you are bound to think of Bally. He ran forever and never lost his edge; he was quick and cute, he was the perfect midfielder. Today, I can only see two people in the Premiership who could come close to him, and they would have to be at their best: Paul Scholes and Cesc Fabregas."

Ramsey saw Ball and Nobby Stiles as supreme water carriers in the service of Bobby Charlton. He asked Ball what happened when a man took a dog for a walk. The man threw an object and the dog ran after it, picked it up, returned and dropped it at its owner's feet. Ball must think of himself as the dog and Charlton the owner. Some dog; some pedigree.

Stiles and Ball were room-mates at England's Hendon Hall headquarters and Stiles recalls vividly the anguish of his friend when, after the opening World Cup deadlock against Uruguay, he was left out of the remaining group games with Mexico and France.

"After Alf's decision, Bally came up to the loft room we shared with some winnings he had collected from the bookmaker. He spread the fivers on the floor and danced on them, saying 'Fuck Alf Ramsey'. But he didn't kid me. You only had to look at his face to see that he was breaking up inside."

It is one of the more significant facts of football history that Ramsey recanted soon enough, recalling Ball for the quarter-final game against Argentina. Ramsey knew what kind of game it would be. It would be won by the bigger hearts and the more relentless willingness to run.

When the great trophy was gathered in, Stiles, who had a crisis of endurance in extra-time, spoke in wonderment of the force and the energy of Ball's performance. He said: "I didn't know where my next step was going to come from and when Bally came running by he shouted: 'Move, you bastard, move'. He was on fire and on that day you had to believe he could have run until midnight."

Soon after he received that last phone call from Bobby Moore, Ball was encountered on Gold Cup day at Cheltenham. He loved racing and golf and he liked a drink, but always you sensed they were by way of substitutes for that thing which had always been at his core.

In a voice that would never lose its high pitch, he talked of "Mooro" and the boys and how it had been when the world was so young and everything that it offered was so full of the highest promise. It was almost as an aside that he speculated on what might win the big race.

When he was chairman of Manchester City, Francis Lee, a footballer of similar heart and bite, desperately wanted his old England team-mate to succeed as his manager. Lee ran a gauntlet of criticism for the appointment of Ball – but persisted with him to the point of relegation. Why? It was not that Ball had built a portfolio of success as a manager or coach. He had had his moments, notably at Southampton immediately before moving to Maine Road in 1995, but he could not claim any trophies, any solid body of work.

Lee admitted it was a gamble, but on what? "I suppose," said Lee, "it's because Bally will always represent something in football that is precious. He cares so much and he is always looking for the kind of performance that he produced every time he ran out on the field."

Maybe Lee and Ball were creatures of their own times, locked into an old ethos that could never work in the age of £100,000-a-week players. But you had to warm to Lee's romantic gesture. He wanted to re-create some of the best of the past of English football.

Soon after his departure from City in 1996, over dinner in the West End, on a night when he may have felt obliged to put on one of his brightest faces, he told a joke against himself.

He said that while leaving a supermarket that day he had seen an old lady struggling with her bags. "Can you manage, love?" he asked. "Probably better than you, Bally," she was alleged to have replied. Everyone laughed – including Alan Ball. But maybe not with his eyes – the ones that always used to glow so fiercely in and around the battle.

PURE DESIRE SECURES CROWNING GLORY FOR PETER PAN OF FOOTBALL

Published: 07 May 2007

At that moment when every small phrase of Sir Alex Ferguson's body language said he knew in his defiantly unfragile old bones that he had completed one of the greatest personal statements in the history of football, when the title he had once believed was nothing so much as his right was won back from the rouble mountain of Stamford Bridge, you were reminded of what it is precisely that makes him utterly unique in the game of today and the past.

It is that he is nothing less than the Peter Pan of football. He acquires years but not age. In 1999, when his young team gathered in the European Cup to go alongside the one won by his admirer Sir Matt Busby 31 years earlier, he ran along the touchline at the Nou Camp stadium like a schoolboy rushing to his summer break.

It was the same at the City of Manchester Stadium on Saturday when United moved eight points clear of Chelsea. He was back in Never Never land.

When his reign at Old Trafford is finally over, when all his triumphs at Aberdeen, where he broke the vice of the Old Firm of Celtic and Rangers, and United are lined up, there will be endless analysis of his phenomenal presence in the front rank of football management.

Was he the most astute tactician, did he have Jock Stein's freakish capacity to go the heart of the weakness of his opponents? Maybe not.

Did he have the grace and the purity of Busby's vision of what the game should mean – and his eye for football genius? Perhaps nobody quite had that.

Did he have the passion and the generosity of Bill Shankly, the other member of the great Scottish quartet to which Ferguson long ago elected himself so irresistibly? In some ways this is the closest match, but then there is a point where the comparisons have to stop.

No one, not Stein nor Shankly nor Busby, was able to maintain the energy and the appetite that Ferguson has carried so triumphantly into his 66th year.

Stein died on the touchline at Ninian Park, Cardiff, while managing Scotland at the age of 62. Shankly, though he would regret the decision until the last of his days, walked away from Anfield at the age of 60. Busby, still haunted by Munich, finally put down the burden of being the Father of United – and some said of all of football – when he was 62.

Ferguson marches on, repelling doubts, indeed making a mockery of all those claims that he should have stuck to his brief conviction that it was time to savour a retirement, watching football at a distance, going to the races and savouring his collection of vintage wine.

His family talked him out of it because better than anyone they knew the essence of him. It was in football and it will always be so.

Despite the crushing disappointment he experienced in San Siro last week, when his most talented players effectively went missing for a night, there was good reason for his elation when on Saturday it appeared impossible for him not to collect his ninth Premiership title.

It was that his triumph over the young pretender José Mourinho ran deeper than the mere count of points – or the fact that United had returned to the top with football of touch and ambition which reminded us that in the two years of their dominance Chelsea had achieved nothing more profoundly than a relentless, power-based efficiency.

United have taken the title with a game faithful to the origins of their great tradition, when Busby's great team of Carey and Rowley and Pearson filled post-Second World War stadiums with entertainment that seemed expressly designed to colour in brilliantly some of those grey areas imposed by the years of war and dislocation.

Now the pyrotechnics of youngsters like Cristiano Ronaldo and Wayne Rooney, and the professional brilliance of veterans like Paul Scholes and Ryan Giggs have created the promise of still another era of virtuosity.

To do this at 65, to have walked away from the crisis of the Rock of Gibraltar affair and the distractions of war with the ruthless, moneyed faction led by John Magnier, and to have survived the arrival of the bottom-line specialists in sporting empires, the American Glazer family, and move forward to new levels of prestige, is surely Ferguson's crowning achievement. So many thought he was suddenly a dead man walking. He was advised to go gracefully, to acknowledge that for him the tide had turned irrevocably.

It was a position endorsed by the arrival of Roman Abramovich, and nor could it have helped too much to hear the Russian's appointment, Peter Kenyon, the man who when he was chief executive of Manchester United was blamed by Ferguson for the bungling of the Ronaldinho signing, announcing that the Premiership would in future be fought out by a "bunch of one." This season Ferguson has not only defied such a smug assumption. He has heaped scorn upon it with the instinct of a natural-born street fighter.

The scale of his victory in terms of football management is more than significant; it is complete. If Mourinho had prevailed in the league it would still have been at enormous cost to his old image as the Special One. Victory would have come with compromises that you could only believe would have been deemed unthinkable by Ferguson.

The Chelsea coach, plainly, has suffered blows to both his pride and his independence.

Abramovich's decision to impose upon him Andrei Shevchenko – and freeze resources which Mourinho deemed essential to overcome the effects of injuries in vital areas of the team – broke the fundamental operating principle of Ferguson, and all the great managers who went before him.

This can be identified easily enough. It is the right to decide on the signing of players and to control the ins and outs of everything to do with the running of the team.

Ferguson, right or wrong, has been able to impose his will. It is the legacy of all his work at United, his extraordinary achievement in turning a club that was dangerously close to being sold for the pittance of something in the region of £12 million into one of the richest sports franchises in the world – and his understanding that he was only as strong as his refusal to compromise on those issues which he deemed of vital importance.

So he made the hugely unpopular decision that it was time to move on the David Beckham celebrity circus. He took the boos and the waves of protest. He broke with Roy Keane, and took another backlash at a time when many of his contemporaries would have kept their heads below the parapet.

He couldn't do that because it was against his nature, against all those beliefs he acquired in the little streets beside the docks and the shipyards of Govan.

Now his reward is another winning battle, another triumph for his belief that age is an impostor as long as you retain the means – and the appetite – to do the job. Whenever it comes, his last victory will be the best. It will enshrine the fact that no football man ever before stayed the course so combatively – or so well.

RONALDO AGAIN FAILS TRUE TEST OF GREATNESS: MAKING AN IMPACT WHEN IT MATTERS MOST

Published: 21 May 2007

It was billed as a coronation for Manchester United and the most celebrated of their stars in the new Wembley fantasy park (sorry, that should be football stadium, despite the dismaying quality of the pitch and most of the Cup final). Instead it was the big reality check for all those who forget some of the basic rules of measuring greatness.

Yes, we're speaking – and without apology – of the latest farcical denouement of some of the more hysterical claims on behalf of Cristiano Ronaldo.

For many Ronaldo was the great magnet of a match invested with the challenge of properly launching another phase in the life of football's ultimately vaunted piece of real estate. But then we have to forget the weight of history; Chelsea full-backs Paulo Ferreira and Wayne Bridge – neither of whom has ever been mistaken for the new Maldini – didn't need the help of such mystique to render Ronaldo so anonymous that Sir Alex Ferguson, once again in a big match, must have been tempted to form a search party.

Great players – and Ronaldo has already been categorised as such even to the point of being compared to Pelé and George Best – embrace such games as Saturday's because they are the purpose of their lives.

Cutting it against some of the Premiership's mediocrities is one thing; taking hold of the big stage, and the toughest opponents in the land, should be a progressively routine test of players who announce they are going to be remembered through the football ages.

Now those who so enthusiastically announced that Ronaldo had already arrived on such a plane surely have enough evidence to think again; to think, mostly that is, of the criteria of performance which separates in the all-time ratings those of the outstanding natural gifts with which Ronaldo undoubtedly has been bombarded and the others who also have the nerve and the vision to make them work under the greatest pressure.

It is in the second category that we find the Bests and the Pelés. It is the first where Ronaldo remains anchored by his failure to confidently negotiate the end of a season in which he had received unprecedently lavish acclaim.

Where was Ronaldo when Didier Drogba, who was one minority choice for the honours which were heaped upon the Portuguese 22-year-old, scored his 33rd goal in all competition so magnificently in the last minutes of extra time? Where was he when Paul Scholes, the game's best player by some distance, and the only one who seemed to know the value of turning on the ball in a truly positive frame of mind, was desperately trying to bring drive and order to his team?

He was where he was rooted throughout the entire match. In the margins. Tepid, without influence or a hint of spark, he was the same Ronaldo who was so becalmed in United's catastrophic performance in the San Siro a few weeks ago.

Ronaldo's crime was not in having a bad game. It can happen to any mortal and ever so occasionally even a great player. No, Ronaldo's offence went rather deeper than some fleeting dip in form and commitment. It was the body language of discouragement that screamed out of him from the moment Chelsea's defence made it clear there would no easy pickings, no suicidal lungings announcing susceptibility to his pace and balance, no hint of fear induced by the tide of wild and sometimes risible praise.

Comparisons? They came like a flock of starlings over the ragged turf. Johan Cruyff, who scored 33 goals for the Netherlands in 48 games, once masterminded a victory over England at the old Wembley with a series of sublime breaks and passes. Some observers swear he never crossed the half-way line.

George Best, whose finest moment at Wembley came with a European Cup-winning strike against Benfica, scored a goal against England at the old stadium that left Nobby Stiles – the man who tamed Eusebio – and Gordon Banks in his wake. Later Stiles reflected: "I shall never forget that goal because it said everything about George's career and life. There he was, with the world falling on his head, drinking, losing touch with what had made his name so brilliantly, but still able to do something that made the little hairs on the back of your neck stand up. I said to him, 'George, I'll never forget that goal – only you could have scored it.'"

We are talking values here that go beyond a player's age or style or character. We are discussing an endless urge to inflict yourself on great events. Sir Stanley Matthews was a teenager when he first lit up the Potteries – he was 38 when he fashioned the 1953 Cup final forever named in his honour. Pelé was 17 when he scored a hat-trick in the World Cup final.

It is only when such standards are equalled that we can rush a 22-year-old through the gates of greatness.

No one would suggest that Ronaldo isn't a player both of bewitching possibilities and also a striking reason for United's first Premiership title in four years. No doubt they deserved their title; they played some excellent, expressive football and applied the pressure on Chelsea through the season. But then, just as in the case of their star player, they were maybe not as good as double triumph would have suggested.

United's most consistent performer – when he was free of suspension – was unquestionably Paul Scholes, and the weight of his contribution, unrecognised at award ceremonies, had never been more explicit than on Saturday. He set a rhythm and a level of professionalism which was never matched by Michael Carrick or Darren Fletcher, and until it is United cannot assume any easy ability to march beyond the restrictions placed upon by them by Chelsea in the last of the domestic action.

United's challenge is the same one that faces the sometimes luminous Cristiano Ronaldo. It is to improve at the critical point of delivering performance when it matters most. Without this, talk of greatness in a team or an individual will always be some kind of folly. Here, especially in the case of Ronaldo, it was as bad as it can be. All the evidence said, after all, that it was a ridiculous misapprehension.

THERE ARE REASONS TO LOVE BENÍTEZ... BUT NOT BECAUSE OF FOOTBALL HIS TEAM PLAYS

Published: 22 May 2007

There are quite a number of reasons to admire, even love Rafa Benítez. In the snakepit occupied by so many overstated and under-principled football managers, in all the hot and often stagnant air and the cold spirit, he is mostly a model of decorum and, even more importantly, decency.

His status in Merseyside football lore is already for the ages. However, if it should happen that he delivers a second Champions League triumph for Liverpool over Milan, in Athens tomorrow night, delight in this quarter, if we are honest, will not be without a few complications.

This will have nothing do with Rafa the man or the motivator. When his team won in such extraordinary, even surreal circumstances in Istanbul two years ago he handled the glory with beguiling modesty.

Unlike that of the most conspicuous victim of his almost eerie ability to neutralise the strength of the most powerful of opposition, José Mourinho, Benítez's reaction to the greatest moment of his career included no attempt to deflect attention from the heroics of his players.

In the post-match dawn he stood away from the microphones and the television cameras, a small, benign smile lighting up his broadly open features as the likes of Steven Gerrard, Jamie Carragher and Xabi Alonso fondled the gold winning medals dangling around their chests.

The cynical might say that it was reality as much as good character which dictated such exemplary behaviour, Liverpool's victory flowing not from a tactical masterplan but an outpouring of physical and emotional strength from the players which could not have been created by even the most brilliant work on the dressing-room blackboard.

However, Benítez wouldn't have been the first coach to cheerfully ride on the fighting instincts of players breaking out of a limited gameplan.

No, the problem has nothing to do with any aspect of Rafa's nature. The trouble is his football. It is not the kind which, beyond admiration for superbly genuine competitive honesty, a not exactly ubiquitous quality in the upper reaches of the game, could possibly lift the soul of a neutral.

If Jorge Valdano's crude assessment that Liverpool's semi-final triumph over Chelsea represented not the beautiful game but "shit on a stick" was excessive, no one could deny that the former football director of Real Madrid had touched on an element of truth. Excrement it wasn't, but nor was it the work of Van Gogh or Cezanne.

The unavoidable fact about Benítez – and one that makes matchwood of one recent assertion that if he delivers a second European Cup in three years, from a standing start in the wake of Gérard Houllier's moribund reign, he is an immediate contender, or better, for the status of greatest manager in the history of British football – is that he puts such a low priority on the ability of outstanding individuals to shape a game.

This was the thrust of Valdano's criticism and, whatever you think of his way with words, there is no question he is a witness of some authority. Few former footballers on earth are better acquainted with the value of a player free to follow, more than any word from the touchline, his own gut instincts. Valdano scored one of the goals that helped deliver the 1986 World Cup to Argentina. He was also permitted a close-up view of Diego Maradona's last touch in his campaign of bewildering force and virtuosity. It was the lacerating pass which finally demolished West Germany's elaborate plan to have Lothar Matthäus mark Maradona out of the game.

Such individual inventiveness, Valdano argues, is not a key part of the game of Benítez, or Mourinho, and the reason for this, he further suggests, is because neither coach reached the upper levels of the game as players. It is a shaky theory when you consider that Arsène Wenger, the author of some of the most beautiful football ever seen in these islands, also failed to get beyond the foothills as a player.

Yet, still, Valdano hits a nerve in any ultimate assessment of Benítez the coach who has produced such brilliant results in the Spanish League and the knock-out tournaments of England and Europe. In that creatively wretched semi-final against Chelsea at Anfield, Benítez chose to leave out Alonso, a player of infinite ambition and lovely touch in his passing when he first arrived at Anfield.

That surely was a statement that the Liverpool effort would be most vitally concerned with stifling Chelsea. That it worked, via the shoot-out, finally brought unconditional joy to Anfield but there were many doubts expressed on the way to the right result.

At Valencia, Benítez also had a habit of benching one of the local heroes, the beautifully talented Argentine Pablo Aimar. Valencia enjoyed fiestas when two league titles were snatched from the jaws of Real Madrid and Barcelona, but the manner of the triumphs lacked a certain flamenco snap.

If the right result comes in Athens, the odds are that the fine points of Liverpool's performance will be relegated to the margins of celebration – and Benítez will have encouraged still more sweeping assessment of his place in the game. No doubt he will again react to the acclaim with his trademark humility, and that will be still another reason for applause.

There should, though, be no loose talk of the greatest achievement ever by a British club in Europe. That is a place in history which, for all the achievements of Bob Paisley, Joe Fagan, Brian Clough, Sir Matt Busby and Sir Alex Ferguson, still belongs to Jock Stein.

When the Celtic manager took his team to Lisbon to break down the "bolted door" of Helenio Herrera's Internazionale in 1967, he declared that his deepest ambition was a victory for football, something to thrill every neutral. He felt he owed that much to the game and he produced his extraordinary gift with 11 players bred in a 20-mile radius of Glasgow.

It would not be Rafa Benítez's style to make such a promise. There are a number of reasons for this. Some of them are good. One of them is bad. It is the fact that nothing in his football would give any weight to such an undertaking.

At critical moments, Stein reached for the stars; Benítez from time to time benches his most creative players. Don't mention it on Merseyside, but, putting aside all the moral questions about whether they should even have been competing in the Champions League this season, a win for the Milan of Kaka and Maldini and Seedorf will also be one for football – as it should be played. Hand on heart, you can say a lot in favour of Rafa – but of his football, not that, not yet.

BECKHAM'S RESCUE MISSION FAILS TO HIDE RIFT BETWEEN McCLAREN AND VENABLES

Published: 29 May 2007

The principle is one of the most basic in football – and any competitive sport – and it still holds good even though it has has been submerged for the past 48 hours in a substance which for delicacy's sake we will call treacle.

It is the one insisting that if the England manager Steve McClaren truly believes David Beckham provides his best option on the right of midfield for a game in Estonia that could decide European Championship qualification, it is nothing less than his handsomely paid duty to put aside all the sickeningly gaudy baggage we know will accompany the player on his hero's flight from Madrid.

Really, it should not have been a matter for "discussion" among background staff, right down to the team psychologist. McClaren is paid several million pounds a year, theoretically for knowing his own mind – and what he is supposed to be doing. But then even when this otherwise impeccable assertion is made, you have to remember quickly enough that we are not talking about common rules of evaluation in sport or anywhere else. We are talking Beckham – or, to put it another way, unbridled moonshine.

There isn't the time or the space – or the stomach – to catalogue here all aspects of the landslide of Beckham Brand advertisements over the past few days. But then let's make a stab at précis. Having accepted an extraordinarily lucrative deal with Los Angeles Galaxy that he would finish his playing career in a Mickey Mouse league, he is apparently now adamant that he be free to continue his England career past the magic total of 100 caps. This has plainly surprised, if not deeply irritated, employers who were led to believe that their capture's last and overwhelming ambition was to be the man who finally conquered football's last frontier of North America, a Daniel Boone or Jim Bowie – please, stifle that giggle – in white soccer shoes.

Rescuing England, less than a year after his embarrassingly tearful exit from the World Cup and his mawkish resignation as captain, apparently quite seamlessly restores his old status in the front rank of English international football. It is a nonsense, of course, but you wouldn't have thought so by the flood tide of reaction yesterday.

It means that two main points have to be made about the meaning of the restoration of David Beckham.

The first is that it has revealed a deep division in the relationship between McClaren and his chief assistant Terry Venables, a partnership which at its birth represented an appallingly transparent public-relations lunge.

McClaren was supposed to be the man to separate England from the years of ultimate futility under Sven-Goran Eriksson – years in which, as long as he went along with every Eriksson move, he was an inextricable part of a moribund regime – and more than ever now it seems that his decision to jettison Beckham at the start was designed to speak of new authority and independence and toughness.

So what was the purpose of Venables, a football man of much greater prestige and infinitely deeper experience than the man he was to serve? To guide? Or to deflect potential criticism by commentators outraged by the appointment of McClaren but also highly respectful of Venables? If this wasn't aimed at dividing and conquering, maybe it just might have been something of a muzzle. Certainly it may just be significant that since the start of a pointed rift between McClaren and his adviser, which became so evident after the catastrophic performances in Croatia and Israel, criticism of the former has been progressively savage.

The other irresistible conclusion is that Beckham is now convinced that he will indeed reach his target of 100 caps and join such as Bobby Moore and Sir Bobby Charlton in the most exclusive corner of English football honour. Here, perhaps, he is entitled to hear a hard word. It is that if he goes on to win not another six but 106 caps he will still be the odd man out up in the top end of the pantheon.

Why? Because Moore and Charlton accumulated more than glass cases bulging with badges of recognition. They also built up achievement that has never been subject to debate. It was written across the football sky. When looking for moments of supreme accomplishment by Moore and Charlton you don't have to go ferreting back to some home qualifying game against Greece. No, you go to the ultimate moments of success in a World Cup campaign against Argentina, Portugal and West Germany. You go up to the football mountain top.

And then there was the "failure" of Moore and Charlton four years later in Mexico. When Moore played so brilliantly in Guadalajara against Brazil that

Pelé rushed to embrace him at the end of the game and insisted they swap shirts. Pelé talked about the honour of duelling with such an opponent.

And then in Leon, Charlton played with such beauty and control in midfield that the West Germany of Franz Beckenbauer were being ushered to defeat before Sir Alf Ramsey decided that his general should be withdrawn from the sapping heat and given a little respite before what seemed a certain semi-final against Italy. Even then Germany progressed only because of the terrible vulnerability of Gordon Banks' replacement, Peter Bonetti.

It is this kind of perspective which shows up the latest Beckham fiesta in its true light. He had five cracks at the glory in five major tournaments and he came up empty each time. Now he is being asked, by a desperate and utterly unconvincing England coach, to put a little bit back into a cause from which he gained so much in all but genuine achievement. Is it too much to ask that he simply does that? Already, we know it is.

BY ALL MEANS GIVE BECKHAM A KNIGHTHOOD: FOR SELF-PROMOTION, NOT REAL ACHIEVEMENT

Published: 02 June 2007

Whatever the pyrotechnics produced by David Beckham in the friendly showpiece at Wembley last night, one certainty was always going to be hidden by days of acclaim that lacked only a full-scale ticker-tape parade. It was that there would be little or no reference to his last performance against Brazil, one that mattered in real football terms.

Remember it? Quarter-final of the World Cup, Brazil, a vulnerable team for whom Rivaldo had found it necessary to stoop to the most outrageous cheating in a group game against Turkey, one goal down beneath the blazing Japanese sun, the door open sufficiently for all of England to believe that this was the nation's best chance of winning the greatest prize in football for 36 years.

A time, surely, for English players of destiny, if ever there was one, but do we all not remember with a wince what happened next? It was the country's great hero jumping so high out of a tackle the Olympic record was imperilled, Ronaldinho dancing down the field before delivering a killer pass to Rivaldo, 1-1 ... door closed, even when Ronaldinho was sent off after he had deceived a tearful David Seaman not with a cunningly flighted free-kick, but, England insisted, a pure freak of nature. Beckham, naturally, was Seaman's chief consoler – bang in centre screen.

You might say it is cruel and petty to resurrect that moment in a week when everybody has gone out of their way to pay homage to the man who blubbed and gave up the England captaincy unilaterally last summer after his fifth largely innocuous appearance in a major tournament. But then, in the real world, any truthful accountancy of achievement is based not on image, not on a handful of decent performances at the end of a season, but the long run of a professional life's work.

Why, though, go back to a point which when ventured here in the past has provoked offers of psychiatric help? Because the problem really isn't David Beckham, a self-advertiser on the eternal make. It is a culture which responds as readily as one of Pavlov's dogs to the often clever promptings of the king of Celebrity Inc's football department.

It is possible to ignore most of it, especially the coarse banalities of *Big Brother*, Sir Alan Sugar and the rest of the dreary parade of reality shows, but sometimes we reach a point when the madness is simply too much, when values are screwed up in such a way that there has to be a cry of protest.

The strengthening rumour that David Beckham will be knighted – that he will get the nod from a government in which he would surely have flourished as a senior minister of spin – is such an example of dire provocation. Knighthoods have been devalued so relentlessly in recent years that one handed to David Beckham by Tony Blair would have the one merit of perfect symmetry: who better to acknowledge an artist of hype than the grand master?

It is dismaying enough that the odds have apparently shortened dramatically on Beckham being told to "Arise, Sir David" – at the age of 32 – but what can we make of plain Mr Jack Charlton's assertion that he will be one of the first to applaud if it happens? A generous statement spanning the football generations? A touch of satire by the rugged countryman? Or one of those light-headed moments which once used to regularly confound his brother, Sir Bobby – most notably when, soon after winning the World Cup, he told a national television audience that he carried around a little black book with the names of players on whom he was planning to wreak physical revenge? Let's be generous to the old and often mischievous warrior. Let's place his approval of a Beckham knighthood somewhere between categories two and three.

Most members of Jack Charlton's generation of authentic achievers will no doubt keep their own counsel on Beckham's apparently now inevitable honour. Jimmy Greaves, bravely in that he might be accused of sourness because his own magnificent career has received not even a passing glance from Downing Street down the years, has spoken against. The late Alan Ball might have been wheeled into some acid aside on the subject of Sir David. He could have spoken for himself, Nobby Stiles, George Cohen, Ray Wilson, and Roger Hunt. They went to the palace to receive their MBEs – the bottom rung of the honours system sometimes accorded to dutiful lollipop ladies – 34 years after winning the World Cup.

When Her Majesty presented Cohen with his medal, she said: "It's been a long time." Cohen, briefed by the master of protocol, nodded politely but later he reflected: "I could have told the Queen that, although we were very happy to receive the honour, in truth we felt it was a proper and necessary thing, it was not as though for one single moment down the years we had ever felt unfulfilled.

"We had something you couldn't mint, and still less dispense in any honours list. We had knowledge of ourselves and something we had achieved, which would hold us against the worst of our days. Of course, it did not provide any proofing against worry or disappointment, or even despair. It didn't remove the possibility of a little envy at the way our livelihood had become awash with what we might feel, in our grouchier moments, had become easy money indeed.

"It wasn't such a great help to me when I was twice told that the cancer had come back – or when I had to pick up the broken pieces of my life without the all-enveloping reassurance and peace that comes with a shot of morphine.

"No, real life is not so accommodating. It tells you that the shelf life of euphoria can be brief. But then sometimes it gives a gift which cannot be taken away. Only 10 Englishmen alive [nine now] know what it is like to win a World Cup, and sadly our number do not appear under imminent threat of invasion, judging by the tournaments in Japan in 2002 and Germany last summer. Having an MBE, quite honestly, didn't affect our sense of achievement too much, but it was nice to have. It took away a rankle, a little tug of resentment which nobody needs."

No rankles or resentment for the putative Sir David, of course. Just, presumably, a surge of satisfaction, underpinned so strongly this week, that he has won most things any man would want: riches beyond reason, almost universal applause, and now, it appears, elevation above the common subjects of the Queen. Pity about that tackle, though.

THAKSIN TAKEOVER SHOWS A GAME BLINDED BY THE COLOUR OF MONEY

Published: 22 June 2007

You might imagine the new chairman of Manchester City is a suitable case for resounding rejection by the quaintly named arm of the Premier League known as the Fit and Proper Persons Test.

You might think the antecedents of Thaksin Shinawatra would provoke the full majesty of an instrument that sounds as though it was made to sift out candidates who do not perhaps carry all the right credentials for ownership of a club which, for all the despair and the angst it has generated over the years, is still one of the most beloved in the land.

But then you will probably have to think again. Why? Because Thaksin, the former prime minister of Thailand who has been accused of corruption by the military government that succeeded him and has been regularly in the sights of Amnesty International and Human Rights Watch, and who has just had more than £1bn frozen in 21 banks, has proved himself eminently capable of command to the hierarchy of City and enough of the club's shareholders.

He has passed the Premiership's only consistently working litmus test. He has quite enough money squirrelled away despite the bank raids – and who cares about the past? Certainly not the man whose first gift to the City fans is expected to be the appointment of Sven-Goran Eriksson.

Thaksin and Eriksson? No wonder there is talk of riot on the streets of Manchester. It doesn't sound so much like a partnership as a condition. Eriksson was something in European club football no doubt, picking up trophies in Sweden, Portugal and Italy, but for five years he scandalised all those who thought him a sensible choice to lead England.

He chased skirts and avenues of imperfectly perceived advancement in what appeared to be a random fever and all the time the England team, when it truly mattered, went from bad to worse. Now it seems he may be foisted on the long-suffering City fan. It is as cruel as it is perverse, but then it does illustrate well enough the reality behind the Fit and Proper Persons Test.

The proper person, we know well enough now, can be someone like Thaksin. He has the supreme virtue of carrying more than enough of the folding stuff. It is, apparently, the ultimate requirement in an examination which is not so much a moral probe as a financial checklist. Human rights and business practice are simply not part of the equation. Have you or one of your companies suffered bankruptcy in this country? No, well fine, march on. Give us your huddled masses of money.

The "test" postdates Roman Abramovich's arrival at Chelsea and did little to investigate the wealth accumulated by the French-based Alexandre Gaydamak, owner of Portsmouth. No matter that the latter's father, Arcadi, a Russian-Israeli businessman, fled France in the face of accusations of illegal arms dealing and tax evasion. Alexandre, we are told, is a business magnate in his own right. So that's all right.

Roll up, roll up, the Premiership will take your money and leave the agonising to more gentle souls, who might just wonder how it was that Abramovich was a man of fabulous wealth in his mid-thirties in a society where professors and eminent doctors can go months without being paid? He won himself so many of the mineral rights of the people who authored the October Revolution.

Naturally, the selling owner of Chelsea, Ken Bates, didn't thrash out the moral imperatives of the man who was about to pay off the club's debts and so substantially augment his own wealth.

Premiership football doesn't work like that. It doesn't worry about the origins of wealth; it just counts the money.

The guardians of City over the last few ill-starred years, the chairman John Wardle and director and chief executive Alistair MacIntosh, plainly have no reservations about the Thaksin takeover. They are so convinced of its virtue they have decided to stay on and enjoy the years of projected plenty, Wardle merely stepping down to vice-chairman, MacIntosh retaining his role as operating chief of a club which had become such an embarrassing inheritor of a tradition which, while always error-prone, had the glory of both a warm past and the eternal potential provided by some of the most loyal and passionate fans in the land.

Inevitably, there now must be a sense of working amorality that is quite stunning. Thaksin may have a dubious past, he may be *persona non grata* in his own country, but he brings the promise of success, of wealth that will make City contenders again. It is the simplest equation: money makes success, money swamps guilt.

When the American Glazer family took over Manchester United there was outrage enough. Fans went to the streets, after a fashion, in their rage that football's most romantic club was in danger of asset-stripping, had been inflicted with huge debt and had had its entire future imperilled.

Reality has been somewhat different, of course. The Glazers, while certainly not delighting fans with a 14 per cent ticket hike, have been exemplary owners, backing their manager Sir Alex Ferguson with a generous budget and, unlike the case of Abramovich, studiously avoiding even a hint of undermining the man in charge of football affairs.

The Glazers know about the dynamics of professional sport and proved it when their acquisition, the Tampa Bay Buccaneers, won a Super Bowl. They know the value of a tough and winning coach. They are businessmen and what they did to United was something so many tried to do, including Robert Maxwell and Rupert Murdoch, and which became inevitable the moment the club declared itself a plc.

So what's the difference between the Glazers and Thaksin? Only that the Glazers take their investment money from the banks while Thaksin is accused of gaining the same facility directly from the people of Thailand.

It takes us to the ultimate question. Will the City fans care how their new wealth and power were gained any more than the denizens of Stamford Bridge when mega-signings like Michael Essien and Didier Drogba put on some unanswerable show of power? Did Pompey supporters fret over the background of their owner when they pushed for the once fantasy ambition of European football?

There are no prizes for the correct answers to such leading questions. They produce only sighs of recognition that football has rarely had a more poignant example of the degree the game has changed than in the annexation of a club which, even more than the late-charging United, was so rooted in the streets of its city.

For many years there was nostalgic regret enough when the action shifted from Maine Road, the theatre of the young Matt Busby, Peter Doherty, Don Revie, Roy Paul, Mike Summerbee, Francis Lee and Colin Bell, to the splendid new City of Manchester Stadium.

But that was merely a journey across town. What happened yesterday took City into another world, one ungoverned by anything less flimsy than the Fit and Proper Persons Test. One, indeed, where only one rule applies. Do you have the money, can we see and feel it? Yes? Well, come on down. What, anyway, does Amnesty International have to do with the grand old game?

TALISMAN WAS JEWEL IN ARSENAL'S CROWN BUT WENGER IS TRUE KING OF THE EMIRATES

Published: 26 June 2007

He could have gone in any way he chose, with all debts paid a thousand times over. He could have made an ultimate hero's farewell. He could even have raised his arms in that familiar gesture and murmured *"C'est la vie"*. Instead Thierry Henry, artist footballer, dug down into the ragbag of mischief and self-justification that never seems far from the reach of any big-time football player, especially when he is on the move.

Yesterday Henry was in the new colours of Barcelona – and another set of fans with whom to pledge deathless fidelity. There was another shirt to kiss, another dream to espouse.

Gunners who live in the real world will surely shrug away the number of times Henry has told them they are the best in the world, that they owned both his heart and his talent not for another day or season but forever.

It is all in the way of today's game, of course. Contracts don't mean much beyond expressing a mood of the moment and if 85-year-old Sir Tom Finney, who heard only mocking laughter from the directors of the one club he ever played for, Preston North End, when he expressed interest in an overture from Italy around the middle of the last century, had read the comments of Henry to the French sports bible *L'Equipe* at the weekend he would have been more convinced than ever that he now occupies an alien planet.

The move, said Henry, was all about his fears for the future of the club who had been paying him £120,000 a week. The club – and his Svengali Arsène Wenger – had been "de-stabilised" by the departure of the manager's ally, vice-chairman David Dein. Presumably, this abiding concern will burn just as fiercely each time he collects the extra £10,000 a week it is reported Barça will pay him.

Henry's comments to *L'Equipe* could be translated into English – and reality – easily enough. He thinks storm clouds are gathering over the Emirates Stadium. So rather than stay around as the father of a young and emerging team, adding the beautiful sophistication, if admittedly fading dynamism, of his game to the strivings of his young team-mates, he flits to the Nou Camp. It is his right, just as it was David Beckham's to take the sweetheart contract offered by Los Angeles Galaxy instead of remaining in seriously competitive football. But why all the larding and the breast-beating? Why not avoid the insult to the intelligence of fans who may just have believed some of the things you have said in the past? No, the style is relentless now. It is not enough for a player to follow his impulse or his convenience or his pocket. He has to dress it in so many different ways. Beckham didn't sign for the Galaxy because it suited his particular needs, and perhaps even more those of his wife, we were told, but because he wanted to face one last challenge in lifting the third-rate American league to world-class status. Henry has gone to Barça not because it eventually suited him, notwithstanding his eternal affection for Arsenal, but because of the imminent break-up of the club his mentor Wenger has come to represent more profoundly, in his values and his impact, than any other contemporary except Sir Alex Ferguson at Manchester United.

The fact is that Henry's departure is for Arsenal more a sadness, a poignant punctuation mark, than a disaster. Under the prompting and the genius of Wenger, Henry's gift to both his club and English football has been sublime. He has drawn new and expanded boundaries around the beauty of the game played in these islands. He has scored a torrent of goals, many of them exquisite. But then who could say confidently that Wenger, as he did with the equally influential Patrick Vieira, has not picked the perfect time to release a talent that, for the moment at least, adds up to his supreme example of inspired assessment of football potential? Henry may have an Indian summer in the company of Ronaldinho and Lionel Messi, but over the last 18 months or so there was evidence that his fire, at least on behalf of Arsenal, was running down into its embers.

Certainly the risk that Wenger, when he measures his strength, and his support, in the boardroom at the end of next season, as a free agent of the utmost allure to any football club on earth, will decide it is time to move on, outweighs hugely the implications of Henry's transfer.

Henry was Arsenal's greatest adornment, but at a time when Wenger was attempting to re-make his team yet again, was he providing the kind of leadership and passion so vital in any transition period? The suspicion, whatever the impression created by the player, is that the manager some time ago decided he was not. Not when he seemed happy to have the club's approach to the 2006 Champions League final in Paris dominated utterly by the question of whether he would stay or go. Not when Wenger was obliged to tell him before a game against Spurs that selection was down to his judgement and not a superstar's whim.

No doubt these are anxious times for Arsenal. Wenger's departure would be the equivalent of the rooks flying away. He has made Arsenal, as much as he made Henry, and it is hard not to believe that even in the absence of Dein there will be enough collective football intelligence in the boardroom to grasp this essential point.

Here, the belief is that Wenger, at 57, is strong enough to write himself another ticket at the club he has shaped so intuitively, perhaps in the company again of a Dein who has been notably anxious to keep his own counsel as the rumblings of American takeover refuse to go away. Certainly it is unlikely that he is too cast down by the loss of Henry to give up the work, and the club, that has defined his brilliance. Would he walk away from all that deeply entrenched achievement for the circus of Real Madrid? It doesn't seem so likely.

Maybe the hugely promising Emmanuel Adebayor, after a season of increased exposure to the rigours of English football, will find his stride. Perhaps Wenger will indeed return to the challenge of Nicolas Anelka, the lost jewel for whom a massive transfer profit was never quite adequate consolation. However it goes, there is one certainty. It is that for Arsenal the loss of Henry, for all that he has done, is really just one of those things. That of Wenger would be, well, almost everything.

LAMPARD REJECTS THE WORLD OF REAL VALUE BY MEASURING RESPECT IN PILES OF MONEY

Published: 03 July 2007

If it should happen that Frank Lampard wins his contract battle at Stamford Bridge, if along with John Terry he pushes his wages up around the £121,000-a-week mark enjoyed by the former superstars Andrei Shevchenko and Michael Ballack, he might do himself a huge favour by jettisoning a trademarked gesture.

You know the one. It accompanies every moment of personal triumph out on the field. He kisses the Chelsea shirt with a reverence rarely seen outside an enclosed monastery. There is no reason, however, why his thumb and his forefinger should be suddenly redundant when he sends the ball into the net.

Instead of using them to pull the precious blue shirt to his lips, he might rub them together in the universal statement of avarice.

This might not be terribly attractive to the more romantic Chelsea followers, assuming any have survived the years of the Oligarch, but then it might well head off a need for a general issue of sickbags. The point is that while it would probably be naive to expect Lampard and Terry to separate themselves from the rest of the Premiership feeding frenzy, it is surely fair to ask them to stop insulting the intelligence of those who have provided them with such extravagant rewards.

It comes down to the plain old truth that even in an age befuddled by celebrity and fake achievement there is a limit to how far you can have it both ways.

Before his desperately clunking performance in last summer's World Cup, few professionals had ever built such an enviable reputation as young Frank Lampard. The son of the excellent old West Ham full-back, Frank Senior, the boy seemed to inhabit older, truer values than so many of his contemporaries. When he was voted player of the year he delivered a speech of touching humility; he talked of his debts to team-mates and all those who had helped him to a position of such prominence in the game that had given him everything.

Then, after a string of dauntingly consistent and relevant performances, he touched a nerve in every football man who remembered how the game had first invaded the imaginations of so many ordinary people.

He said he would always be a Chelsea fan, always be utterly devoted to the club. Indeed, such feeling would stretch beyond his days as a player and possibly even a coach. No, it would be a lifelong romance, the one between him and Chelsea. He could see himself as an old man walking down the King's Road alive with hopes for the team's next game.

So much for such dreamy idealism. As Chelsea currently give every sign of a club in the throes of appalling misdirection, when the owner Roman Abramovich denies, at least until a dangerously late hour, his apparently profoundly disliked coach José Mourinho the means to strike back at Sir Alex Ferguson's Manchester United strengthened by a £50m spending surge which has now netted England midfielder Owen Hargreaves, Lampard and Terry fight indignantly for their right to be Chelsea's best-paid players.

They imply that new offers of £120-odd thousand a week constitute an insult. Not only have they been short-changed but disrespected. Where has all that shirt-kissing ended? In a brusque request to kiss the seat of the designer jeans worn by one of the richest men in the world. Heart-rending – or gut wrenching. You pay your money – or you don't.

Lampard, particularly, seems to believe that he is suffering a terrible shortfall in respect. He wasn't so much angered as shocked by the level of criticism he and his under-achieving England team-mates faced after their miserable effort in last summer's World Cup. Simple respect for past achievement should have prevented such a disgraceful reaction. Such bizarre thinking is entrenched in Lampard's current pay demands. Looking at himself, he has plainly mistaken impressively worthy professional standards for something entirely more elevated. He believes he deserves the rewards of a truly great player, and as he does so bemuses plain-talking and thinking football men who believe they know the difference between a player of strength and determination and one who has the capacity to turn any game at however high a level.

When you consider all of this it is hard not be reminded of an early morning collision between one of the truly great Chelsea players, Roy Bentley, and a young colleague at his new club, Fulham, the future World Cup-winning full-back George Cohen.

Fulham were in a Bristol hotel on the dawn of a league match. Bentley knocked on the door of Cohen's room, demanded he got dressed and accompany him on a walk through the empty, early-morning streets. They hiked all the way out to the Clifton suspension bridge. The veteran, an old Navy man, pointed out the beautiful piece of engineering and said to the rather bemused young pro: "Remember George, however great you think the challenge of playing football, think of how it must be to build a bridge like that." Many years later, after winning his World Cup medal, making and losing business fortunes, winning battles against life-threatening illness three times, Cohen said: "Roy Bentley was a wonderful player and a great colleague and he taught me so much about the game, he was a great striker and then he played in midfield with tremendous touch and vision when he lost some of his pace.

"But he never taught me anything so valuable as on that morning when we walked out to the great bridge." What Roy Bentley taught George Cohen was that there was a big wide world of achievement out there beyond the boundaries of a football field, a place where respect could be measured by so much more than loadsamoney.

BECKHAM AN INNOCENT ABROAD WHEN IT COMES TO FULFILLING THE AMERICAN DREAM

Published: 14 July 2007

Why was it possible to tremble for the Beckhams, with all their wealth and their celebrity and their apparent total happiness in their carefully burnished skins, when they made their hugely heralded landfall in Los Angeles this week? It was, strangely enough, because of their innocence. Their innocence, that is, of an American sports culture that – however much it is diverted these next few days by the bangles and the profile of immigrants from another world, and another set of values – will not waver one inch from an ultimately hard-core judgement.

This insists that no form of main-line American sport offers stardom by reputation gathered in other places or achievement that is not instantly overwhelming; and do not, for a New York or even an LA nanosecond, believe that there is any point in lecturing the Americans on the subtleties of the world game, how virtue in a team sport does not necessarily involve the ability to run past the opposition like Walter Payton or O J Simpson or jump as high and as athletically as Michael Jordan.

For this unchanging perspective we can go back a quarter of a century, when football's Last Frontier was invaded by a force which makes the Los Angeles Galaxy's £28m investment in the 31-year-old Beckham seem a solitary straw blowing in the wind.

We can go back to the executive box of the New York Cosmos when, in the wake of the retired Pelé, Franz Beckenbauer made his debut at the Giants' Stadium.

"What the hell is the Kraut doing at the back of defence?" the club president demanded to know. He was told it was where the great German player had exerted vast influence throughout his career. "Not here, he won't," snapped the president. "Tell him to get his million-dollar ass up front."

The old North American Soccer League, which keeled over and died a few years later in 1984, was already experiencing the tightening of the noose. Even Lamar Hunt, scion of Dallas oil tycoons, felt a chill in his blood and, though he would never lose his passion for a game that enthralled him during the 1966 World Cup, over the years, and after the investment of countless millions into the game in his homeland, he was bound to accept that if "soccer" could conquer every other corner of the globe it would always face stubborn resistance in large areas of the American psyche.

Hunt, who also founded the World Championship Tennis circuit and owned the Kansas City Chiefs NFL franchise, had some soaring moments, along with the rest of that first wave of pioneers. His Dallas Tornado lifted the Soccer Bowl in 1971 and his exuberance at a party he threw in his Texas mansion lingers powerfully in the memory. A black pianist, dressed in a white suit, sat at a grand piano on the front lawn and an army of waiters served champagne and mint juleps. The benefactor, though, remained undistracted. He wanted to talk of great soccer players; he wanted to envisage their final conquest.

Heaven knows, there was no lack of quality in the army recruited by Hunt and his fellow NASL owners, who at the league's optimistic peak totalled 24, stretching from Vancouver in the Pacific North-West across to Rochester in upstate New York, down through the Mid-West and Philadelphia, into California and the Deep South. You could hardly go through a North American airport then without encountering a footballer of both celebrity and the highest class: George Best and Johan Cruyff found their way to LA, Pelé was installed with the Cosmos, along with talent like Carlos Alberto, Beckenbauer and the craggy Dutchman Johan Neeskens. Bobby Moore arrived in Florida, Rodney Marsh became something of a folk hero in Tampa, Alan Ball and Rudi Krol joined forces in Vancouver and Charlie Cooke and Alan Hudson had some profitable years in California and Seattle respectively.

There were moments when scepticism was thrust into abeyance. Once it was stunning to see New York sports news telecasts being headed by a report of a Giorgio Chinaglia hat-trick against the Tulsa Roughnecks, and this on a day when Reggie Jackson, Mr October, had clobbered a couple of homers for the Yankees.

Best, though deep into an alcohol-fuelled decline, performed a similar feat when he ran through the opposition to score a goal for the San José Earthquakes. The sequence was rerun for several days. George poured himself a vodka, grinned and conceded: "Crap defence." Astonishingly, Montreal Manic drew a crowd of more than a 100,000 to the Olympic Stadium. Some chose to call it a breakthrough. Soon enough, the guardians of the established games, baseball and basketball and gridiron, were declaring it, no doubt with some relief, "a novelty freak". The problem was that soccer might cause passing interest in a sports-obsessed land but it couldn't engage the heartland of the blue-collar soul.

The American sports fan demands, more than anything, continuous, high-pitched action – and scoring.

He also – let's be honest about this – demands of his great stars a degree of red-blooded masculinity, an authentic combativeness. Mrs Beckham might once have trilled that her husband was a gay icon, but if this had a certain commercial value in the hyping of clothes and other heavily sponsored products, it is not likely to play so well in the macho land of tail-gate parties. Dennis Rodman, it is true, survived a penchant for make-up and the wearing of the odd little cocktail number, but it wouldn't have meant much if he wasn't so ferocious in snagging rebounds. Carl Lewis, arguably America's greatest Olympian, was widely derided for his refusal to wear the clothes and the stereotype of a traditional sports hero.

Has anything fundamentally changed in the American sports outlook? Distaste for steroid abuse has plainly affected the current popularity of baseball, the game of such heroes as Babe Ruth and Micky Mantle and Joe Di Maggio – the last of whom wedded sport and glamour in America in a way never to be rivalled when he married Marilyn Monroe – but it remains deep in American affection, awaiting, perhaps, a periodic cleansing. Basketball is suffering a post-Jordan lull, but the gridiron goes from one level of strength to another.

The NFL is, surely, the sold-out nemesis of Beckham's hope of North American conquest. Phil Woosnam, the former Welsh international who was commissioner of the NASL, had a rush of blood that provoked him to declare his league would surpass the NFL in 10 years – it was dead in half the time – and today such round-ball yearnings seem as remote as ever.

Down the years the NFL has entrenched the American myths of the masterful male warrior, and the result is an impregnability written in blood and a kind of gunfighter's authority. When Jack Lambert, the fierce linebacker, lost one game he was so annoyed he cut his jeep in two with a hacksaw. It took him an entire weekend.

The great quarterback Joe Namath was brilliant and laconic. Once he was interviewed in a studio on the West Side of New York while filming a pantyhose advertisement. He was chewing tobacco and from time to time volleying a wad into an ashtray some distance away. Admiringly, one observed that he was six-for-six, and he smiled and said how much he hated interceptions. He was of Hungarian blood, but like so many of alien stock he had embraced all the style and the tradition of a new world – and a unique sports environment. Famously, when he was asked what he thought of astro-turf, he said: "I never smoked it". Namath was American sport in a way that not even Pelé or Cruyff, Best or Beckenbauer could ever be.

So what price David Beckham? In some ways it doesn't bear thinking about.

WENGER'S DARK HORSES CAN CONJURE A TRIUMPH FOR THE PURISTS

Published: 10 August 2007

Sometimes in football, as in life, it is necessary to make an act of faith. Ideally, though, it is accompanied by a thread of logic and a set of beliefs about what is right and wrong, what deserves success and what doesn't.

Most of all, if you are detached just a little from the apparent need of so many to have their team at the centre of their existence, the hope is for something that does most for the general good, in this case the spirit and the horizons of the money-loaded, morally poverty-stricken Premier League.

What am I saying? Two things. One is that nothing would be more uplifting to the debate about how a football team should be run, what its priorities should be, and how it plays, than for Arsenal to return to the peak of English football and win another title for their allegedly embattled manager Arsène Wenger.

The other is that, despite the widespread dismissal of their chances by the bookmakers who have them 10-1, they are eminently capable of doing it.

Their chances should certainly not be dismissed, and least of all by the man who has so brilliantly reinvented their greatest rivals, Manchester United. Sir Alex Ferguson, claims that he has his strongest ever squad, which is of course what he would say. What he cannot suggest is that Arsenal are necessarily crippled by their youth. With great courage he made nonsense of such a theory, and the infancy of Alan Hansen's career as a pundit, when he released Ryan Giggs, Paul Scholes, David Beckham, the Neville boys and Nicky Butt. Hansen declared that you can't win with kids. Fergie proved him wrong and won the title, as his great predecessor Sir Matt Busby did, four decades earlier with his unforgettable Babes. It simply depended on the quality of the kids.

Relatively speaking, does Wenger hold the same kind of hand as Busby and Ferguson? Do the likes of Cesc Fabregas, Gael Clichy, Emmanuel Adebayor and the potential powerhouse Abou Diaby, and the physically and psychologically maturing Robin van Persie, Eduardo da Silva and Bacary Sagna suffer too much in comparison? Not in the bright light of a new football dawn.

When you feed in the experience of William Gallas, whose substance was underlined by the strength of the reaction at Stamford Bridge to his noisy journey across town, and Kolo Toure and Gilberto, and consider the potential of such as the lurking young Brazilian Denilson, you have to question the rampaging belief that Arsenal, as serious contenders, are shot through.

Why is the suspicion so entrenched? Largely, it seems, because Thierry Henry is gone. In truth, it is the fantasy of Henry that left for Barcelona. The reality of him was scarcely present last season – and certainly not when Adebayor scored a beautifully sculpted goal at Old Trafford for the first of Arsenal's two Premier League victories over the champions-elect.

When Henry was operating at his best for Arsenal the idea of his leaving was unthinkable. He was the spirit and the genius of the side that played so beautifully and, so staggeringly, went a whole season undefeated. That Henry was precious and irreplaceable. He illuminated both the game and the sky. The one that finally packed his bags was much less than that. Some of his aura slipped away in the Champions League final a year last spring. He had the perfect chance to pull the trigger against Barcelona but his instincts froze. So, you had the sense, did his willingness to continue as the supreme guiding light of an emerging young team.

Now those taking the Arsenal odds in preference to those against United, 11-8, Chelsea 6-4 and Liverpool 9-2 have to take the leap on which all of Wenger's immediate hopes depend.

They have to believe that in a way Henry's absence is not a blow but an incentive.

An incentive, this is, for a whole team to grow up, to grasp that potential is a diet on which you can exist only so long without losing a certain strength and panache. Last season Wenger yearned for signs of such dawning knowledge and that it came so spasmodically was no doubt the greatest source of his frustration. Sometimes you could look at his face and see that he ached for a sign of a new force creating the old alchemy.

Fabegras, at 20, has already expressed his desire to be captain of the club. There is nothing wrong with this as long as it is underpinned by a consistent body of work. Some older heads might mutter about an upstart's pretensions – but not those who recognise the kid's extraordinary ability to shape a game, to invite responsibility with the moral courage to get on the ball and make things happen. This is a rare quality in a modern midfielder and Fabregas's progress is still another tribute to the insight and the operating style of his manager.

There were times last season when a popular view was that Wenger was losing it. His touchline capers smacked of desperation. But then Wenger's vision of football has always been that of an artist and it has to be noted that, unlike Vincent Van Gogh, he has yet to cut off an ear... or the lifeblood of his success.

Wenger would no more dream of stocking his team with players he has never seen – as Sven-Goran Eriksson has done in his wild punt with Manchester City – as spend half a training session practising long throw-ins. Wenger is about the certainties of knowing and believing in his players, and whatever the internal politics at Arsenal – and whether or not his friend David Dein will return to the fold in the company of vast amounts of American money – we can be sure that his priorities will remain undisturbed. Yes, we know he is a wretched loser, in some ways worse than Ferguson, but how much in the end does it matter? What is more forgivable? A fierce, and sometimes dislocating, hatred of defeat for the team you have made and whose best values you cherish? Or a desire to win for its own sake and at the expense of all that creates the excitement and the beauty of the game which has given you so much? We should know, by now, where Wenger stands on this most important question of all.

We certainly know that Wenger, no more than Ferguson or Rafael Benítez, would not still be in his job if his club had behaved towards him as Chelsea have recently treated José Mourinho. Mourinho has buried, at least publicly, his angst at the appointment of owner Roman Abramovich's nomination Avram Grant to the coaching staff and, in the context of the Russian's wealth, a cruel pegging back of his ability to spend on the players he wants, but there has to be the strongest sense that the Special One is reduced, for the first time in his extraordinary career, to papering over cracks in what was once a fortress. He walked away from Benfica, the most important club in his own football culture, because they wanted him to surrender some of his independence. Now, whatever he says, he is Abramovich's compliant servant – a status that Wenger, we have to believe, wouldn't countenance for a second.

Of course, Chelsea are still formidable, and not least because of the players' devotion to their embattled coach, but the plague of injuries, and the sense of divided command, says here that they will again be a stride short of the mountain top.

United, augmented by Owen Hargreaves, Nani and Anderson, remain the team everyone has to measure themselves against. Ferguson's confidence is founded solidly enough, but there are still vital questions to be answered. Will Cristiano Ronaldo produce the full range of his talent in the most important matches – something he failed to do last season despite a blizzard of acclaim – and will Wayne Rooney achieve with Carlos Tevez the chemistry that was once or twice so thrilling when he travelled briefly in the company of the old but still bright star Henrik Larsson? Will Rio Ferdinand, for all his gifts, be able to banish another wave of doubts about his defensive resolution? Positive answers to any of these questions will lift the bar for United's three significant challengers, not least Liverpool, who may know that Fernando Torres is a major acquisition but are unlikely to be too sure of their best line-up before Christmas.

There is maybe just one certainty in the coming season. It is that Arsenal will play as they always do, which is to say with artistry and intelligence and a wonderful ambition. That, and the anticipation that Fabregas will make his most serious challenge thus far as everyone's idea of a footballer of the year, surely makes the blood run fast. The hunch is that it will do so all to way to triumph, for both Arsenal and football, in the spring.

BEAUTIFUL GAME WILL ALWAYS BE A FANTASY IN THE EYE OF A PRAGMATIST LIKE MOURINHO

Published: 11 August 2007

Beauty, the new José Mourinho tells us, is a controversial concept in football, adding: "But for me it has a lot to do with having control". These tablets of stone from the Stamford Bridge mountain top must surely provoke two overwhelming reactions. One is that Mourinho is once again talking not from his heart but an extremely dicey relationship with his paymaster and boss, Roman Abramovich. The other is that there is no new Mourinho, just one paying a little lip service to the absurd proposition first handed down to the Chelsea chief executive, Peter Kenyon, from the owner's box.

You may remember the comic effusion from Kenyon. It was when Claudio Ranieri was on his last legs as manager. Kenyon said Chelsea wanted more than victories. They wanted spectacular 5-0 trouncings, long-distance goals, and, presumably, if he was available, Roy of the Rovers.

It was a statement so detached from the realities of modern football, some pointed out, that it should not be a surprise; how would a former shirt salesman like Kenyon know anything about the game that occasionally required Sir Alex Ferguson to take a swig of Scotch and exclaim: "Bloody football!" The truth was that Kenyon was parroting the views of his boss, who also plainly didn't know the first thing about the game he had bought into so hugely.

If he had, and if he really wanted a fantasy team to match the football of Real Madrid or Barcelona, Arsenal or Manchester United – and so stoke up his popularity in his new theatre of operation – he wouldn't have gone for Mourinho.

Mourinho is not about fantasy football; never has been, and never will. He sees football in a certain practical way and has the strength of will and personality to produce its maximum effect with the services of strong and able footballers. You could see this when his Porto overcame the Monaco of Didier Deschamps in the Champions League final of 2004 in Gelsenkirchen. Porto played a game built on strenuous defence, high work rate and opportunism. Their most important player was Deco, who like Frank Lampard, the top midfielder at Stamford Bridge, slaves in the engine room of the game without ever giving a hint that he is capable of the brilliance of a Kaka or the tactical nous of a Paul Scholes or a Cesc Fabregas.

The "new" Mourinho also says: "I want more. It's good for the club that we play differently. Against a big team like ours, the tendency is for our opponents to close down, so our tendency must be to be open. With the quality of wingers we have, we have to use them."

Why didn't he use Damien Duff and Arjen Robben when they were itching to display their wares three seasons ago; why did he field them only sporadically as out-and-out wide men, so often preferring them to tuck 10 to 15 yards from the touchline? It's because it is the way he thinks, and has always had his teams play.

Now are we to believe that Florent Malouda and Shaun Wright-Phillips offer him better options? Malouda has shown some flashy touches but the verdict on Wright-Phillips, apparently one of the brightest prospects in English football a few years ago, had to be bleak after the Community Shield game. His time at Stamford Bridge seems to have drained what little confidence he had.

But then it is not just about wingers and tactical formations. It's about touch and feel and subtlety of intention.

When Chelsea were overpowering the Premiership – and Abramovich was scowling over the fact that his money had bought mere muscularity and power rather than those qualities which separate football from every other team game in its potential to produce skill and imagination – there was an inclination to believe that the self-proclaimed Special One was merely laying down foundations. But the robust, ugly duckling remained just that. That it would stay so became evident when Rafael Benítez outwitted Mourinho in the Champions League semi-finals in 2005 and Frank Rijkaard's Barcelona outplayed Chelsea a year later. This year, in one of the most wretched games seen at this level, Mourinho again failed to get the better of Benítez in a Champions League semi-final. Mourinho resorted to the long ball, as he had two years earlier.

Now he talks about a sudden infusion of beauty? Where is it going to come from? Malouda? He should give us a break on this one. Malouda has pace and skill and trickery, but a player to transform Chelsea from functionalism to fantasy? Hardly. Michael Ballack was widely seen as a superstar before he arrived at Stamford Bridge, but if you had asked any old football man he would have told you that Ballack was not a product of the beautiful game, not somebody who will get on the ball and make flowing movement. He was a hard-running guy who got up into the box and scored goals. Yes, another Frank Lampard.

Whatever you think of his behaviour when everything was going so swimmingly in the early going at Chelsea, when he bent the truth so frequently and projected himself without any restraint, it is hard not to feel a certain sympathy for the Special One. He has lost so much of his old independence and panache. He is talking about beautiful football when all he thinks, and knows, is winning football.

He is in the wrong place at the wrong time and why that is so, given his standing in the game, is something of a mystery. Maybe he likes the London life. Maybe he likes his big fat contract. Maybe he thinks he can truly make both beautiful and winning football. You just have to wish him good luck, because it is something he has never tried before. He talks beauty but, the suspicion must be, he is thinking desperate. It can happen when you forget who you are.

IRAQI VICTORY A REMINDER OF THE POWER AND MAGIC OF WORLD'S GREATEST GAME

Finally, and only a tad out of chronological sequence, a note of uplifting optimism, a delighted nod towards the eternal appeal of football, which still has the capacity to offer hope for the future in a cruel and increasingly cynical world.

Published: 31 July 2007

The next time somebody tells you football isn't worth the chequebook it's written on, that it is rotten beyond redemption, just show him a picture of the kid. The Iraqi kid, that is, the one who for once is smiling despite the clatter of gunfire; smiling because his team have just won the Asian Cup.

We don't know if he is Sunni or Shia, Kurd or Arab. We just know he is a kid who loves football. The world, if anyone making such a mess of the place cares to look, is full of them.

You see the power of the game wherever you go. Youngsters play in the slum streets of Africa and Asia and the poorest corners of Europe and the Americas and even the former minefields of Bosnia and the killing fields of Cambodia, but you take it as much for granted as the sunrise. Then you are reminded of its capacity to stop the world for 90 minutes when you see the smile of the Iraqi kid and ask yourself what else could put the misery of his ravaged country on hold, however heart-breaking the brevity of the interlude, quite like the universal game. A Middle Eastern foray by the new man of peace, Tony Blair? A burst of platitudes from Camp David by George Bush and Gordon Brown? Maybe not.

Of course there are too many wounds in Iraq to be healed by one night of euphoria – there were at least 120 serious new ones when a car bomb went off among fans celebrating out in the street the semi-final victory over South Korea, and there were also 50 new graves to dig – but if football will never on its own stop hate or war in the Middle East, no more than it did in the trenches of the First World War after the fabled Yuletide kick-about by German and British soldiers, it will always be capable of a profound comment.

It will always make for itself the point that in its beauty and freedom of expression, when it is played beyond the cheating and the corruption that have been heaped upon it so relentlessly in recent years by those who profit from it

An Iraqi boy celebrates at the Asian Cup final in Jakarta
©ADEK BERRY/AFP/Getty Images

most, it sends the powerful message that even sworn enemies have more in common than they may think.

For those who know and love the game there is no revelation in the picture of the smiling young Iraqi, only huge reinforcement of the view of the great writer Albert Camus that he learnt more about life and character while playing in goal for the University of Algiers than he ever did hobnobbing with the Left Bank literati.

We have all seen the power of football. Ian St John, the great striker of Liverpool and Scotland, a man of such fierce combativeness his adoring manager Bill Shankly once said he would have made a potential world middleweight champion if he had pursued his promise as a fighter rather than signing for his local club Motherwell, knew much exhilaration in his title-winning career. But when he talks of the great experiences of his life he still counts among the highest his walk back from the stadium in Buenos Aires in 1978 after watching Argentina beat the Netherlands in the World Cup final. Argentina, under the rule of the generals and heading for the disaster of the Falklands War, was not the happiest place but St John recalls a delirious city where for a few hours all the misery in the world seemed to have been sluiced into the South Atlantic.

"I had to walk miles with the traffic at a standstill," said St John, "but I didn't begrudge a yard of it. I just felt so proud to be part of football, to feel the warmth and the power of it to touch people. I danced with an old lady."

Sir Bobby Charlton tells similar stories, reports the emotion that comes when he sees kids emerging from shanties in Nairobi glowing in their football kit.

The face of the Iraqi kid reminds us that there is no game like football, nothing that captures the yearnings for distraction and joy for quite so many people.

It is true, hooliganism has ravaged the image of football for nearly half a century now but football didn't create the problem, society did, and the professional game that has over the years waxed so fat, has never seen its role as a protector, still less an exemplar of all that is best in sport. It has been too busy accumulating power and hoarding the profits. The resulting crimes cannot be placed at the door of the game which has this week again proved its ability to entrance the world.

That talent was perhaps never better expressed than one evening during the 1982 World Cup when the Brazilian team staged a training session in a little town in the hills above Barcelona.

The atmosphere was of fiesta, and the young boys who were invited to join in a pick-up game with such stars as Socrates and Roberto Falcao and Zico had eyes that you had to suspect would shine forever.

Because down the years football has attracted so much avarice and indiscipline and arrogance the temptation to assign such memories to a gilded past has maybe never been stronger. But then it is always the way with football that when you least expect glory, it produces a force, and a spontaneity, to lift almost any heart. It did in 1998, when a brilliantly organised World Cup was won by the "rainbow" French, inspired by a Zinedine Zidane who grew up in the most notorious high-rise slum in Marseilles. Brazil became the glory of world football when it finally absorbed brilliant black players represented most perfectly by Pelé.

Maybe, then, it was more than a random fact that the coach who inspired an Iraqi team riven by ethnic and religious rifts to victory over the sumptuously accommodated and meticulously prepared Saudi Arabians just happened to be a Brazilian. Jorvan Vieira said that he had fulfilled his contract by "bringing a smile to the Iraqi people". He had used something beyond the means of any politician. He had released the power and the magic of the world's greatest game.

ACKNOWLEDGEMENTS

Many debts have been accrued while travelling around the country and the world covering sport and over the last seven years these have accumulated most heavily in the offices of *The Independent*. The editor, Simon Kelner, has never been less than encouraging and I'm most grateful to the constant support of two sports editors there, first Paul Newman, and since 2004, Matt Tench.

Nick Duxbury, assistant sports editor, and Chris Maume, sports news editor, have always been cheerful and kind however pressing the deadlines, and there are too many sub-editors who have rescued me from serious error to list here. All of them have my deepest gratitude.

The cast of those who helped me before I arrived at the 'Indy', somewhat windblown perhaps but still insanely eager to have my say, is again too large to mention individually, but I'm especially indebted to such as David Emery, the former sports editor of the *Daily Express* who brought me back to that newspaper after a stint in North America, and his successors Alex Butler, Des Kelly and Mike Allen.

Beyond the trenches of my own newspaper, the friendship and wisdom of such colleagues as Hugh McIlvanney, Ken Jones, Jeff Powell, David Miller and the late Ian Wooldridge have been the source of great encouragement and warmth – as has the toleration and kindness of a new generation of sports writers, not least that of my colleague Sam Wallace, the *Independent* football correspondent.

A crucial good fortune has been the ability to consult regularly with some of the men within football who have been most significant influences in my attempts, such as they are, to understand the funny old glorious game. They include John Giles, Ian St John, Nobby Stiles, Sir Bobby Charlton, Joe Jordan, George Cohen, Bob McNab, and my first mentors – and let's be honest, heroes – Malcolm Allison and the late Bill Shankly.

My wife Linda once attended a match at Crystal Palace and declared that she had done her duty in respect of my interest in football. In all else her support over more years than she would want me to mention has been indispensable.

James Lawton, September 2007

PRAWNS IN THE GAME
HOW FOOTBALL GOT WHERE IT IS TODAY!

Paul French

£9.99 softback
224 pages
ISBN: 978-0-954684-38-9

Something grotesque is going on in the beautiful game. Money rather than sport now rules the roost. Stadium names are sold off to the highest bidder and players often seem no more than overpaid and over-sexed celebrities. Their every action, both on and off the pitch, is fodder for the tabloids as the players themselves argue over whether it's £100k or £120k a week in their pay packets. Written by a fan for the fans. You'll laugh, you'll get angry and you'll find out: how did the prawn sandwich brigade take over the national sport?

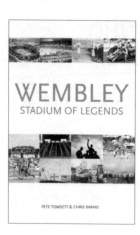

WEMBLEY
STADIUM OF LEGENDS

Pete Tomsett & Chris Brand

£12.99 hardback
160 pages
ISBN: 978-0-954684-39-6

Wembley: Stadium Of Legends combines remarkable archive images with fascinating information: tales of enigmatic entrepreneurs and entertainers, courageous athletes and odds-defying sportsmen. Through unique photographs, the later chapters tell of the transition from old to new, from the faded grandeur of the old stadium, through its demolition, especially the heartbreaking destruction of the twin towers, to the construction of the new building and its dramatic arch.

www.dewilewismedia.com